IMAGES
of America

PARSIPPANY TROY HILLS

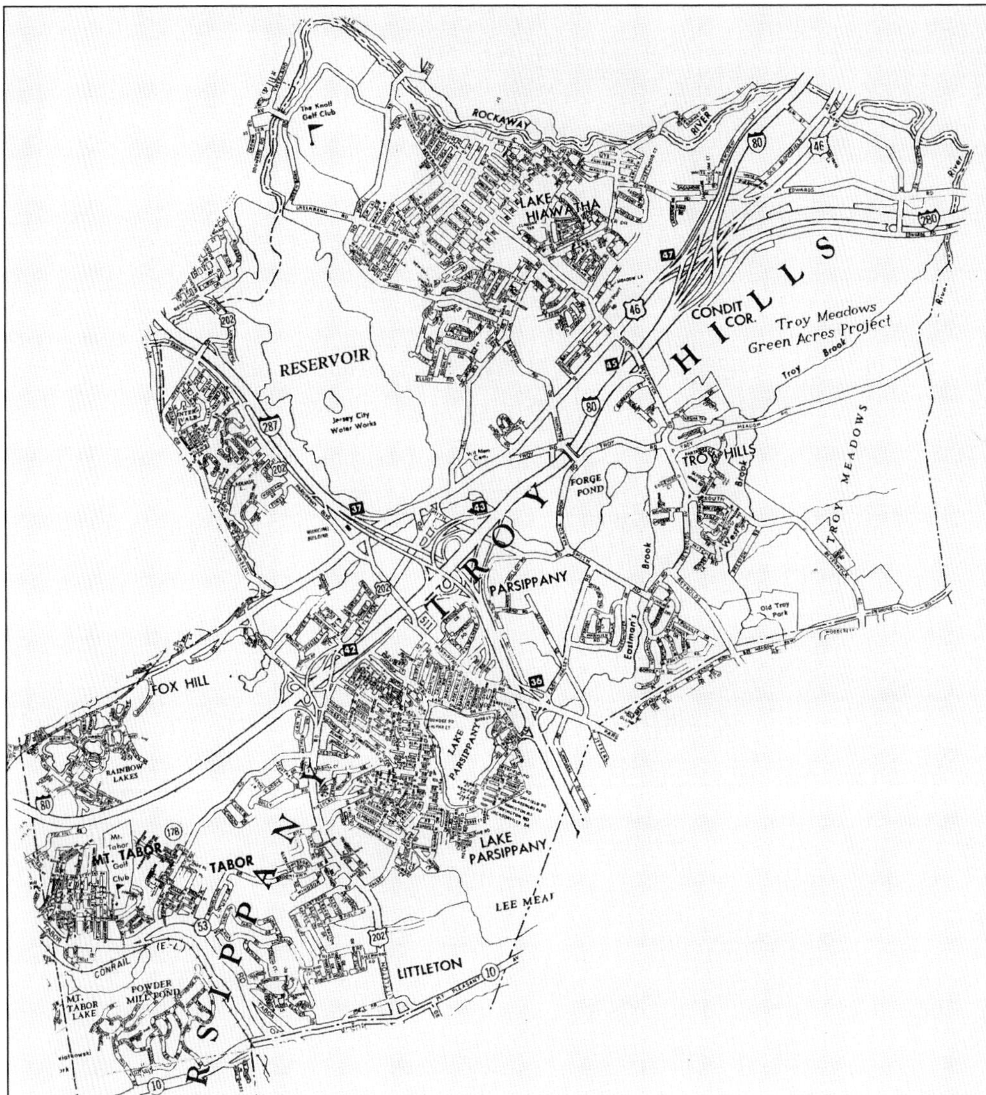

A current Parsippany-Troy Hills map. (Parsippany-Troy Hills Township.)

IMAGES
of America

PARSIPPANY TROY HILLS

The Parsippany Historical
and
Preservation Society

ARCADIA
PUBLISHING

ISBN 978-0-7385-8963-3

Published by Arcadia Publishing
Charleston, South Carolina

Printed in the United States of America

For all general information contact Arcadia Publishing at:
Telephone 843-853-2070
Fax 843-853-0044
E-mail sales@arcadiapublishing.com
For customer service and orders:
Toll-Free 1-888-313-2665

Visit us on the Internet at www.arcadiapublishing.com

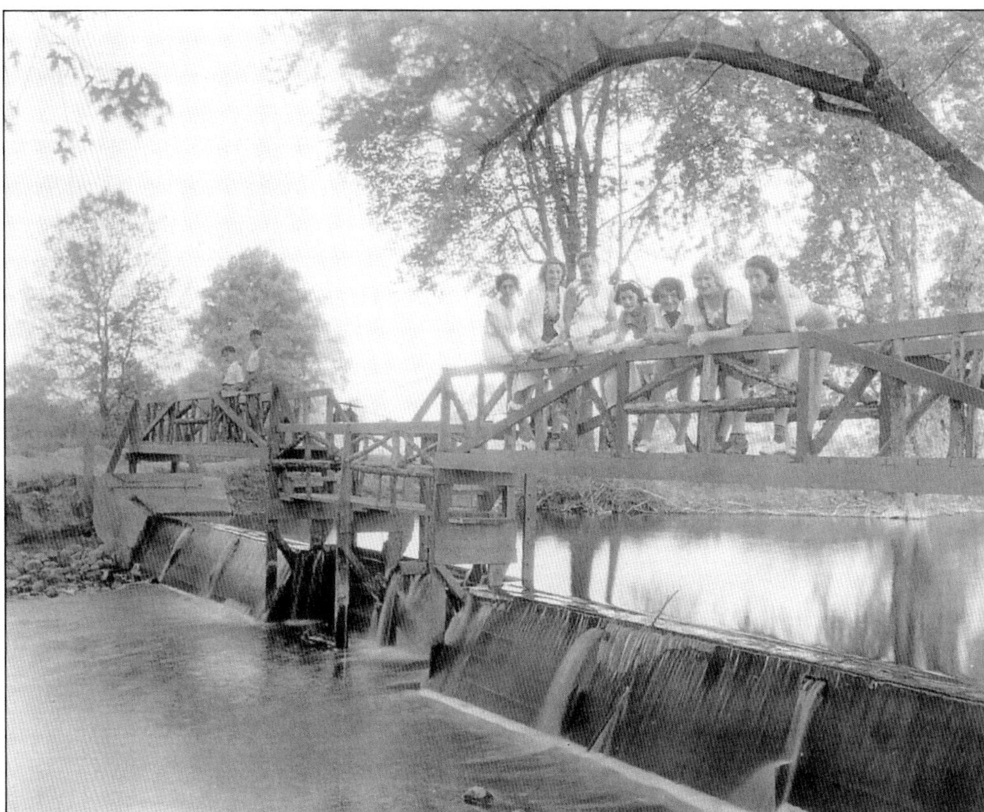

Front cover: The bridge over the Rockaway River in the Lake Hiawatha area, *c.* 1930. The women were models and the boys were local children. (Parsippany Historic Museum.)

Contents

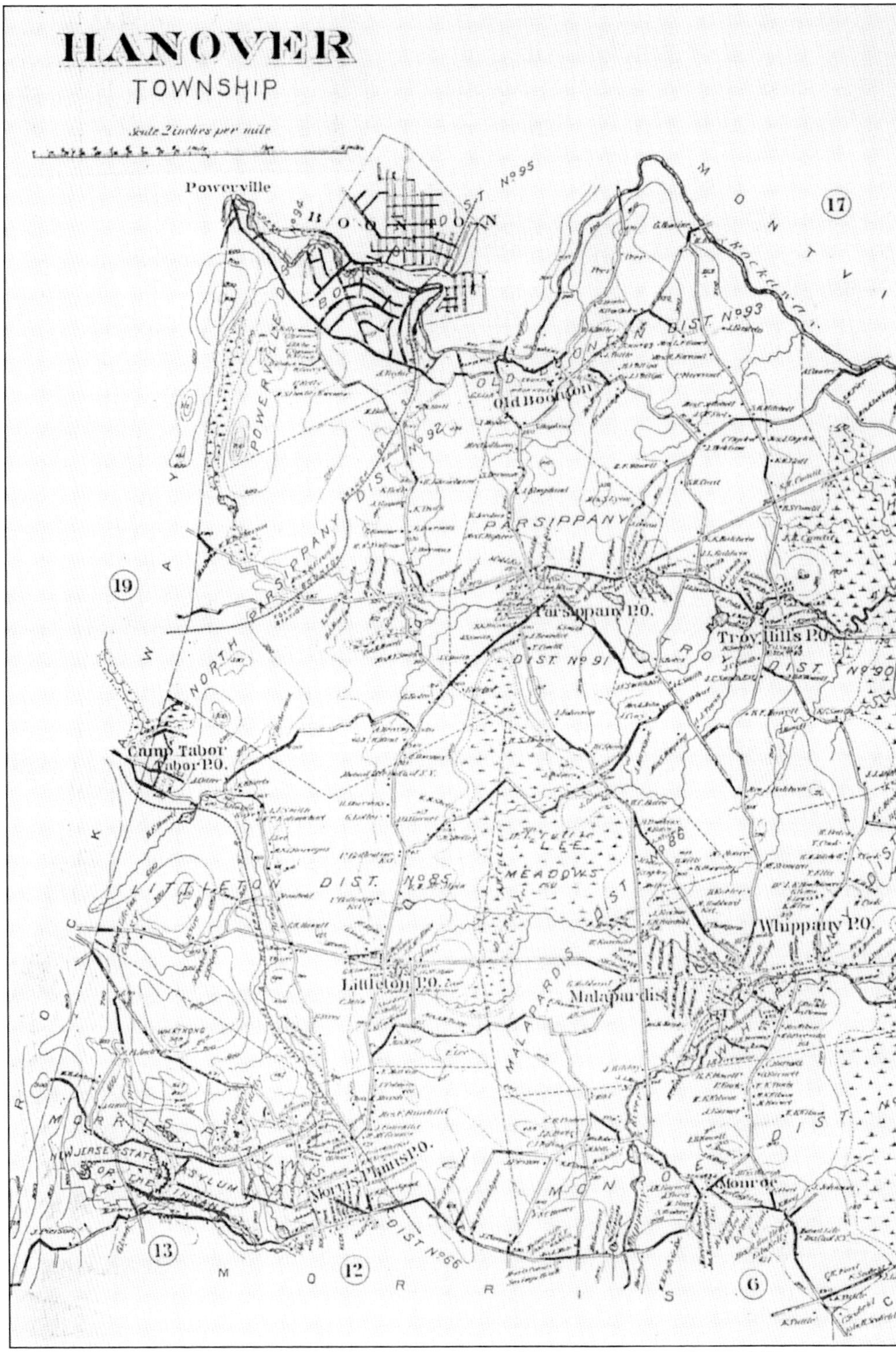

Detail of Robinson's 1887 map of Hanover Township. Parsippany-Troy Hills was part of Hanover Township until 1928. (Morris County Library.)

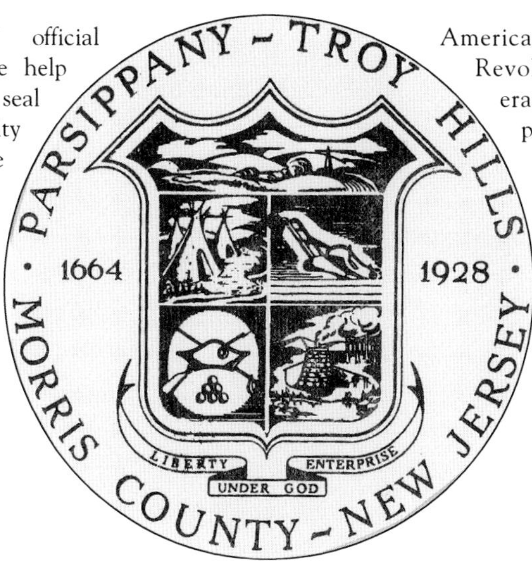

Parsippany-Troy Hills' official seal. Designed with the help of Estelle Condit, the seal portrays the community from the time of Native Americans through the Revolutionary War to the era of farming and dairy production. (Parsippany-Troy Hills Township.)

Introduction

The 25 square miles of Parsippany-Troy Hills is about 27 miles west of New York City. For thousands of years it was the home of the Lenni-Lenape Indians grouped into tribes called Whippanongs, Rockawacks, Hopatcongs, and Parsippanongs. The tribes' artists left a memento of their presence in rock drawings, called petroglyphs, off Park and Ellen Roads.

European settlers arrived in the eighteenth century and found excellent land, iron ore, many lakes and streams, and ample woodlands. They used timber for building homes and making charcoal (essential in processing iron). By 1743, John Cobb was operating a forge at Forge Pond in present-day Troy Hills and others swiftly followed his example. One of the first agricultural settlements was established by James Bollen, who owned 1,666 acres along today's South Beverwyck Road. The Motts, Smiths, Ogdens, Farrands, Mitchells, Howells, Cobbs, Tuttles, Baldwins, Condits, and Kitchells were original settlers. Some of their descendants still reside in Parsippany-Troy Hills.

From 1779 to 1780, General George Washington headquartered in Morristown. Since the Lucas von Beverhoudt estate was directly on the route from Morristown to West Point (a major military station), it became a favorite stopping place for the general, his officers, and his couriers. So frequently was this route traveled that Beverwyck Road was called Washington's Trail. Von Beverhoudt's wife, Maria, hosted gala balls at Beverwyck Mansion which were attended by Revolutionary War luminaries such as the Marquis de Lafayette, Alexander Hamilton, Brigadier General Henry Knox, and George Washington.

At the top of Pigeon Hill (Watnong Hill) was a beacon that was used to alert local militia of the approach of the British. This beacon site is number thirteen of twenty-three such historic markers left in New Jersey. The steps leading to the beacon off Mountain Way still remain.

From 1776 to 1780, New Jersey's first governor after the United States achieved its independence, William Livingston, made his home in what is today known as the Livingston-Benedict House. Here an assassination attempt on Governor Livingston was foiled. Located in a cozy corner of Old Parsippany Road, the home is owned by Helen Benedict Dutton, a Farrand descendant.

Rhoda Farrand became a local folk heroine when her husband, Lieutenant Bethuel Farrand, wrote to her that the troops in Morristown were desperate for warm socks. Acting immediately,

Rhoda got into an oxcart, and driven through the countryside by her son Dan, she exhorted her neighbors to knit stockings. All the while Rhoda knitted at a furious pace, completing one pair of hose each day. In one week she succeeded in motivating the ladies to knit a record 133 pairs. The soldiers were very grateful.

The town helped the patriots: farmers supplied produce; iron mill owners made shot, cannon, and kettles; and local men became soldiers. As testimony to this, there are eighteen valiant veterans of the Revolutionary War buried in the Parsippany Presbyterian Cemetery.

Built in 1870, the Condit house (located on the northeast corner of Beverwyck Road and Route 46), is listed on both the Federal and the New Jersey State Registers of Historic Places. This fine example of Gothic Victorian architecture has, unfortunately, fallen into disrepair.

Greystone Park has been caring for the mentally ill since 1876. Based on the humane treatment of the insane advocated by Dorothea Dix, Greystone holds the distinction of being the second institution of its type opened in New Jersey.

The Powder Mill section of town was home to Gustav Stickley and his Craftsman Farms. Settling here in 1911, Stickley is renowned for his "Mission"-style furniture, distinctive for sturdiness and simple beauty. Craftsman Farms is a federal landmark.

On the northwest side of Route 46 is a massive reservoir which serves Jersey City. Parsippany-Troy Hills gets its water from underground wells. In 1904, engineers flooded millions of gallons of water over Old Boonton, the iron works, Samuel Ogden's elegant home, and the Morris County Poor House.

The infirm, indigents, and orphans all lived together in the Poor House until February 4, 1882, when the twenty-two children were transferred to the Morris County Children's Home, once a mansion called Ailanthus Hall. The Children's Home was situated across from where the Jersey City Reservoir stands today and remained open until 1929. Orphans who died while in residency at the home were buried in the Little Lost Cemetery. This tiny plot of land, located behind the District 6 Firehouse, is the sole remnant left of the Children's Home.

Parsippany-Troy Hills, as a rural area in close proximity to metropolitan centers, was an ideal summer getaway. Taking advantage of the bucolic locale, Methodists established the Mount Tabor campground in 1869. Families came for rest and religious pilgrimage, renting tiny 16-by-25-foot tent sites. Accommodations were generally austere, although some of the wealthier visitors rented multiple sites and brought servants. In later years, cottages were substituted for tents, and the land was leased for ninety-nine years to each family. This charming community, with many gingerbread homes, is now inhabited year-round. The Mount Tabor Camp Meeting Association still leases, not sells, the land to residents.

After World War I, even more people were attracted by the area's rustic quality. The growth spurt led to the community's separation from Hanover Township, and in 1928, Parsippany-Troy Hills was born. Houses sprang up all around: in Rainbow Lakes (1922); Manor Lake and Lake Hiawatha (1930); and Lake Intervale and Lake Parsippany (1933). The *New York Daily Mirror* offered 20-by-100-foot lots on Lake Parsippany for $98.50 as a bonus with a six month subscription to the newspaper. In 1949, an industrial complex and the Sedgefield development were built on the former estate of Newark brewer Peter Ballantine. With increasing frequency summer homeowners converted their houses into all-year residences.

The opportunity for jobs in the community, its close proximity to major cities, the improved and modernized modes of transportation, and city housing shortages during the 1940s and '50s brought increasing numbers of people into our area. Thus began the commuter lifestyle of our community.

Today, Parsippany-Troy Hills is a thriving town of 48,478 inhabitants (according to the 1990 census). There are 5,657 rental apartments, 1,289 condos, and many private homes. Parsippany-Troy Hills is a hub of major highways (Routes 53, 202, 80, 46, 287, 280, and 10) and the headquarters of numerous national and international businesses.

But, this book is dedicated to a Parsippany-Troy Hills remembered in simpler times.

One

Founding Families

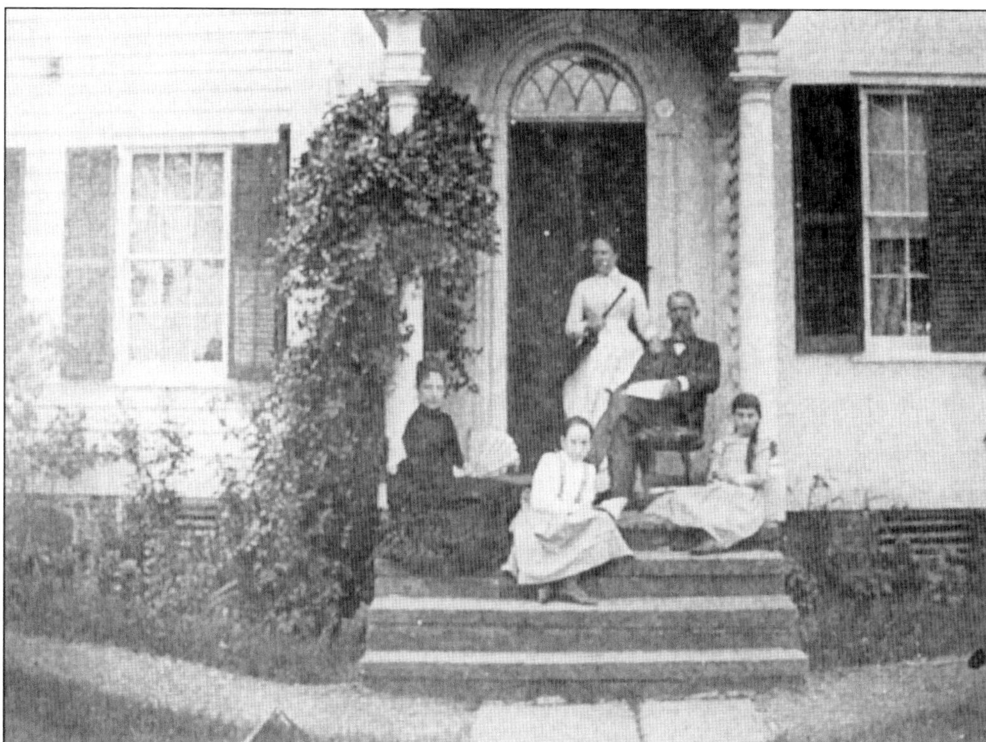

The Richard Smith family on the front porch of their home at 460 South Beverwyck Road in Troy, New Jersey, c. 1886. Mr. Smith was the grandson of Colonel Hiram Smith and Eleanor Parrott Smith, and the son of Hiram Smith Jr. and Mary Allen Osborn Smith. (Mr. and Mrs. Richard S. Baldwin.)

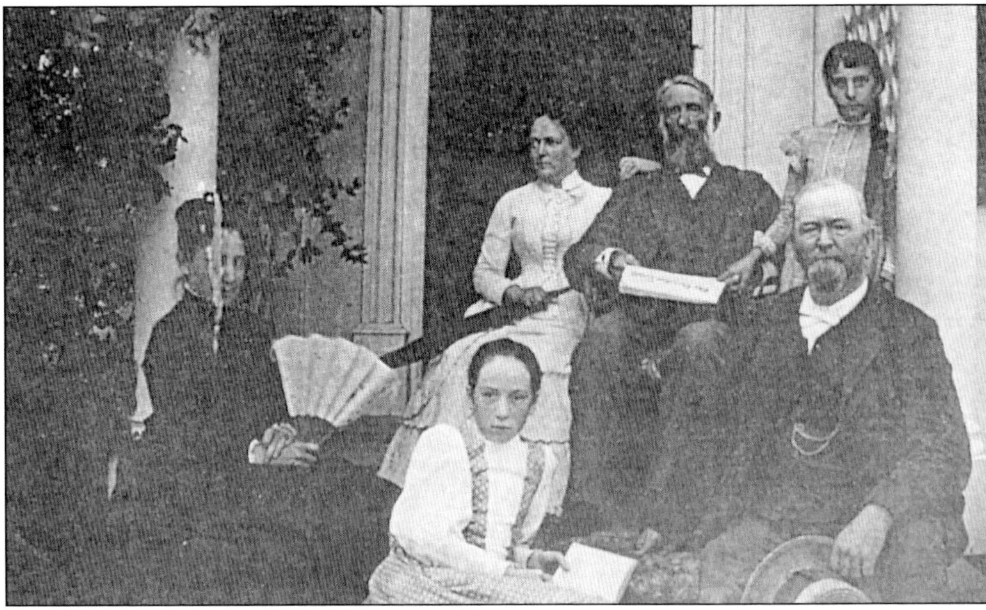

The Smith family. From left to right are as follows: (front row) Mary Smith (1844–1939), Emily C. Smith (1876–1956), and unidentified; (back row) Emily W. Smith (1849–1904), Richard Smith (1838–1891), and Marjorie White Smith Baldwin (1878–1952). *See Historic Homes.* (Mr. and Mrs. Richard S. Baldwin.)

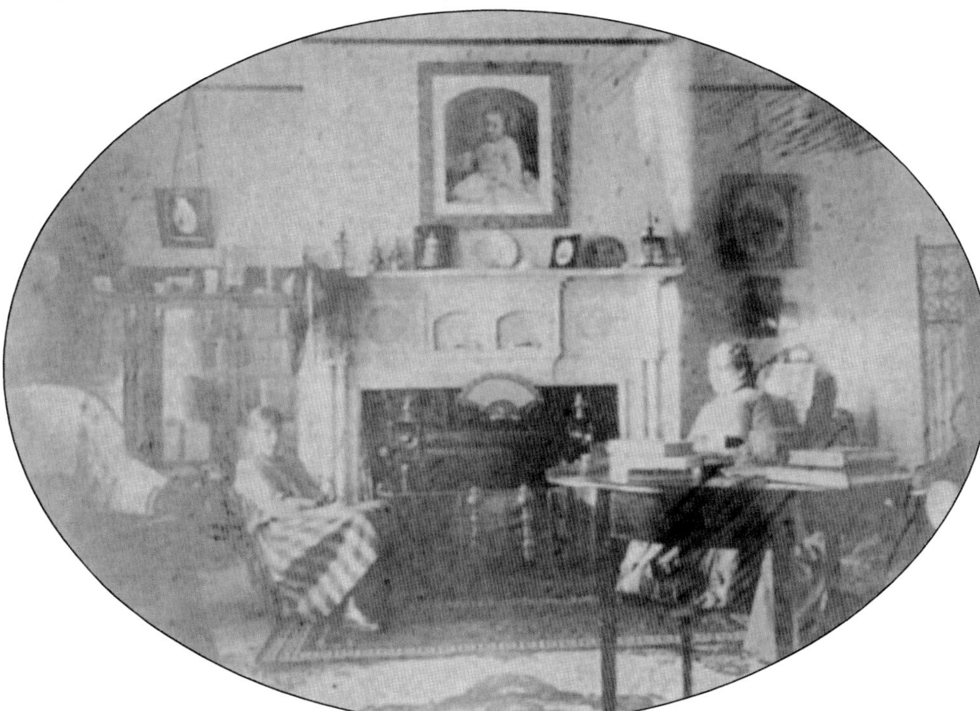

The back parlor at the Old Home (the Smith-Baldwin House). Shown here are Marjorie S. Baldwin and her mother, Emily W. Smith. The house still has the original fireplace mantle. (Mr. and Mrs. Richard S. Baldwin.)

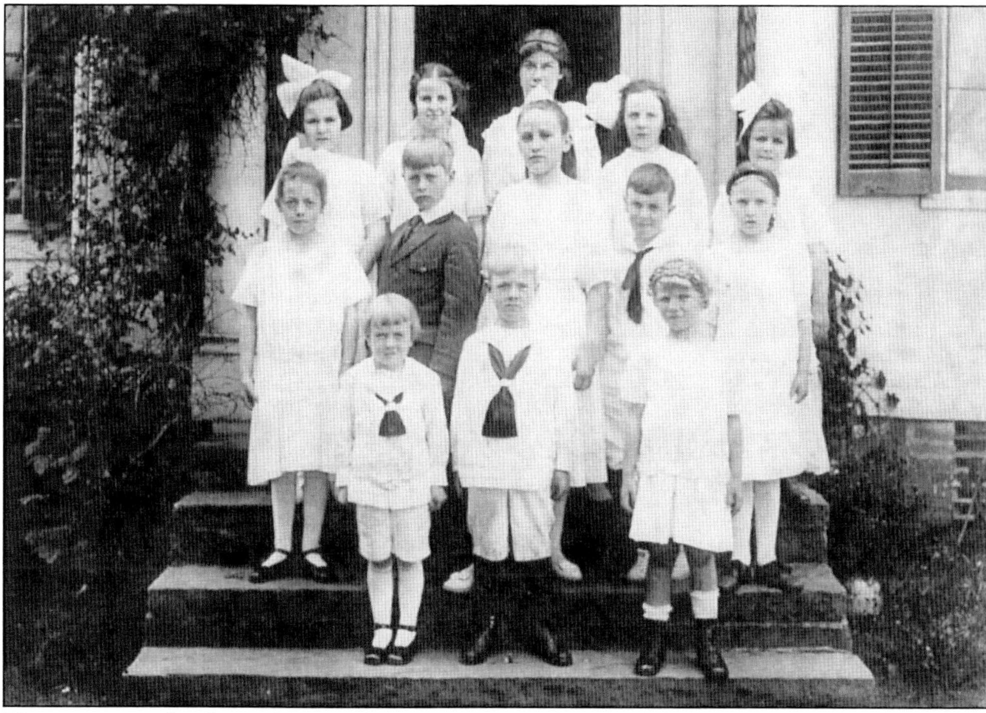

The private school at the Smith House, June 1916. From left to right are as follows: (front row) Arthur Paulniere Jr., Jack Crowell, and Elizabeth Mitchell; (middle row) Florence Condit, Fred Crowell Jr., Irene Kitchell, Horace Paulniere, and Adelaide Baldwin; (back row) Frances Cobb, Emily Baldwin, Florence Howell Prish (teacher), Margaret Brown, and Katherine Mitchell. (Mr. and Mrs. Richard S. Baldwin.)

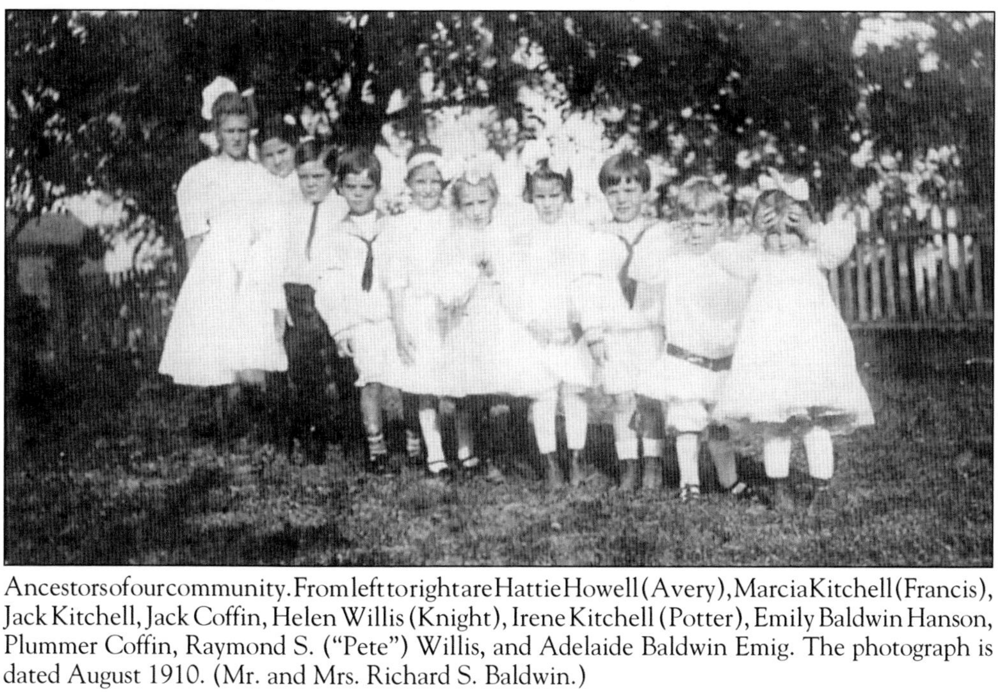

Ancestors of our community. From left to right are Hattie Howell (Avery), Marcia Kitchell (Francis), Jack Kitchell, Jack Coffin, Helen Willis (Knight), Irene Kitchell (Potter), Emily Baldwin Hanson, Plummer Coffin, Raymond S. ("Pete") Willis, and Adelaide Baldwin Emig. The photograph is dated August 1910. (Mr. and Mrs. Richard S. Baldwin.)

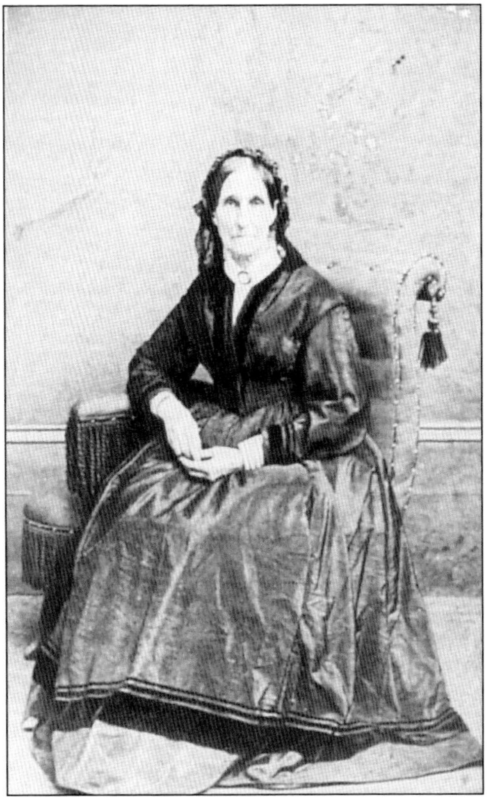

Hyla Mitchell Ogden (1806–1882), wife of Samuel Farrand Ogden (1806–1835). These 2-by-3.5-inch photographs, called *carte de vistes*, were left as calling cards when visitors stopped at the house of a friend. The photographs were usually placed in a receptacle in the foyer of the home. *See Historic Homes*. (Parsippany-Troy Hills Public Library, Condit Room.)

Mary Caroline Ogden Pierson (*c*. 1815–?), wife of Aaron Pierson and sister of John and Samuel Farrand Ogden. On the right is Mary's son, Steven Pierson. The Piersons were a long-established family whose members intermarried with other well-known families of the area. (Parsippany-Troy Hills Public Library, Condit Room.)

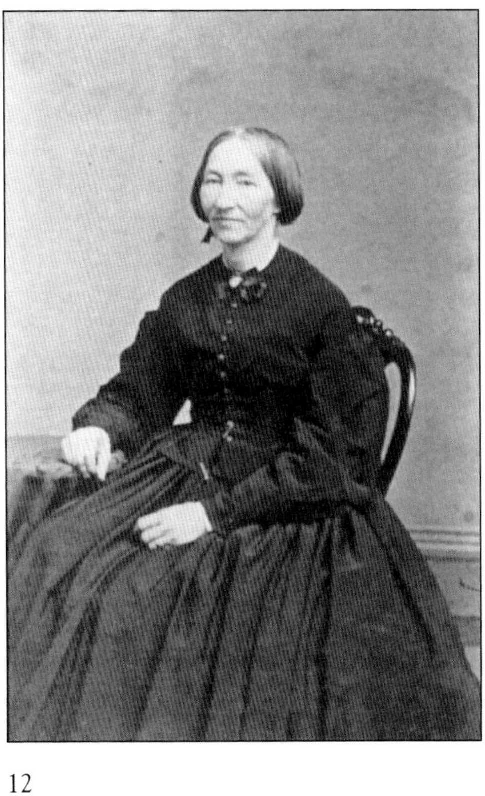

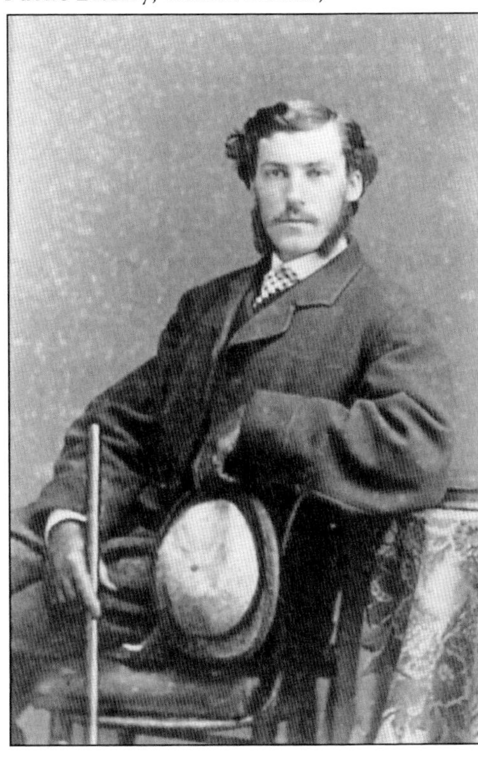

John Ogden (1817–1885), brother of Samuel Farrand Ogden and Mary Ogden Pierson. John married Frances Ford, daughter of Reverend John Ford and Caroline S. Darcy Ford. (Parsippany-Troy Hills Public Library, Condit Room.)

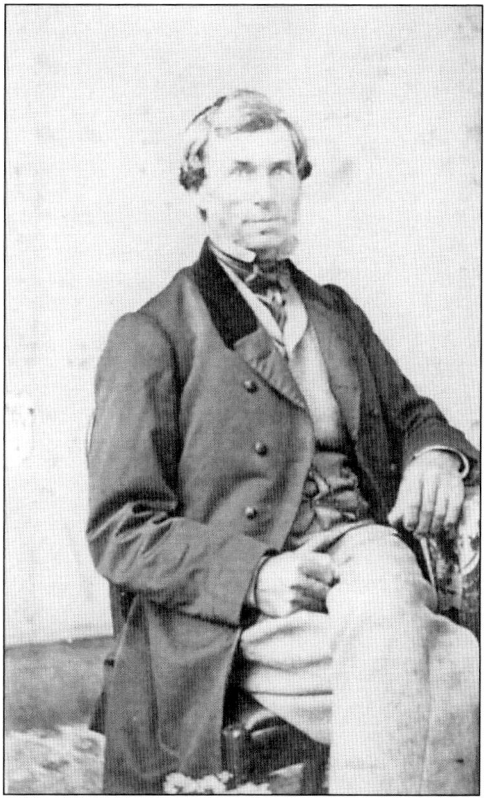

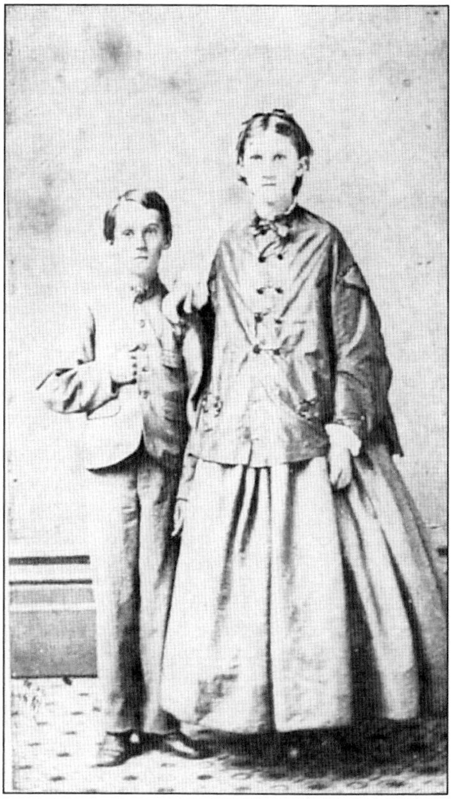

Sue Ogden (1851–1916) and John Ogden II. Sue was married to Phineas Farrand (1838–1915), and was the daughter of John Ogden and Frances Ford Ogden. (Parsippany-Troy Hills Public Library, Condit Room.)

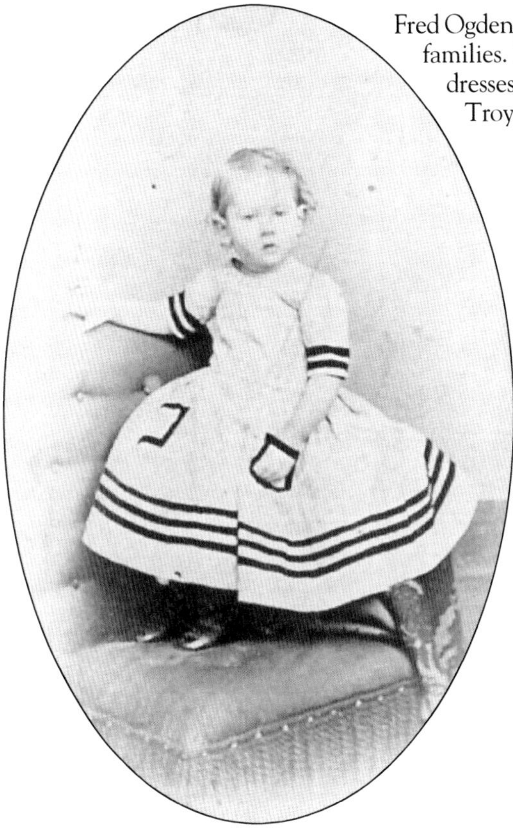

Fred Ogden, *c.* 1880. Ogden was related to prominent local families. It was the custom of the time for boys to wear dresses sometimes up until the age of five. (Parsippany-Troy Hills Public Library, Condit Room.)

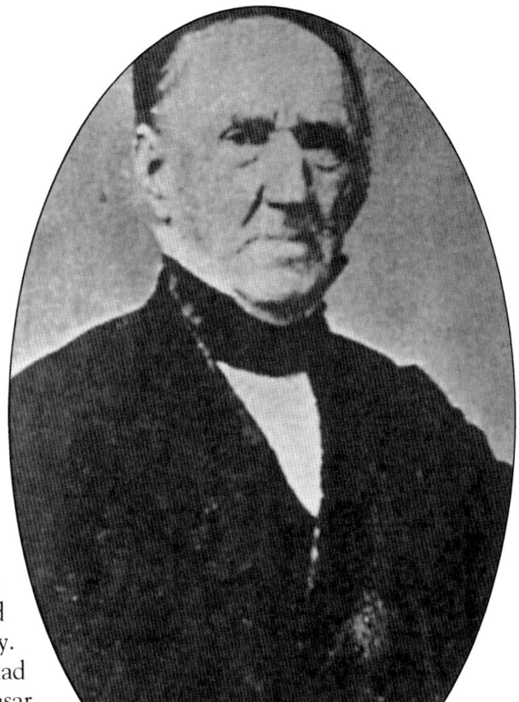

Reverend John Ford (1787–1872). Ford's first wife was Caroline S. Darcy and his second was Jane Howell. He was a graduate of Princeton (officially called The College of New Jersey until 1896) and was minister of the Parsippany Presbyterian Church from 1816 to 1857. From 1816 to 1825 Reverend Ford served as principal of the African School, an institution that prepared young black men for the Presbyterian ministry. One known graduate of the school, which had seven students in 1819, was Gustavus V. Ceasar. This unique facility never flourished; the school closed in 1825 and its work was transferred to the African Education Society in New Brunswick, New Jersey. (Fran Kaminski.)

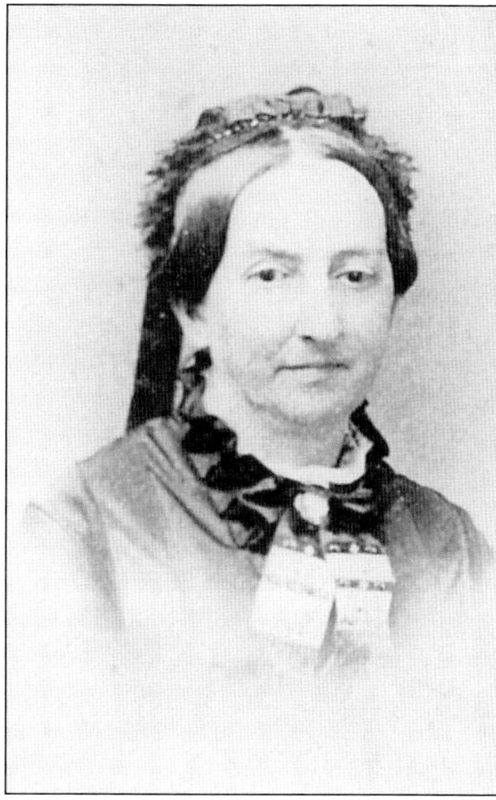

Mary Ford Condit (1821–1906), c. 1870. Mary Ford was the daughter of Reverend John Ford and the wife of William Condit (1816–1881), farmer and elder of Parsippany Presbyterian Church. Mary Ford Condit was active in the church and a charter member of the Daughters of the American Revolution (DAR). (Parsippany-Troy Hills Public Library, Condit Room.)

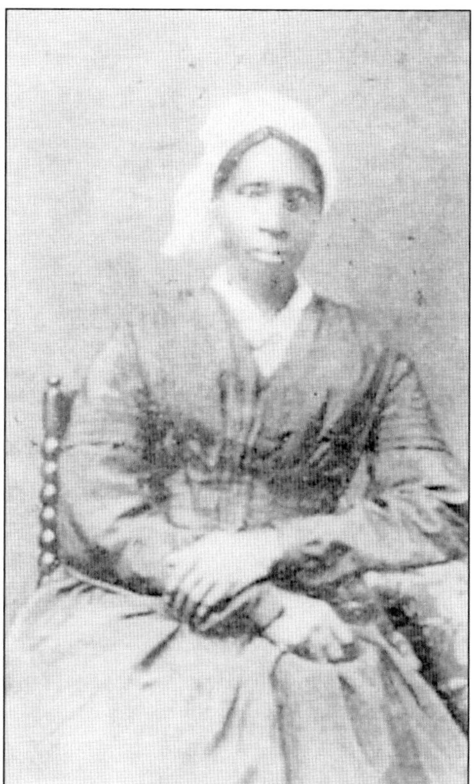

"Aunt" Peggie. Written on back of this photograph is the following: "Aunt Peggie's picture taken when I [Mary Josephine Condit] was a girl. She and her family lived with grandfather Ogden. her [*sic*] children were borne [*sic*] there, a large family." When Rebecca Farrand (1784–1848) married Aaron Ogden (1783–1848), she received Peggie as a wedding gift from Lucas Van Beverhoudt. During the ceremony, Peggie carried the train of her new mistress's gown. Later in 1829, even after being given their freedom papers, "Aunt" Peggie, her husband Cuff, and their children preferred to remain on the estate with the Ogdens. (Parsippany-Troy Hills Public Library, Condit Room.)

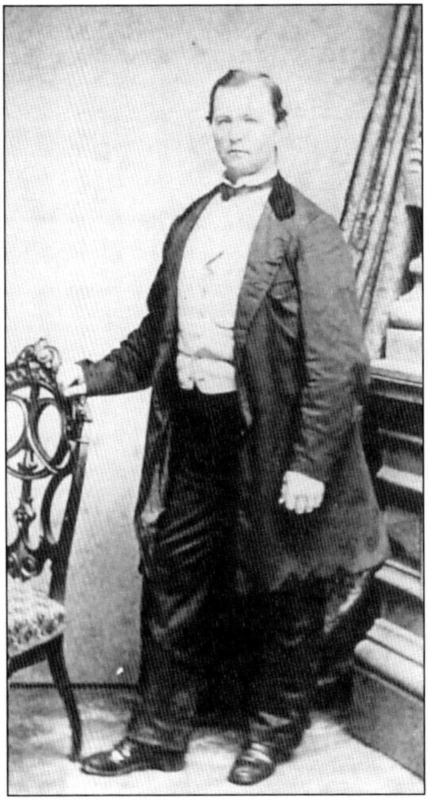

Thomas O. Smith (1825–1892), brother of Richard Smith. Smith's first wife was Mary Green and his second was Annie Ogden. *See Historic Homes*. (Parsippany-Troy Hills Public Library, Condit Room.)

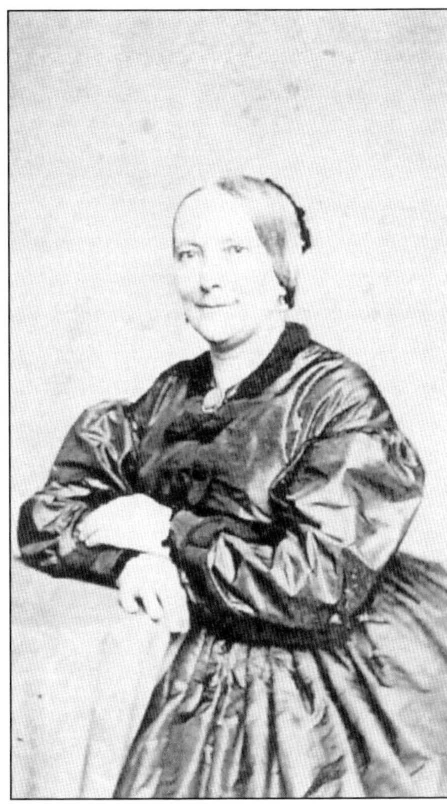

Ann R. Ogden Smith (1833–?), second wife of Thomas O. Smith. Ann was the daughter of Samuel Farrand Ogden and Hyla Mitchell. (Parsippany-Troy Hills Public Library, Condit Room.)

Thomas (Tom) Smith Jr. (1865–1925), son of Ann and Thomas O. Smith. Tom married Mary Eliza Condit (1867–1958), daughter of Melvin Smith Condit of Boonton. Tom and Mary are buried in the Parsippany Presbyterian Cemetery. (Parsippany-Troy Hills Public Library, Condit Room.)

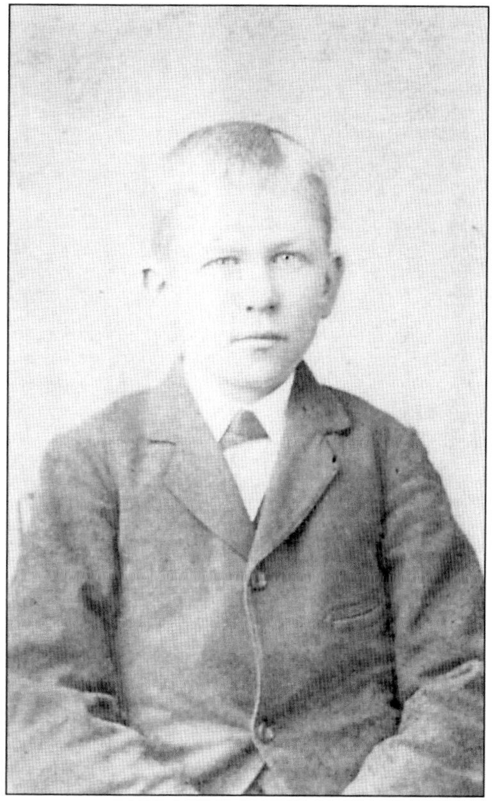

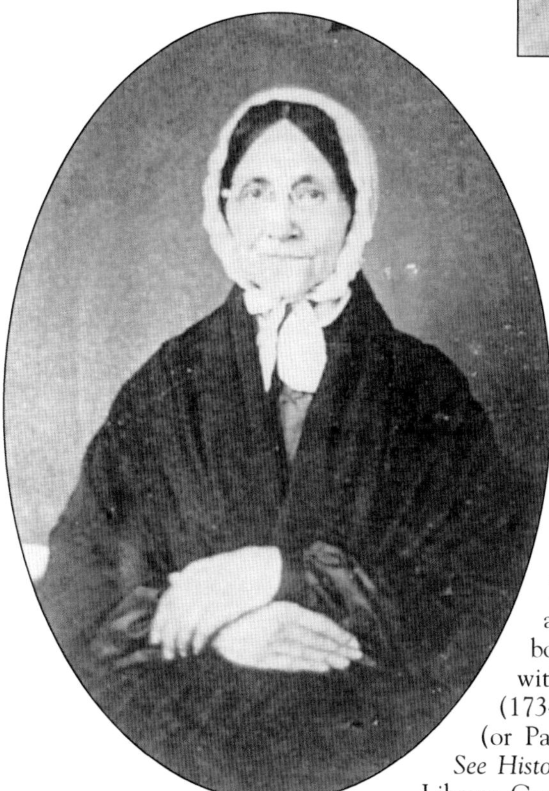

Sarah (Susan) Farrand Condit (1788–1854), wife of Benjamin L. Condit (1782–1852) and mother of William Condit. Called "Sucky," Sarah was the daughter of Mary (Polly) Howell Farrand (1759–1832) and Samuel Farrand (1757–1788). She was born on the day her father died. She lived with her mother and grandparents, Ebenezer (1734–1807) and Rebecca (1738–1883) Parrott (or Parritt), in the Farrand-Condit-Ball home. *See Historic Homes*. (Parsippany-Troy Hills Public Library, Condit Room.)

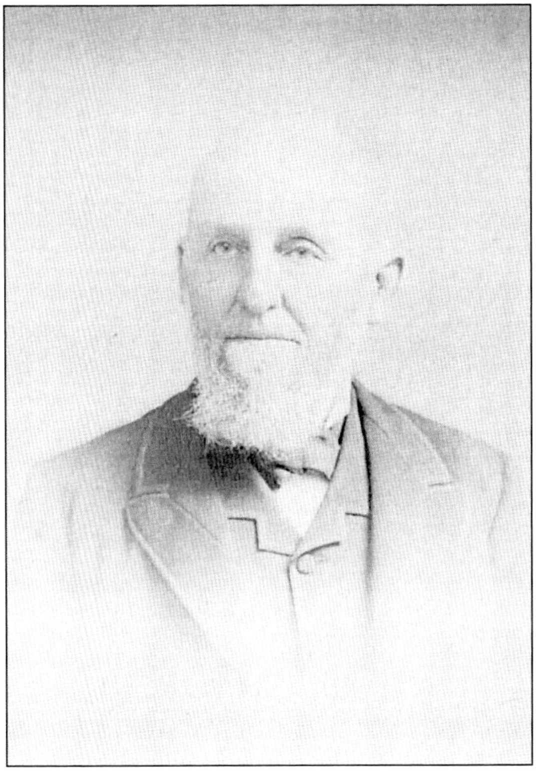

Benjamin Smith Condit (1832–1903), husband of Sarah Augusta DeHart and brother of John Howell Condit and Stephen Hobart Condit. Benjamin was given the same name as a brother who had died at the age of two, a common practice of the time. He was a farmer, and lived with his family in the Beverwyck Mansion. *See Historic Homes*. (Parsippany-Troy Hills Public Library, Condit Room.)

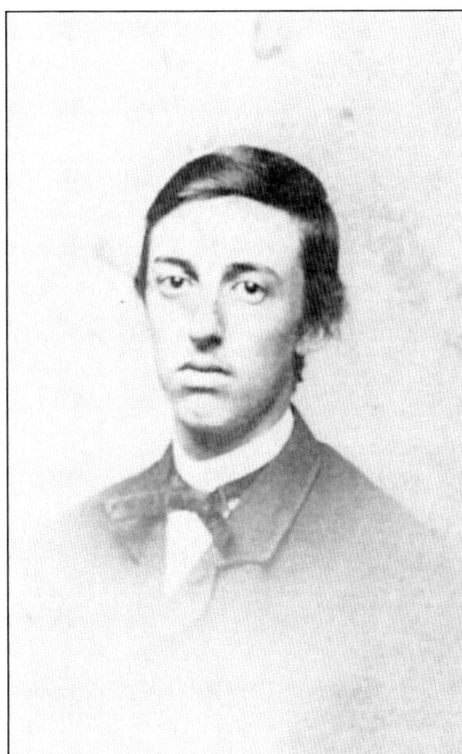

Charles DeHart Condit (1870–1947), husband of Florence Bates and son of Benjamin S. Condit. Charles lived in the Beverwyck Mansion. His daughter, Florence Bates Condit, was the last Condit to occupy the mansion. (Parsippany-Troy Hills Public Library, Condit Room.)

John Howell Condit (1835–1902), husband of Caroline Bostedo and brother of Benjamin Smith Condit and Stephen Hobart Condit. (Parsippany-Troy Hills Public Library, Condit Room.)

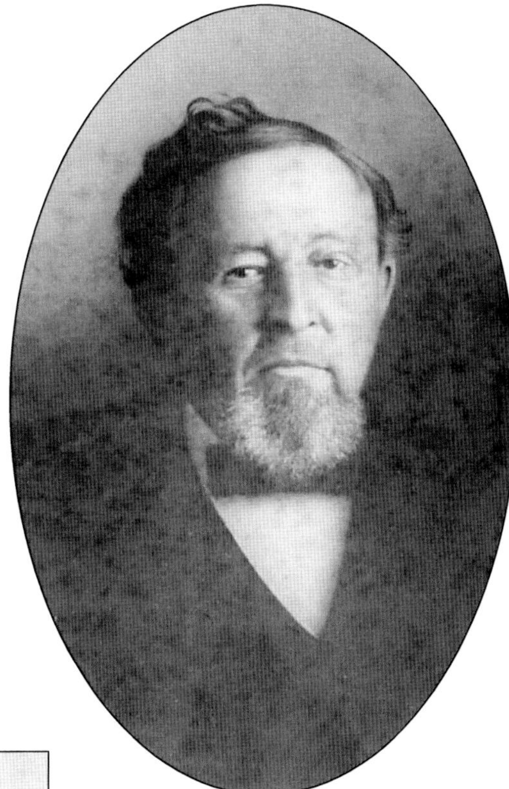

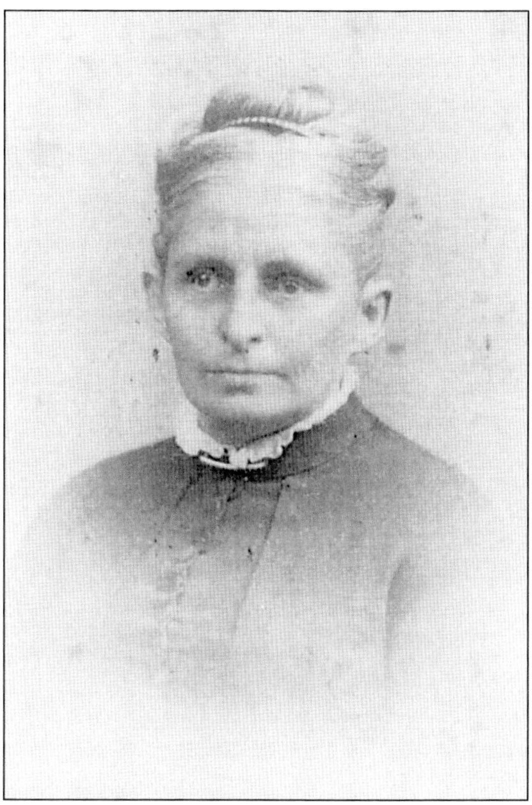

Susan Margaret Condit (1833–1906), wife of Charles F. Ogden (1832–1914) and sister of Stephen Hobart Condit, Benjamin Condit, and John Howell Condit. (Parsippany-Troy Hills Public Library, Condit Room.)

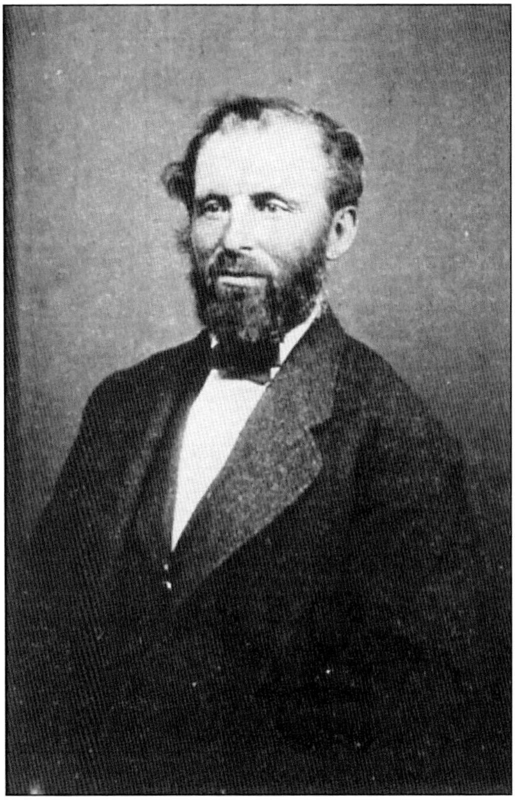

Stephen Hobart Condit (1830–1909), husband of Mary Josephine Ogden and grandfather of Stephen Hobart Condit. He was beloved by all, and known as "one of the most successful farmers in Morris County during the 19th century." Stephen built the Condit House at 41 North Beverwyck Road. *See Historic Homes*. (Parsippany-Troy Hills Public Library, Condit Room.)

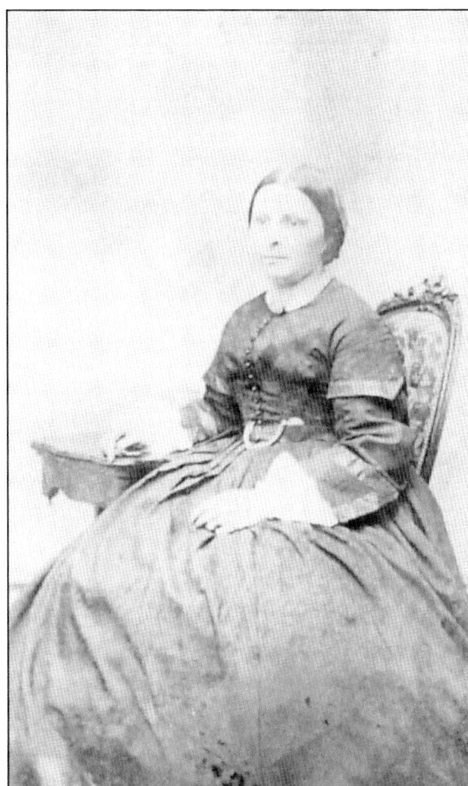

Mary Josephine Ogden Condit (1835–1916), wife of Stephen Hobart Condit and daughter of Samuel Farrand Ogden and Hyla Mitchell Ogden. (Parsippany-Troy Hills Public Library, Condit Room.)

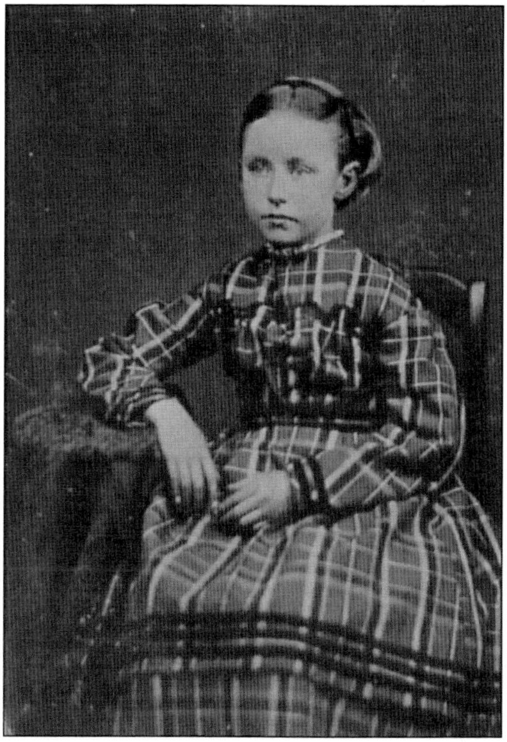

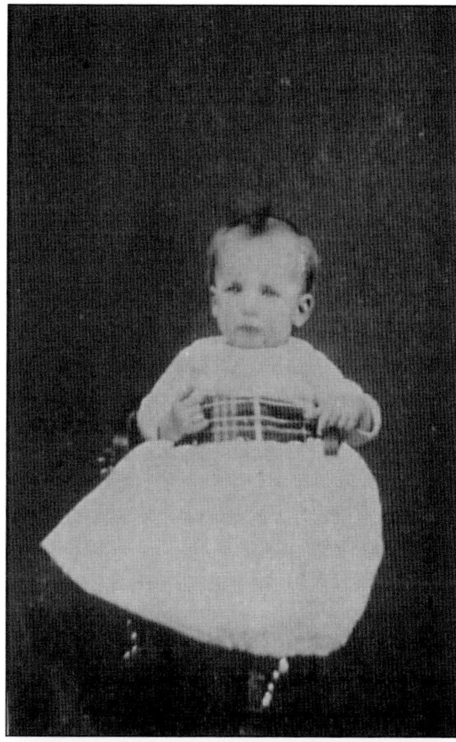

Children of Mary Josephine and Stephen Hobart Condit, *c.* 1872. On the upper left is Elizabeth Smith Condit Mitchell (1862–1924), wife of Stephen Hobart Mitchell, and on the upper right is Harry Hobart Condit (1871–1941), who married Julia A. Osborne. To the lower right are John Ogden Condit (1866–1888) and Judd Condit (1868–1936). (Parsippany-Troy Hills Public Library, Condit Room.)

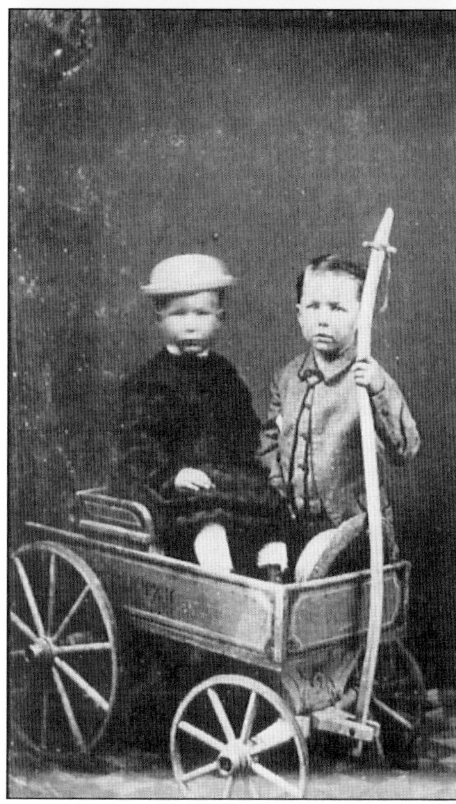

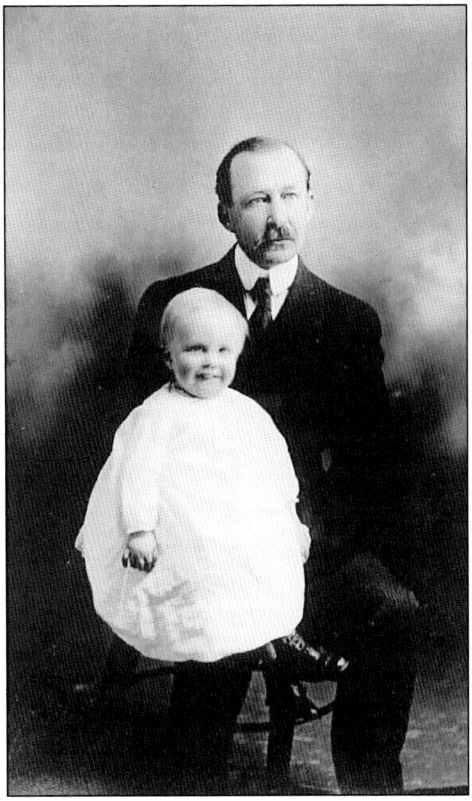

Judd Condit, husband of Estelle Bleu Turquand, and his son, Stephen Hobart Condit, c. 1910. As a member of the Hanover Township Committee (Council), Judd was actively involved in the drive for the separation of Parsippany-Troy Hills from Hanover Township. He inherited 41 South Beverwyck Road. *See Historic Homes*. (Parsippany-Troy Hills Public Library, Condit Room.)

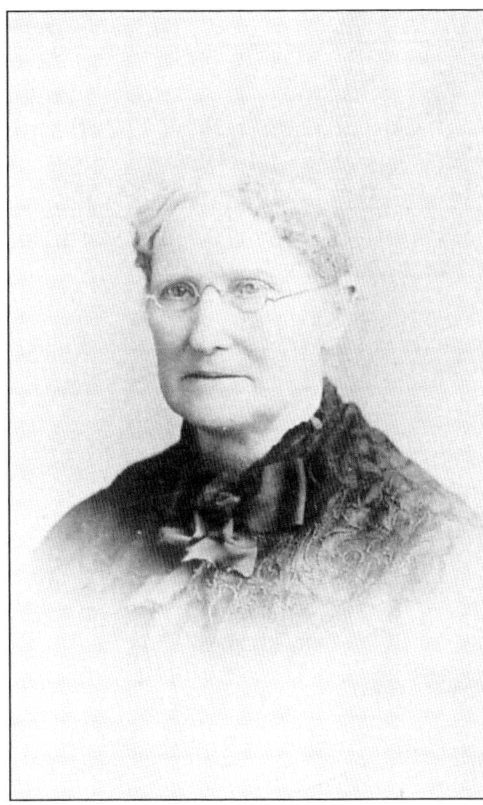

Sarah Elizabeth Bleu Turquand (1817–1895), wife of Paul Leonard Turquand and grandmother of Estelle Condit, c. 1890. (Parsippany-Troy Hills Public Library, Condit Room.)

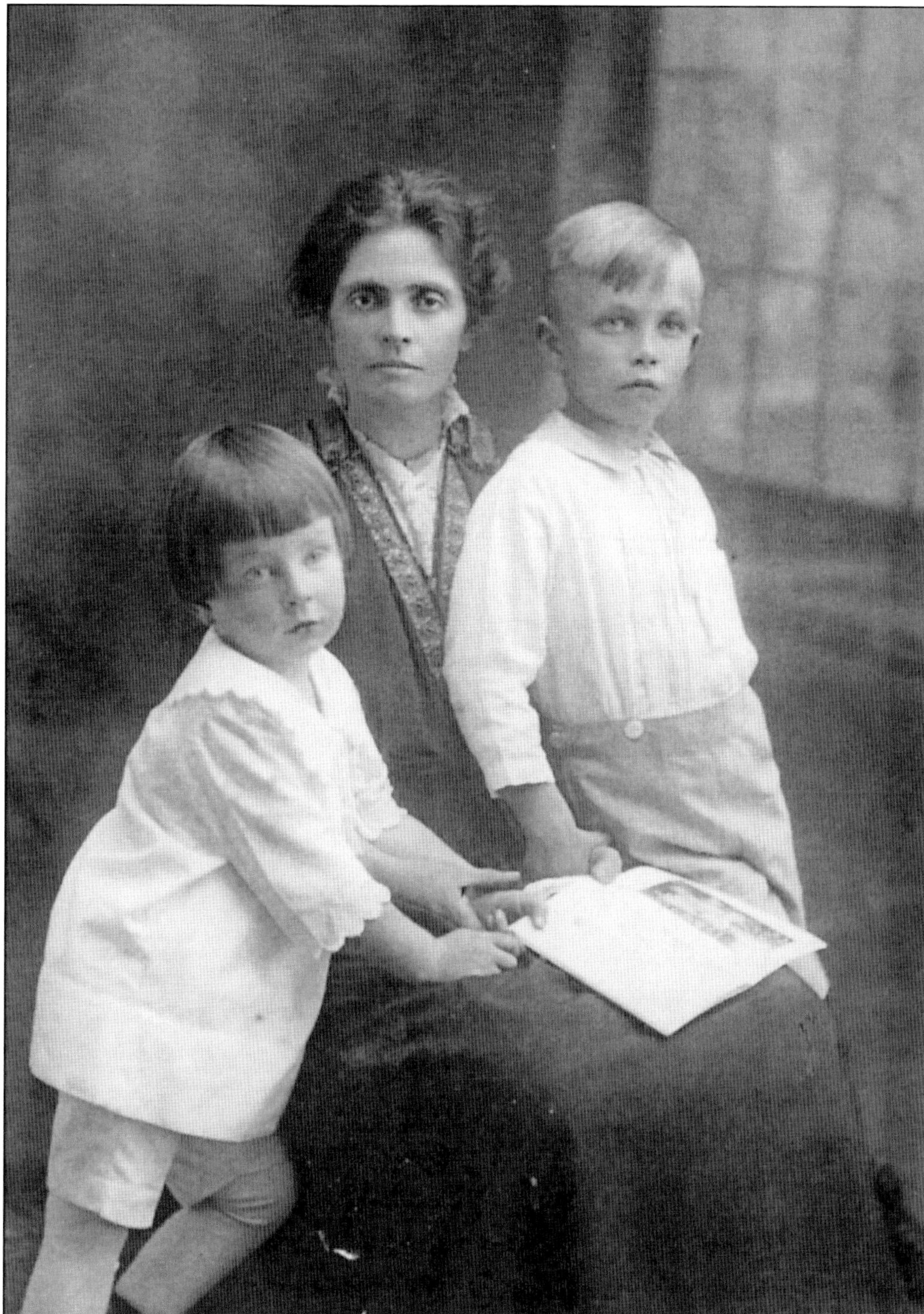

Estelle Turquand Condit (1878–1969) and her sons, Paul Hobart (1912–1930, to the left) and Stephen Hobart (1909–1983, standing), *c.* 1920. She was a schoolteacher, regent, and historian of the Parsippany DAR, as well as the wife of Judd Condit. (Parsippany-Troy Hills Public Library, Condit Room.)

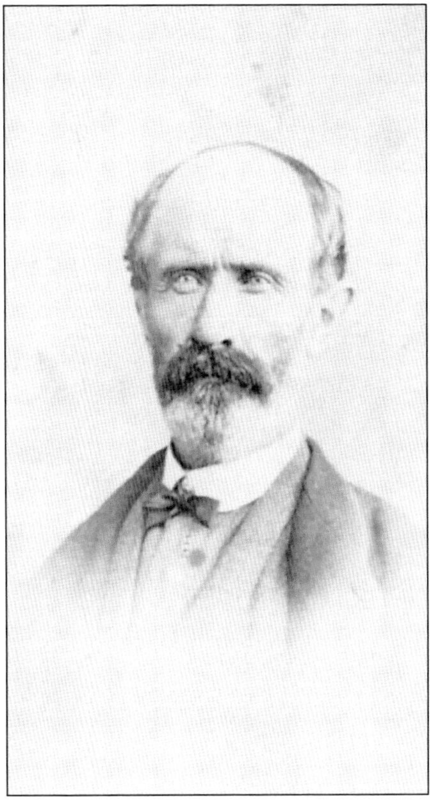

John Mitchell, who was related to prominent local families. (Parsippany-Troy Hills Public Library, Condit Room.)

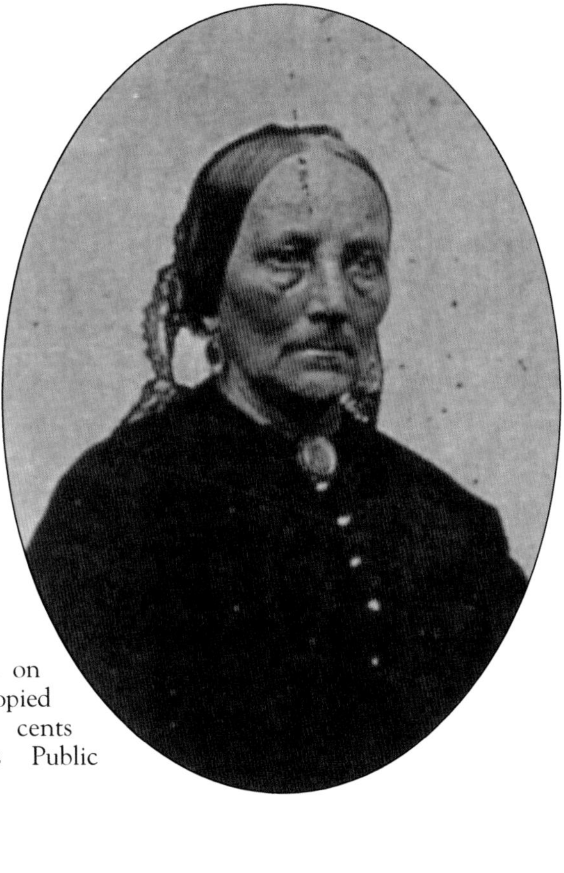

Mrs. John Mitchell, *c.* 1875. Written on the back of this image, which was copied from a tintype, were the words "25 cents per dozen." (Parsippany-Troy Hills Public Library, Condit Room.)

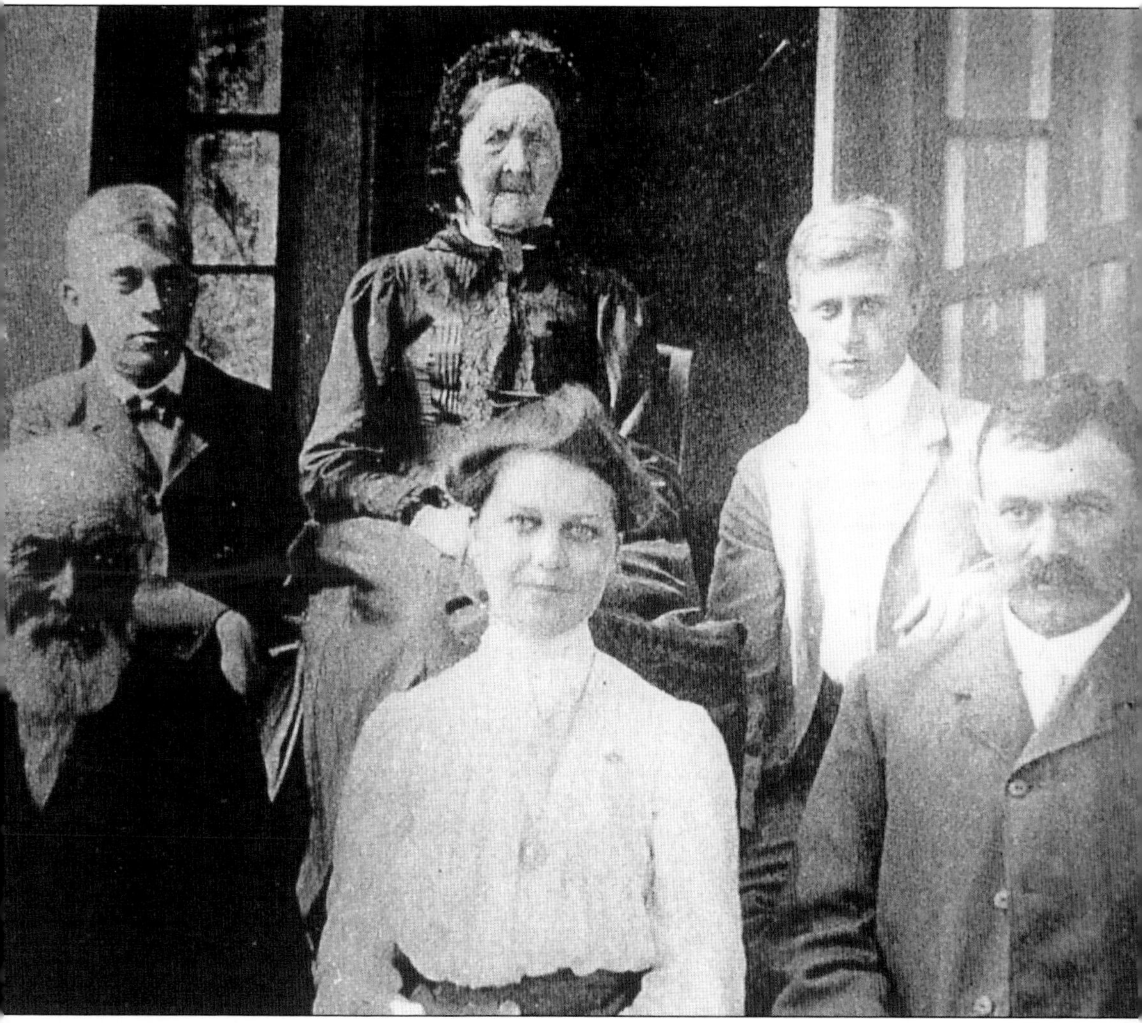

The Doremus family in a photograph dated 1903. From left to right are as follows: (front row) Abraham Doremus (Sarah's son, with beard), Naomi Doremus (sister of Elias), and John August Doremus (father of Elias and grandfather of Donald); (back row) John Munson (cousin, with bow tie), Sarah Hall Doremus, and Elias Doremus (father of Donald Doremus). The Doremus family lived at 243 Intervale Road, were farmers, and raised sheep on 200 acres of land. (Muriel Berson.)

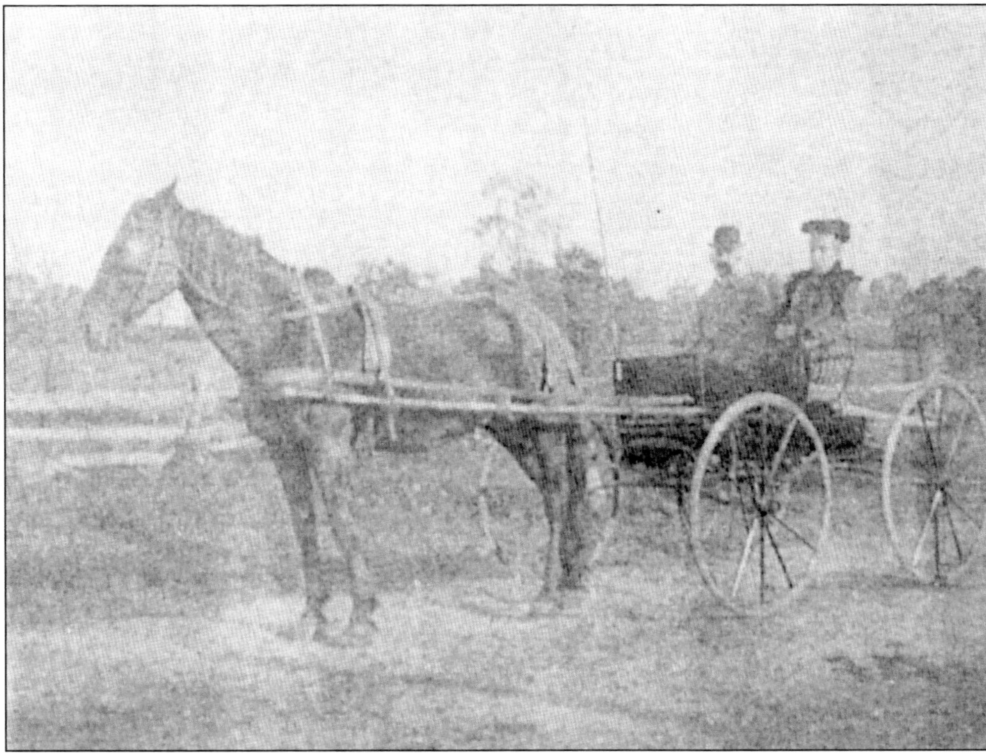

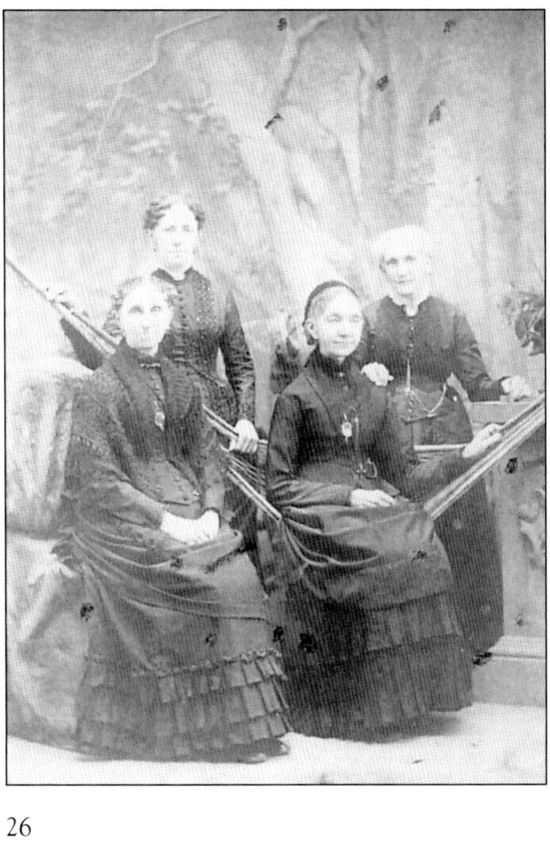

Edward Halsey Ball and Annette Cotton Howell Ball, grandparents of Harold O. Farrand, c. 1860. Annette Ball wrote a history of her church and was active in the DAR. E. Halsey Ball (1855–1941) was a farmer, the proprietor of a general store, active in civic affairs, and tax collector of Hanover Township for twenty years. (Harold O. Farrand.)

The Stevens sisters (relatives of the Farrands), c. 1880. From left to right are Ann Newell, Caroline Smith, Harriet Farrand (the wife of Dr. R.S. Farrand), and Maria D. Stevens. (Harold O. Farrand.)

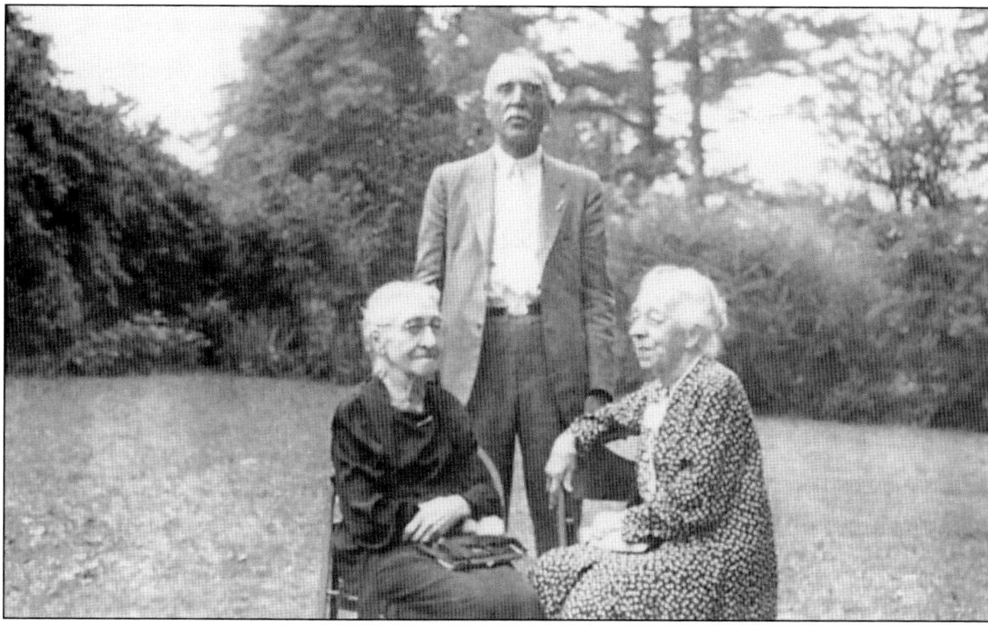

Grandchildren of Benjamin Howell. From left to right are Elizabeth Howell Mitchell (1857–1943), Richard Howell (1870–1943), and Annette Cotton Howell Ball (1850–1947), who was the author of the *History of the Presbyterian Church*. This photograph was taken c. 1930. (Harold O. Farrand.)

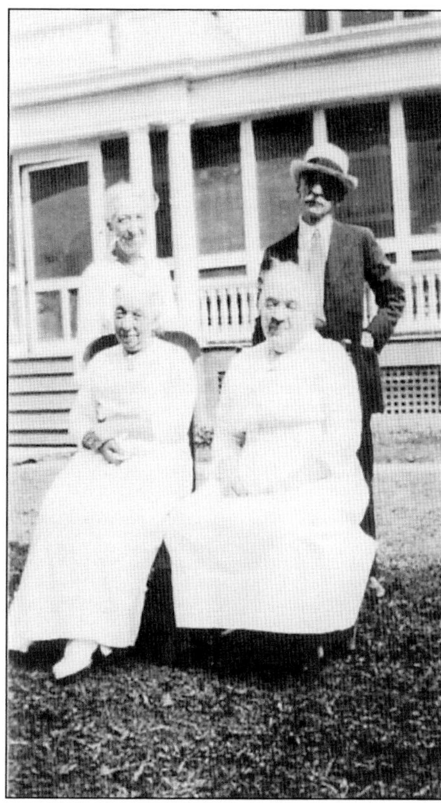

Monroe Howell II (1860–1927) and his sisters. Howell was the first property owner to allow electric lines to cross his property at 420 South Beverwyck Road. He was also postmaster of Troy Hills. Initially the area was simply called Troy, but mail was so often misdirected to Troy, New York, and vice versa, that to avoid this confusion Troy became Troy Hills. Sitting from left to right are Annette Cotton Howell Ball and Maria ("Aunt Cliff") Clifford Howell Kitchell (1865–1930). Standing from left to right are Elizabeth Howell Mitchell and Monroe Howell. *See Historic Homes*. (Harold O. Farrand.)

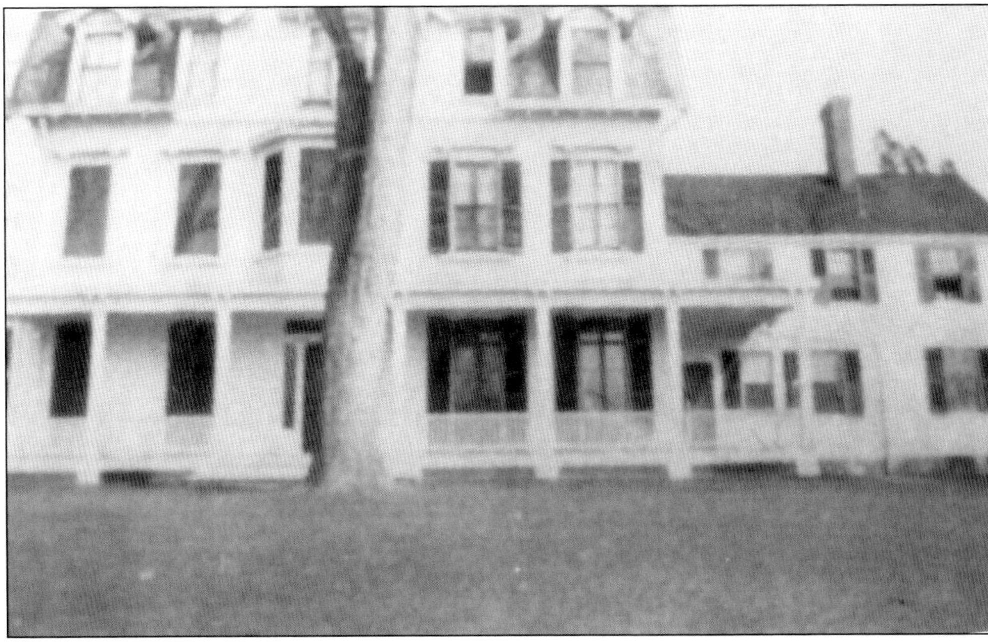

The Silas Condict House on Littleton Road (Route 202), built *c.* 1810. Silas Condict was a farmer, a patriot in the Revolutionary War, a member of the Continental Congress, and speaker of the Jersey House of Assembly from 1792 to 1794 and again in 1797. The last bear to be sighted in this area was seen from the kitchen window of the Condict House. (Joint Free Public Library of Morristown and Morris Township.)

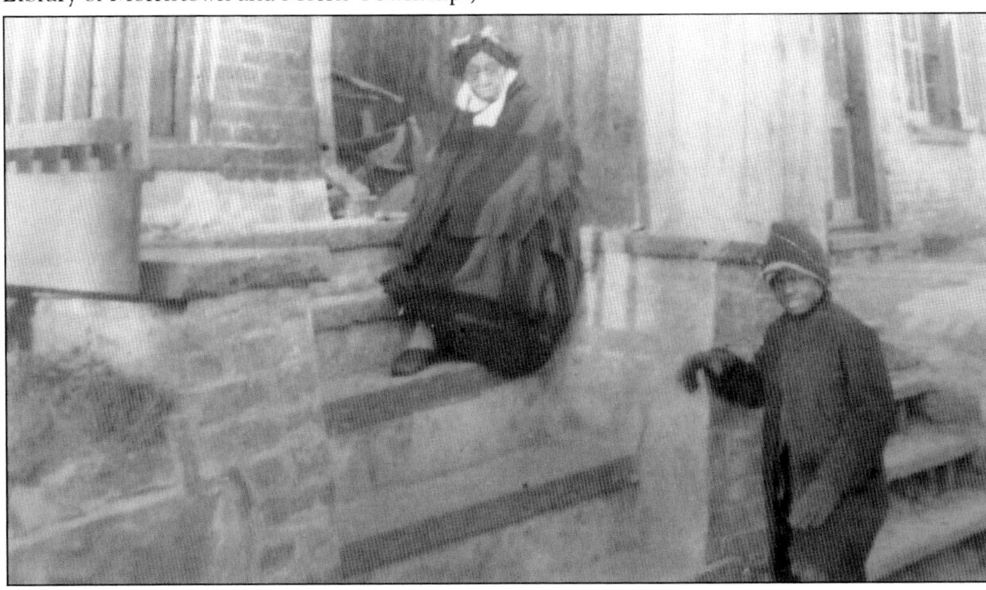

Old Silvey, a slave of Silas Condict (the original spelling of Condit), b. 1785 and shown here in a photo dated December 25, 1890. She received her freedom before the Civil War but remained with the family and became salaried. When she got too old to work, the family supported her for the rest of her life. She was a member of the first Sunday school in Morris County (the Littleton School), which was run by Mrs. Silas Condict. *See Founding Families.* (Joint Free Public Library of Morristown and Morris Township.)

Grandma Bowlsby, who was related to prominent local families. *See Historic Homes*. (Fran Kaminski.)

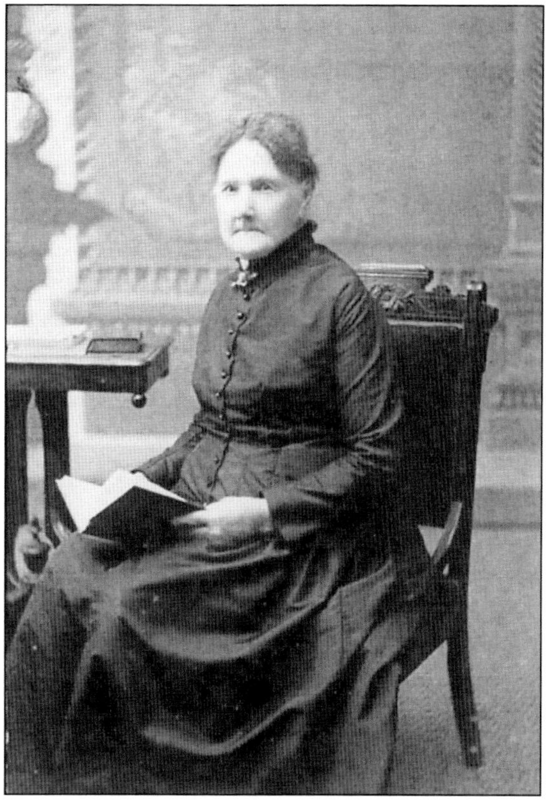

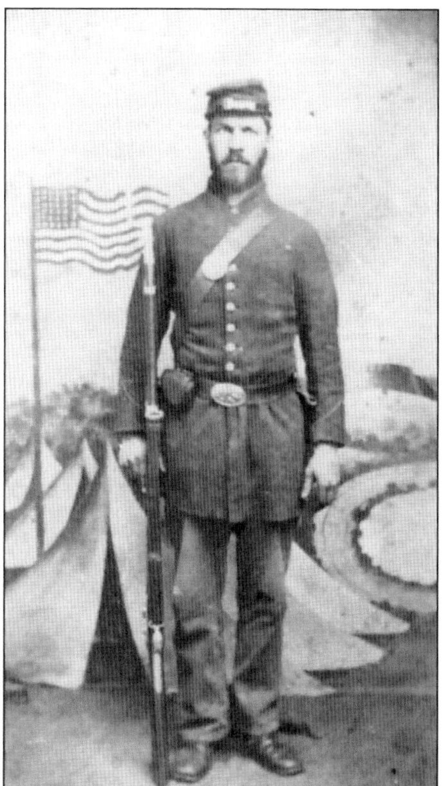

Private William Van Fleet (1836–1864). Van Fleet left his wife, Anna Doremus, and three small daughters to enlist in Company H (later Company K) of the First New Jersey Volunteers. He died at Spotsylvania Court House, Virginia, on May 12, 1864, one of 12,000 Union casualties of the campaign. The battle at Spotsylvania Court House was the only one he fought in; he was twenty-eight years old. (Fran Kaminski.)

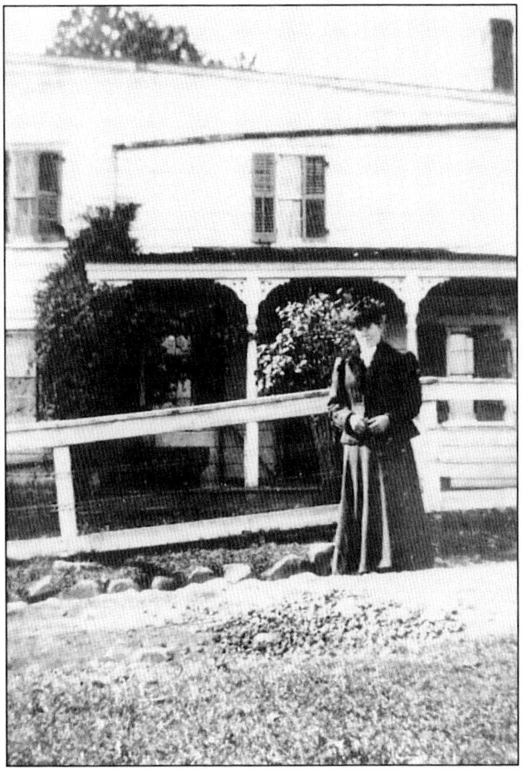

Bessie McGovern Smith from Ireland (mother of Florence Smith), in front of the Keeler House on 755 Smith Road, *c.* 1891. The Cases owned the home until the 1980s. The house is still standing. (Muriel Berson.)

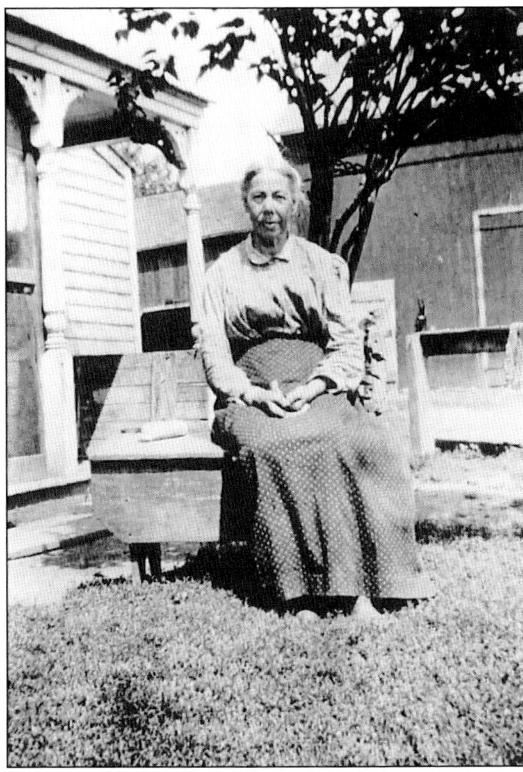

Grandma Smith Corey in front of the George Smith-Corey House. George Smith was a laborer at the Jersey City Reservoir (see p. 105), where his daughter Florence would bring him his lunch pail every day. (Muriel Berson.)

Two

Historic Houses

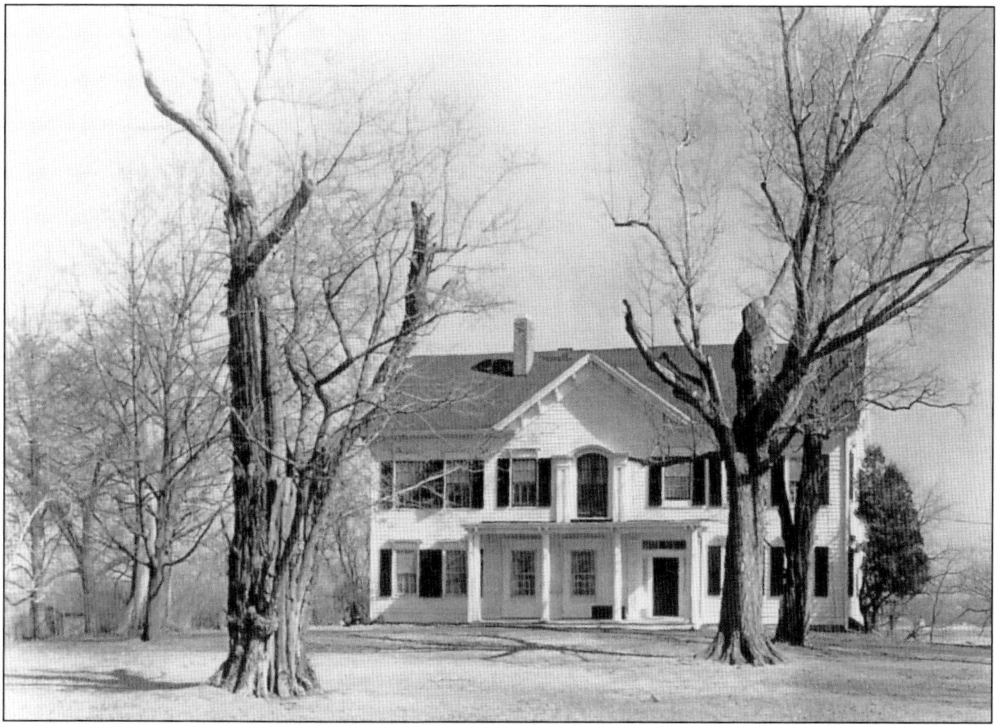

The Beverwyck-Lucas von Beaverhoudt Mansion, built *c.* 1745, located on the southeast side of Route 46 and South Beverwyck Road. This 2,000-acre plantation was visited by such famous dignitaries as George Washington, the Marquis de Lafayette, and Nathaniel Greene during the Revolution. In front of the mansion stood one hundred slave cabins called the Red Barracks because of their color. The mansion was destroyed by fire on August 24, 1971. (Robert Benson.)

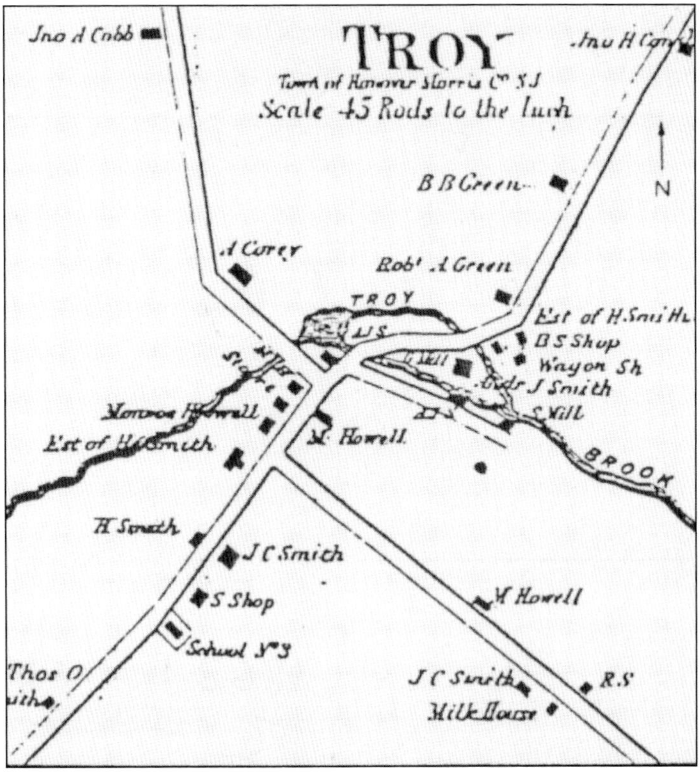

Beers Map of Hanover Township, Morris County, 1868. The map shows the intersection of South Beverwyck Road and Troy Road along with the names of the homeowners in this area. *See Founding Families*. (Parsippany-Troy Hills Township.)

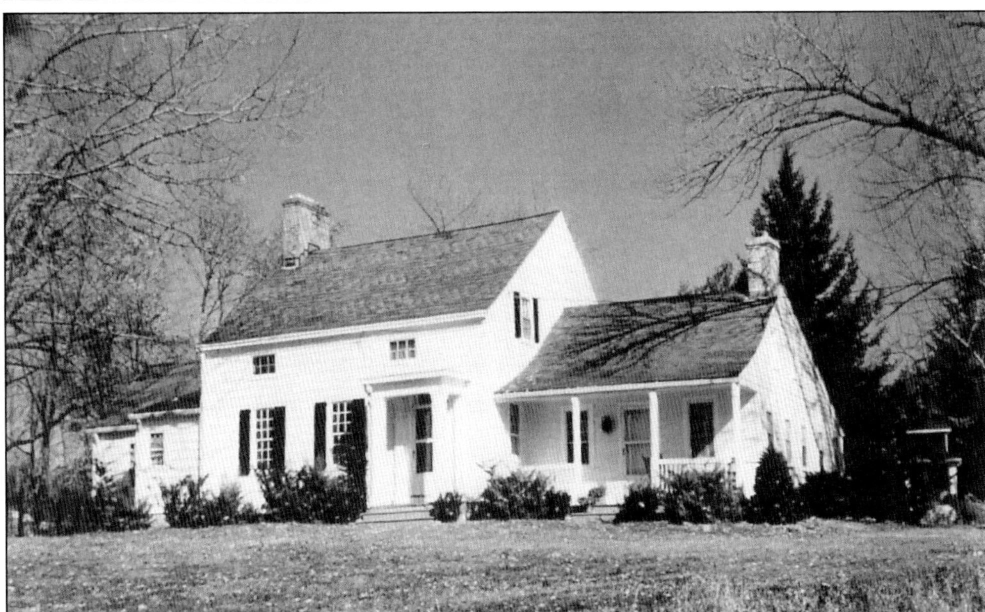

The Robert Green House, built *c.* 1750 at 330 South Beverwyck Road. Situated on a knoll overlooking mill ruins along Troy Brook, the home's left addition dates from *c.* 1790, with its Greek Revival entrance from *c.* 1835. Robert Green owned the home in late eighteenth century, and during the Revolutionary War served as a soldier and pamphleteer. His father, Jacob, had operated a fulling mill on Troy Brook. (Fran Kaminski.)

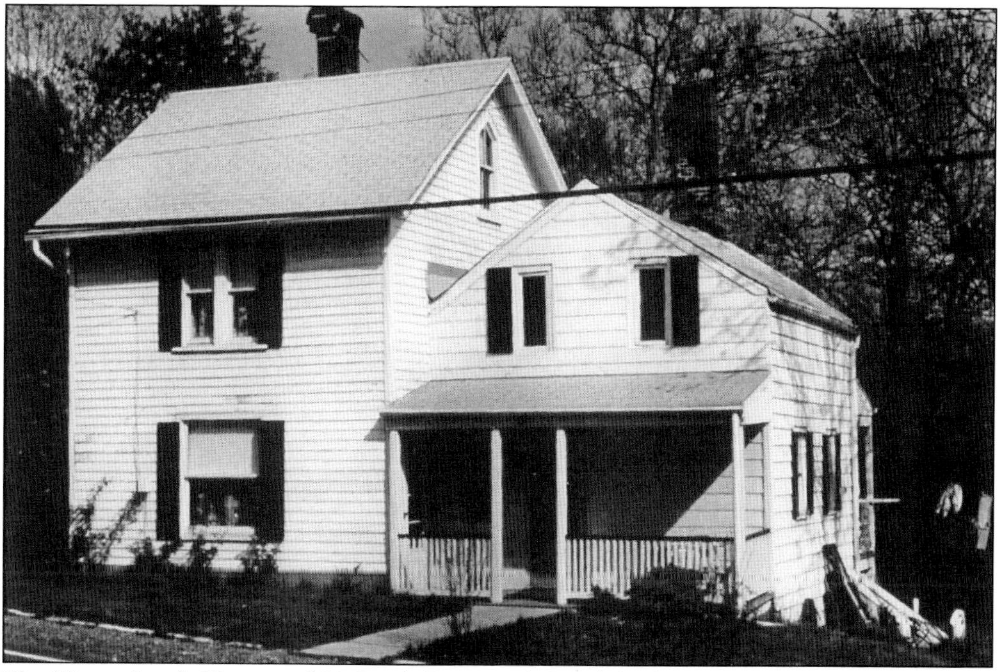

The Hiram Smith House at 331 South Beverwyck Road, built *c.* 1845. Two houses were put together about 1900 to form one. Built by Hiram Smith Jr. for the caretaker and blacksmith of the grist mill, the house was part of an industrial complex that included a distillery, a shoe factory, a flour mill, a general store, two cotton mills, a sawmill, a tannery, and a jail. (Fran Kaminski.)

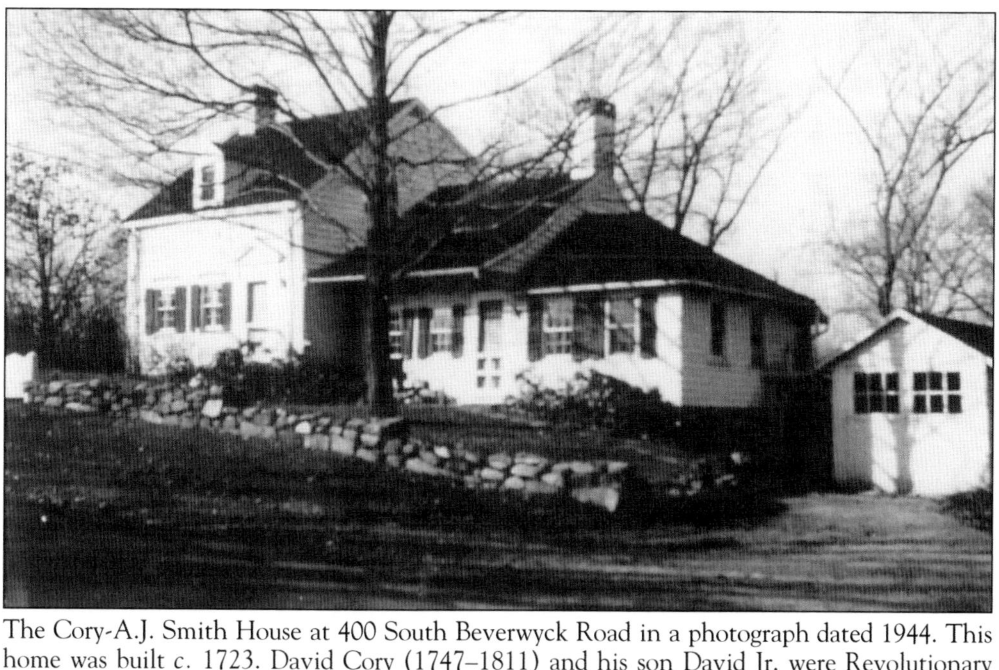

The Cory-A.J. Smith House at 400 South Beverwyck Road in a photograph dated 1944. This home was built *c.* 1723. David Cory (1747–1811) and his son David Jr. were Revolutionary War soldiers. The home was later owned by Emily Smith Baldwin, who called it Bybrook. The oldest section was replaced after fire gutted the home *c.* 1960. (Anita Baldwin.)

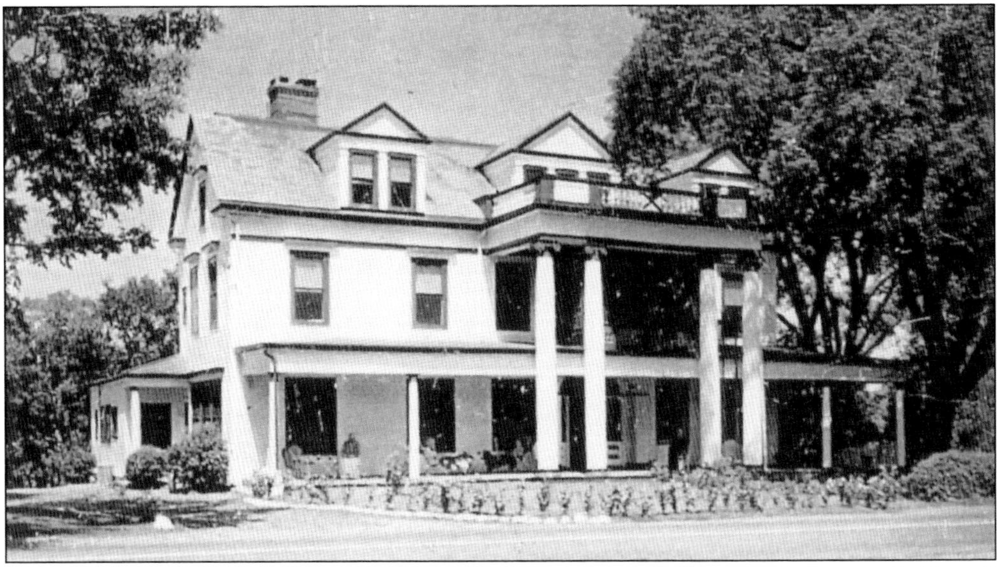

The Troy Hills Nursing Home at 420 South Beverwyck Road, built by Benjamin F. Howell c. 1780. The structure was purchased by Monroe Howell in the mid-1800s from the estate of his mother, Elizabeth Cobb Howell. In the 1930s, Charles Edison converted the residence into a club and restaurant called the Beverwyck Inn. Charles was the son of Thomas A. Edison, and famous in his own right as secretary of the navy and governor of New Jersey (1941–1944). Around World War II the building's pillars and portico were removed; later the home was used as an apartment building. *See Founding Families.* (Robert D'Alessandro.)

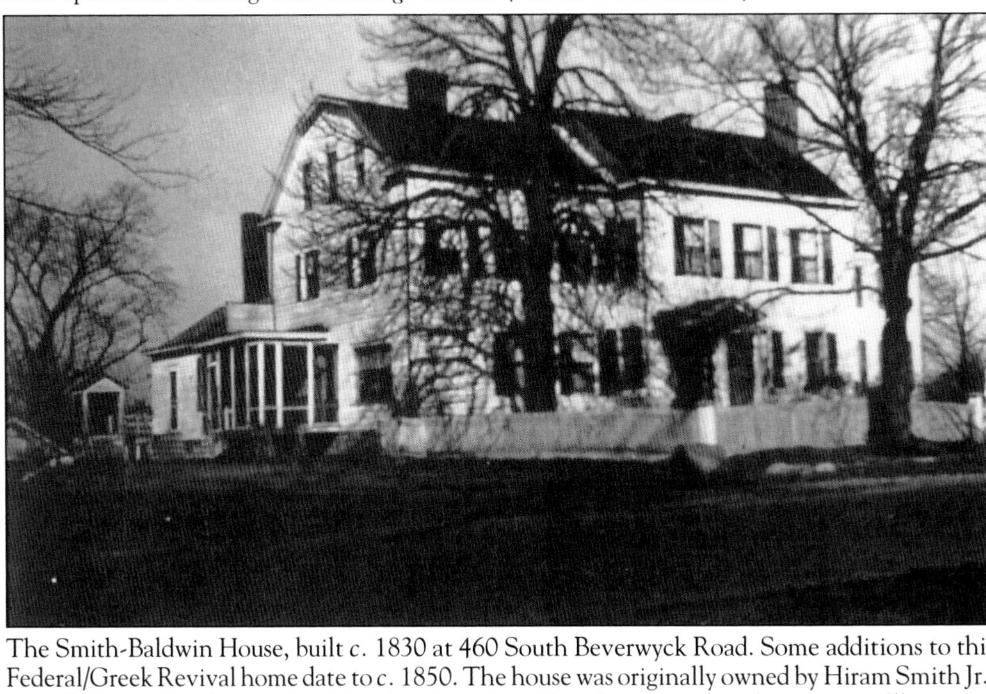

The Smith-Baldwin House, built c. 1830 at 460 South Beverwyck Road. Some additions to this Federal/Greek Revival home date to c. 1850. The house was originally owned by Hiram Smith Jr., son of Hiram Smith, a colonel in the American Revolution and an honorary pallbearer at the funeral of George Washington. It is currently owned by Hiram Smith Jr.'s great-grandson, Richard Baldwin. *See Founding Families.* (Anita Baldwin.)

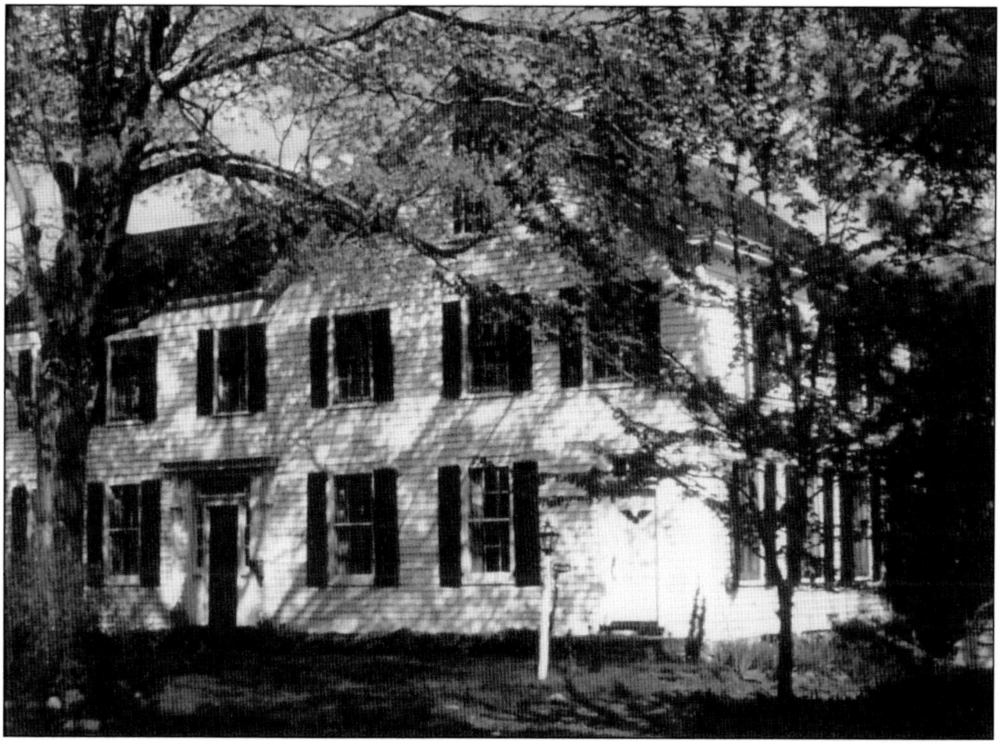

The John Condit Smith Home at 489 South Beverwyck Road, built *c.* 1771. John Condit Smith, a son of Hiram Smith Jr., owned the home about 1868. In later years, it was owned by his brother, Thomas O. Smith, who delivered milk to customers in New York. Thomas Smith kept the milk cold by immersing it in the brook that runs alongside the home. An unusual feature of the house is its double front door: a subsequent owner attached a complete second section to the original dwelling. (Fran Kaminski.)

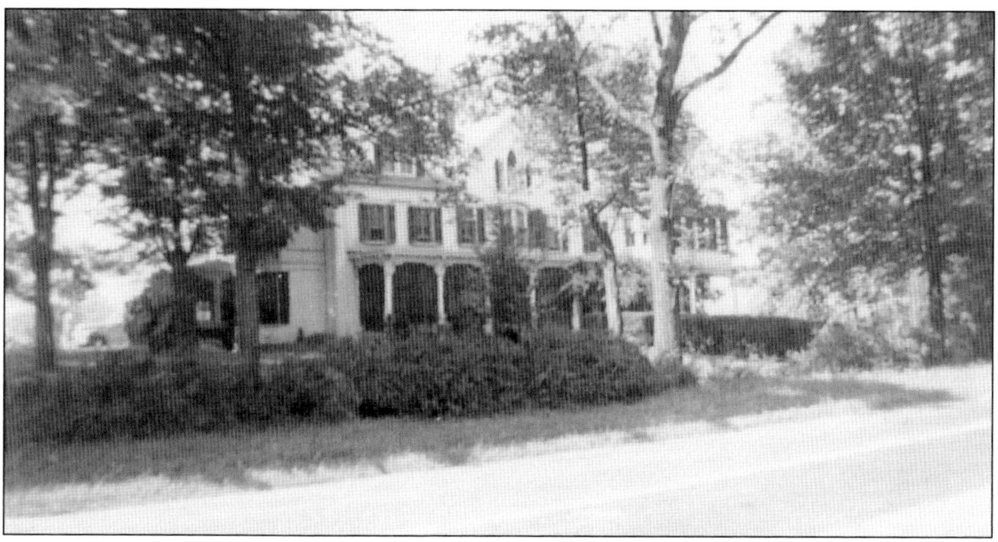

The Schaible House, built *c.* 1800 on S. Beverwyck Road just north of the fork with Reynolds Avenue. The Schaibles owned this home, once possibly a Smith house, in the 1930s. It was torn down in the late 1950s. (Connie Schaible.)

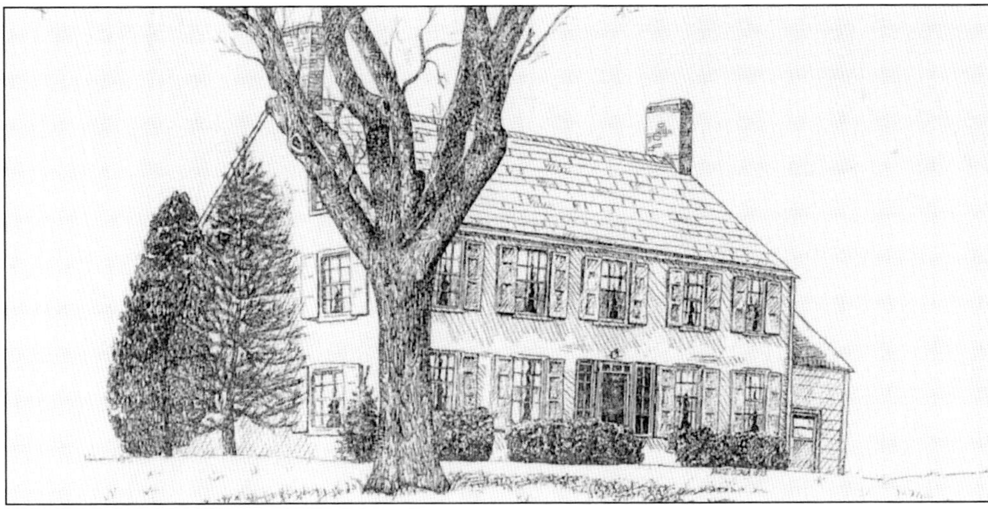

The Benjamin F. Howell House at 709 South Beverwyck Road. Benjamin F. Howell (1725–1798) acquired the 160-acre farm from Gershom Mott for £68 in 1760 and built the home in 1763. He built on an addition in 1793. Howell was the owner of a large sawmill, a justice of the peace, a member of the Committees of Correspondence in 1775, and host to General Washington and his aides in 1779–1780. The house remained in the family for six generations until 1944. The property was subsequently purchased by John Sheehy, a former superintendent of Parsippany-Troy Hills Schools, in 1961. Within the house are two corner fireplaces, unusual features for that period. The home is listed on the state and federal historic registers. (Diane Cicala.)

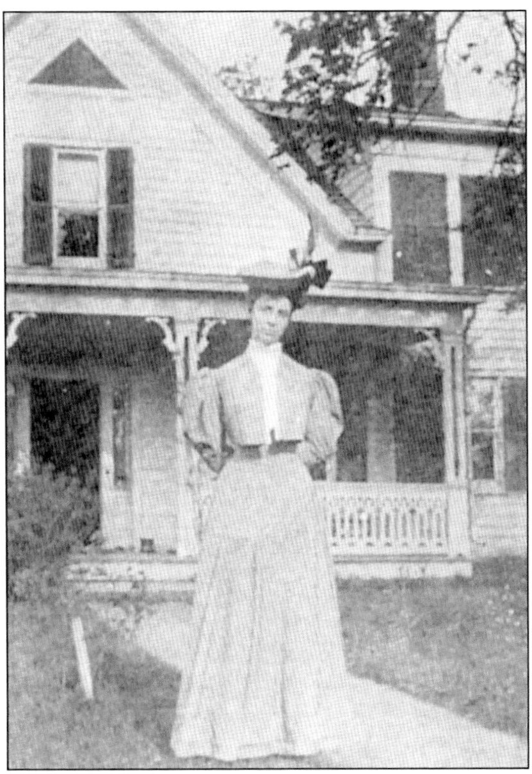

The Farrand-Condit-Ball House at 85 North Beverwyck Road. This house was built for Ebenezer Farrand Sr. in 1788. Close to the day Ebenezer and his wife Rebecca were to move into this home, their son Samuel died after catching a chill while baling hay in the rain. The very same day, Samuel's wife, Mary, gave birth. Mary and daughters Rebecca and Sarah lived in the North Beverwyck house with Mary's in-laws for many years. Sarah Farrand married Benjamin Condit. In 1885, E. Halsey Ball and his wife, Annette, acquired the home from the Condits. This photograph features Ethel Morse, a Ball family friend. *See Founding Families.* (Harold O. Farrand.)

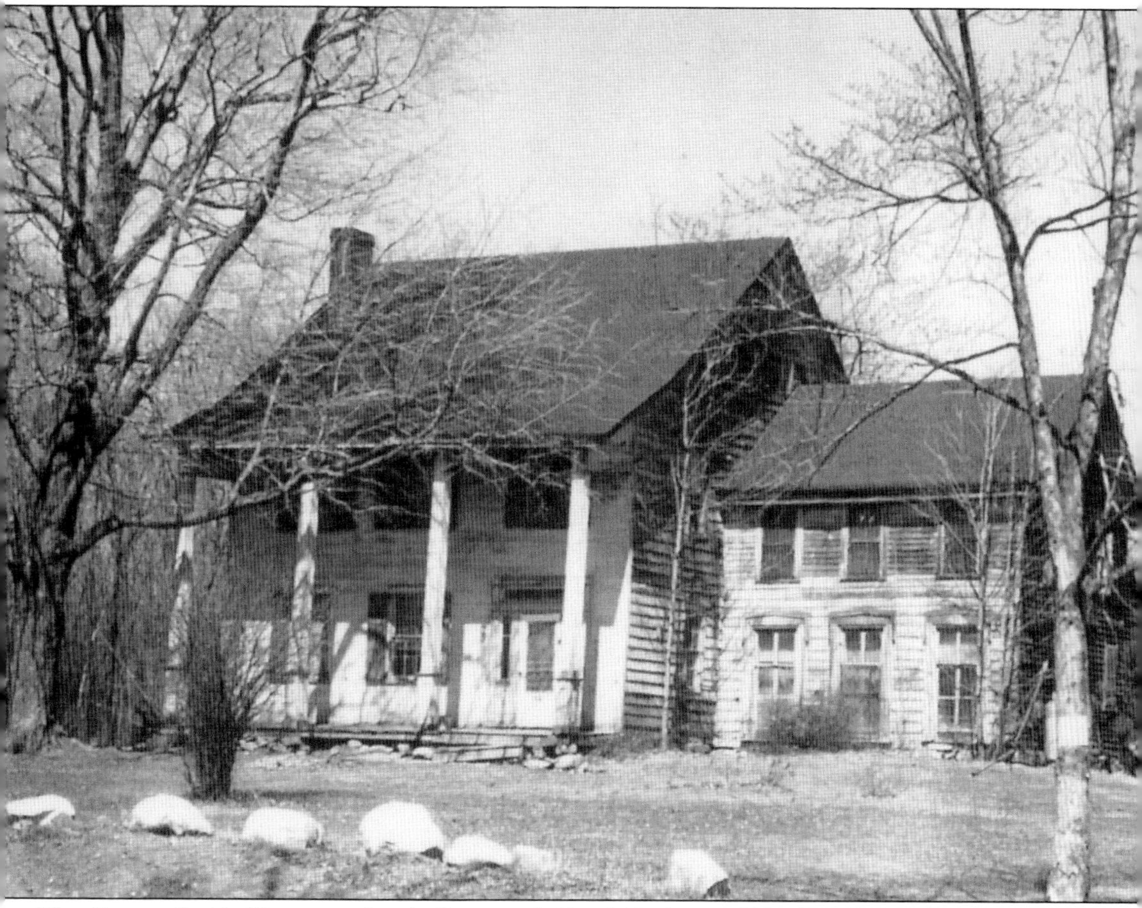

The Parrott-Smith House on South Beverwyck Road. Built in 1738, this elegant home was erected by Dr. Samuel Parrott. When Dr. Parrott died in a boating accident, his death became cause for gossip. He and another man, Tobias Boudinot, were both courting the same girl, Adrianna von Beverhoudt. When only Boudinot returned from a rowing trip the two had taken together, rumors of foul play arose. Tobias did indeed later marry Adrianna. Dr. Parrott's only daughter, Eleanor Parrott (1779–1810), married Colonel Hiram Smith. The house was destroyed by fire in 1974. (Fran Kaminski.)

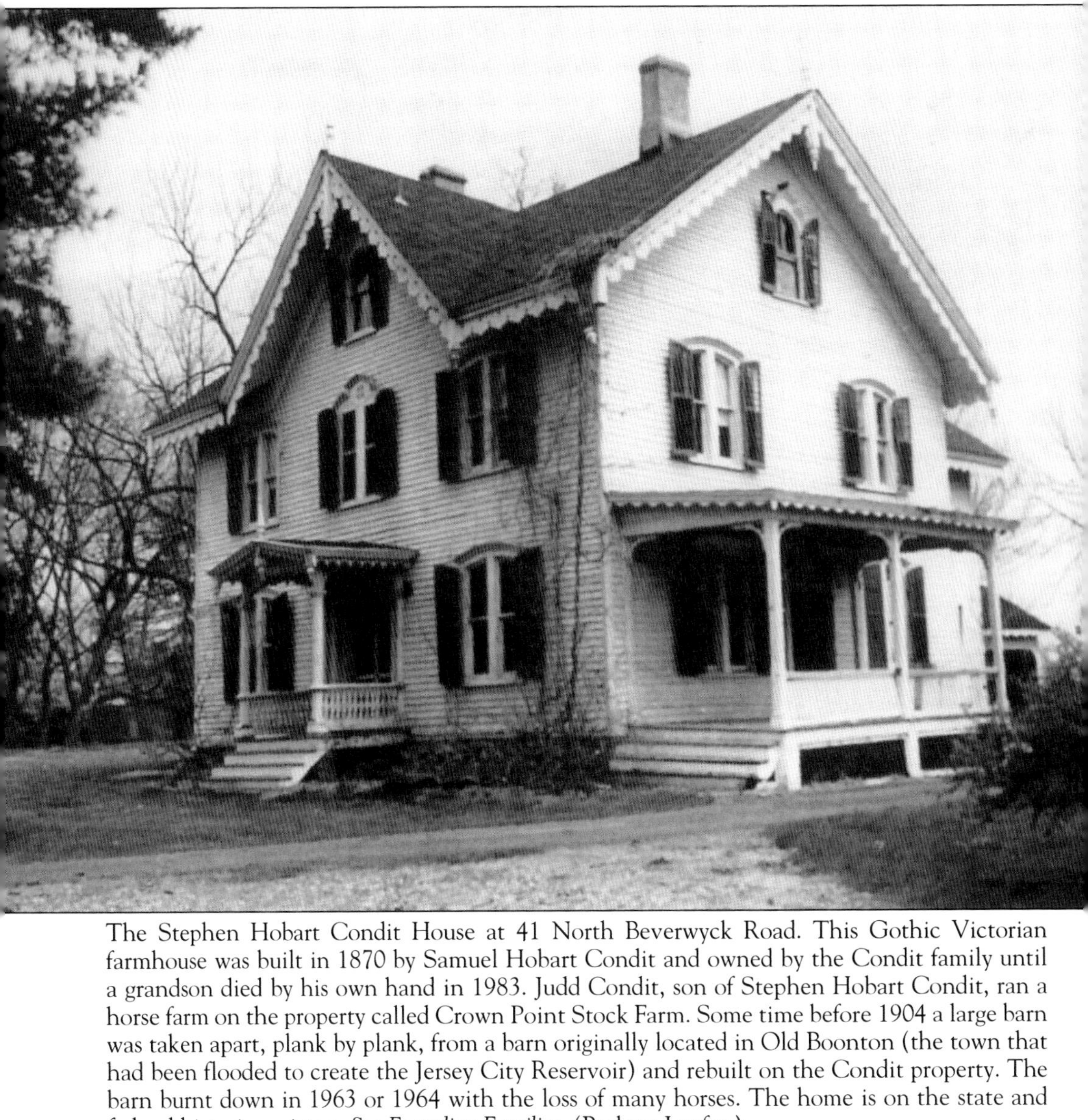

The Stephen Hobart Condit House at 41 North Beverwyck Road. This Gothic Victorian farmhouse was built in 1870 by Samuel Hobart Condit and owned by the Condit family until a grandson died by his own hand in 1983. Judd Condit, son of Stephen Hobart Condit, ran a horse farm on the property called Crown Point Stock Farm. Some time before 1904 a large barn was taken apart, plank by plank, from a barn originally located in Old Boonton (the town that had been flooded to create the Jersey City Reservoir) and rebuilt on the Condit property. The barn burnt down in 1963 or 1964 with the loss of many horses. The home is on the state and federal historic registers. *See Founding Families*. (Barbara Laufer.)

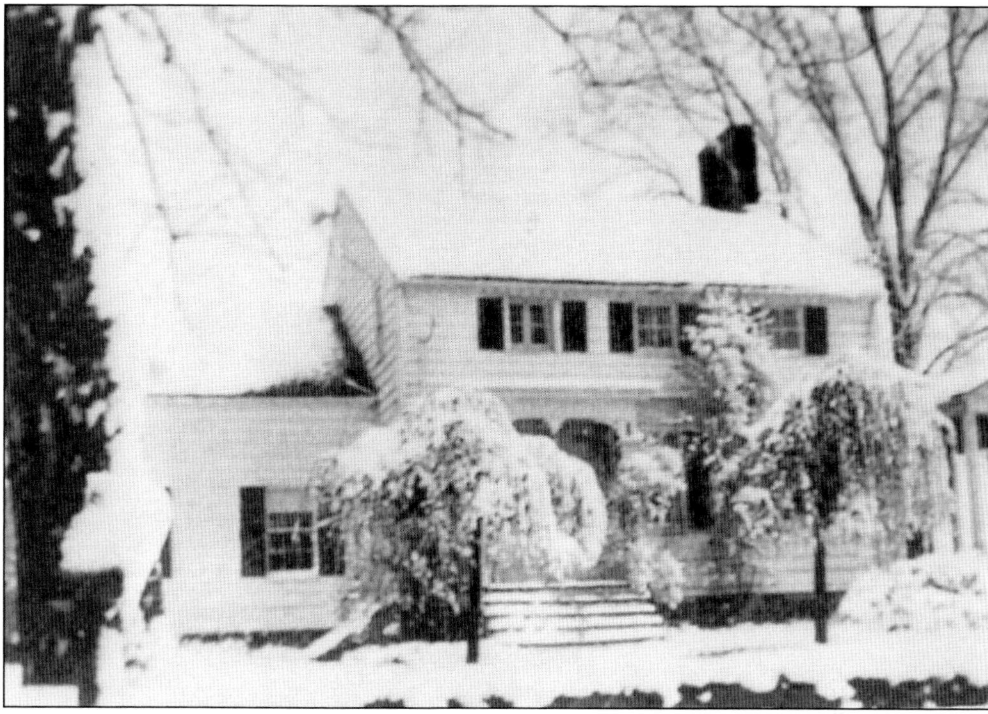

The Farrand-Ogden House at 260 North Beverwyck Road. The older part of this Federal/Vernacular home (left) was built in 1803; the newer portion was erected by Samuel Farrand Ogden in 1832. *See Founding Families*. (Fran Kaminski.)

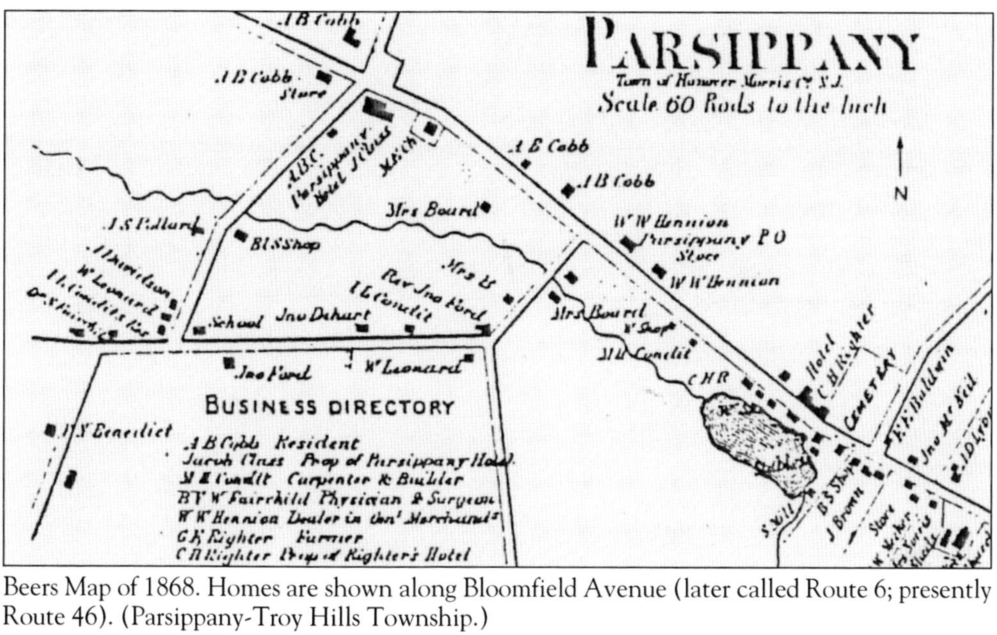

Beers Map of 1868. Homes are shown along Bloomfield Avenue (later called Route 6; presently Route 46). (Parsippany-Troy Hills Township.)

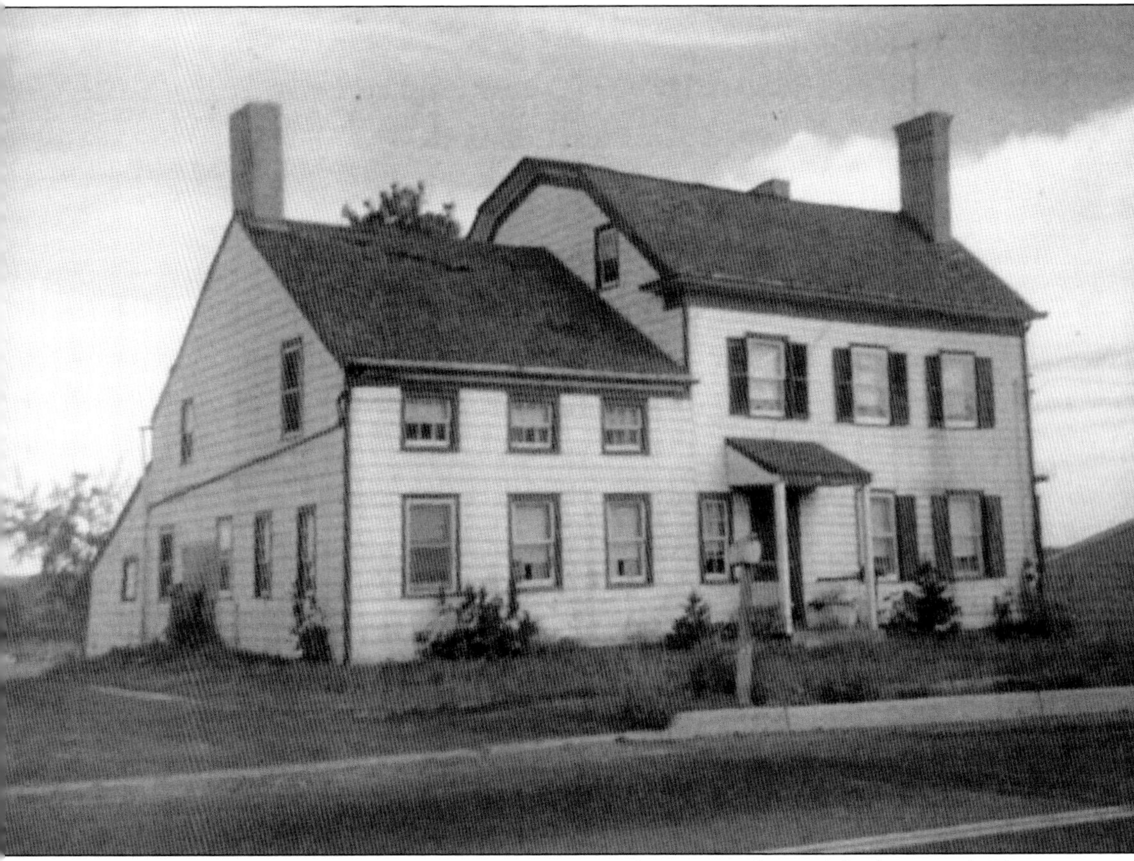

Sunnybrook (also called Sunnyside) Farm on North Beverwyck Road, built *c.* 1806. This estate was built for Aaron Ogden (1783–1848) and his wife, Rebecca Farrand Ogden. The home was passed down to their son, John Farrand (1817–1885), to his daughter, Susan Farrand (1852–1916), to her son, William Ogden Farrand (1881–1958), and finally to Harold O. Farrand. Harold sold the property to the developers of Rickland Village in 1964, and the house was then demolished. There is a legend about a tree on the property. Called the Snoozin' Tree, it was special to landowner Ebenezer Farrand (1734–1807), Rebecca Farrand Ogden's grandfather, for he took his daily nap there. When the land was sold, a stipulation was included in the deed that this tree was never to be uprooted. *See Founding Families*. (Charles Bates.)

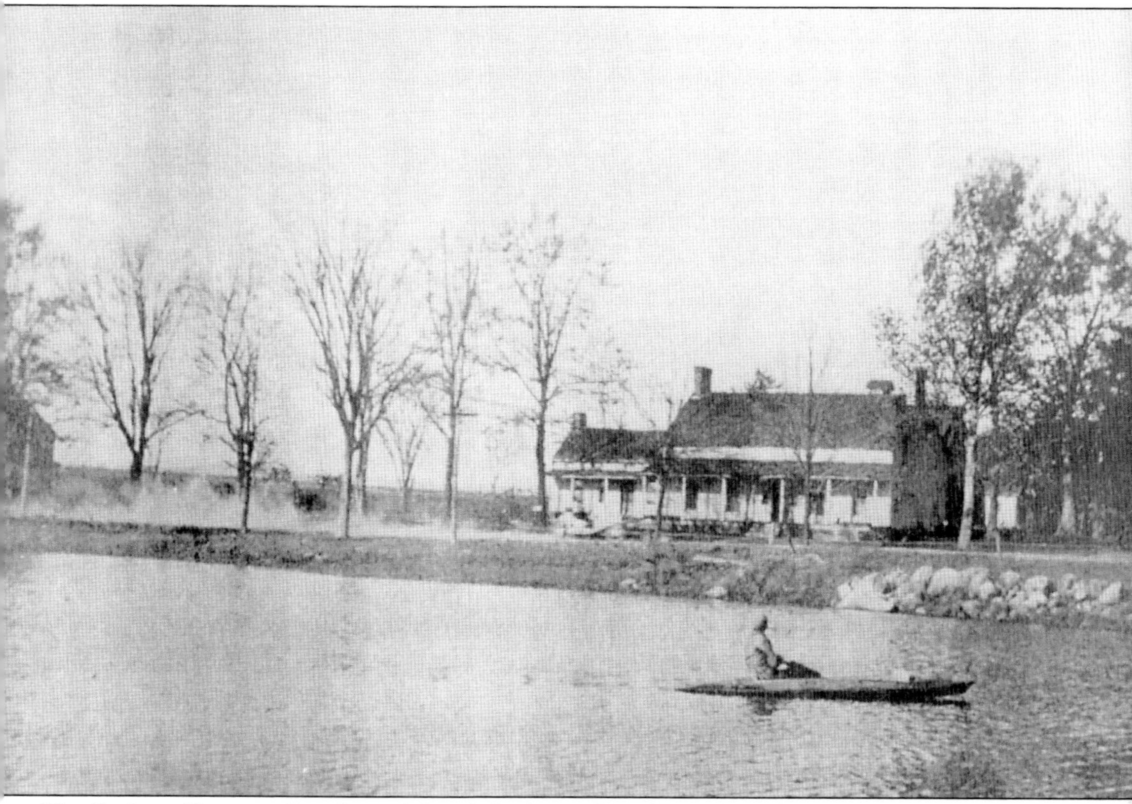

The Righter House at Brookwood Pond, built c. 1770, located at the corner of Vail Road and Route 46 West. The home was originally a stagecoach stop on the Parsippany-Rockaway Turnpike (presently Route 46). Located northwest of the Parsippany Presbyterian Cemetery, it is still used today as the home of the caretaker of the cemetery. Righter's Hotel stood west of Righter House and was run by Charles H. Righter. (Parsippany-Troy Hills Township.)

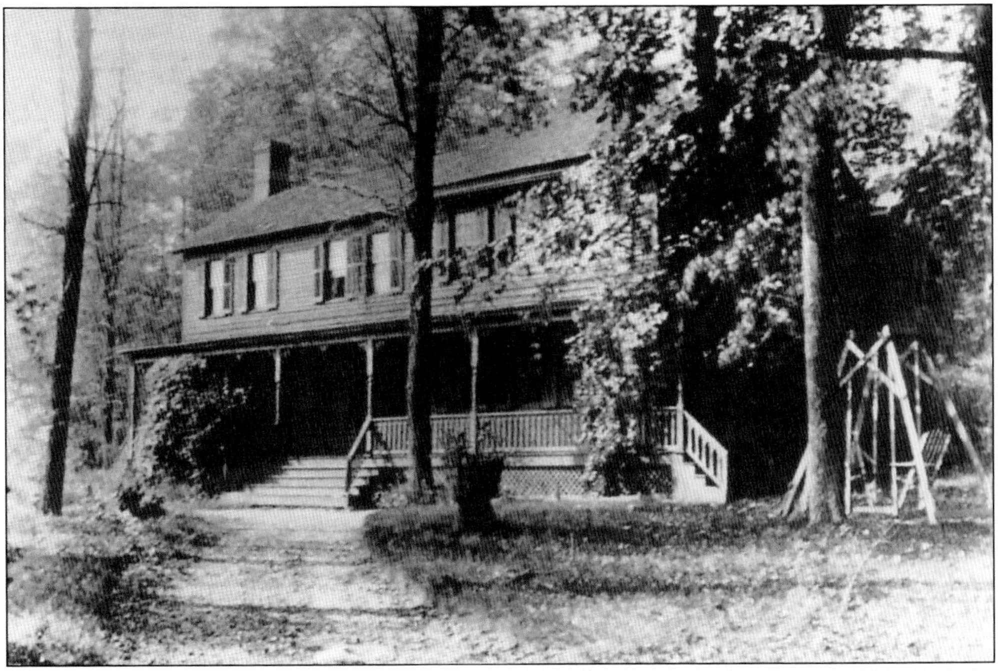

The Ogden-Faesch House (also known as the Old Lafayette House), built *c.* 1800. Built by Samuel Ogden, owner of the iron works in Old Boonton, this house was renowned as one of the most elegant homes in the area during the eighteenth century. Famous people, such as the Marquis de Lafayette and Royal Governor William Franklin, were guests at this home. Governor Franklin remained a confirmed Loyalist despite the fact that his father, Benjamin Franklin, was an ardent Patriot. The house was demolished to make way for the Jersey City Reservoir. (Fran Kaminski.)

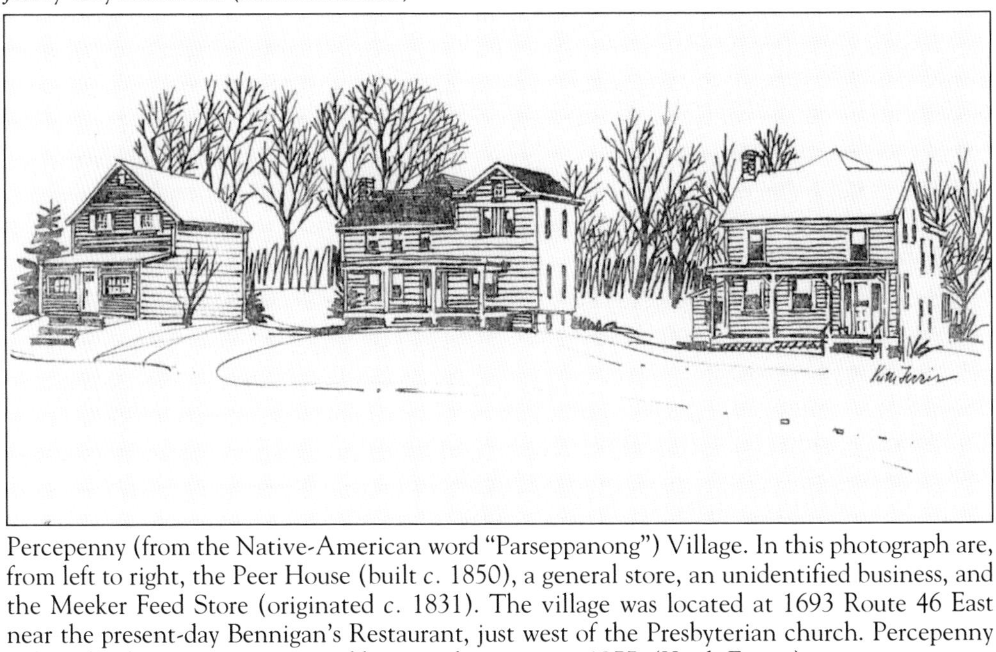

Percepenny (from the Native-American word "Parseppanong") Village. In this photograph are, from left to right, the Peer House (built *c.* 1850), a general store, an unidentified business, and the Meeker Feed Store (originated *c.* 1831). The village was located at 1693 Route 46 East near the present-day Bennigan's Restaurant, just west of the Presbyterian church. Percepenny Village has been a state registered historic district since 1977. (Keith Ferris.)

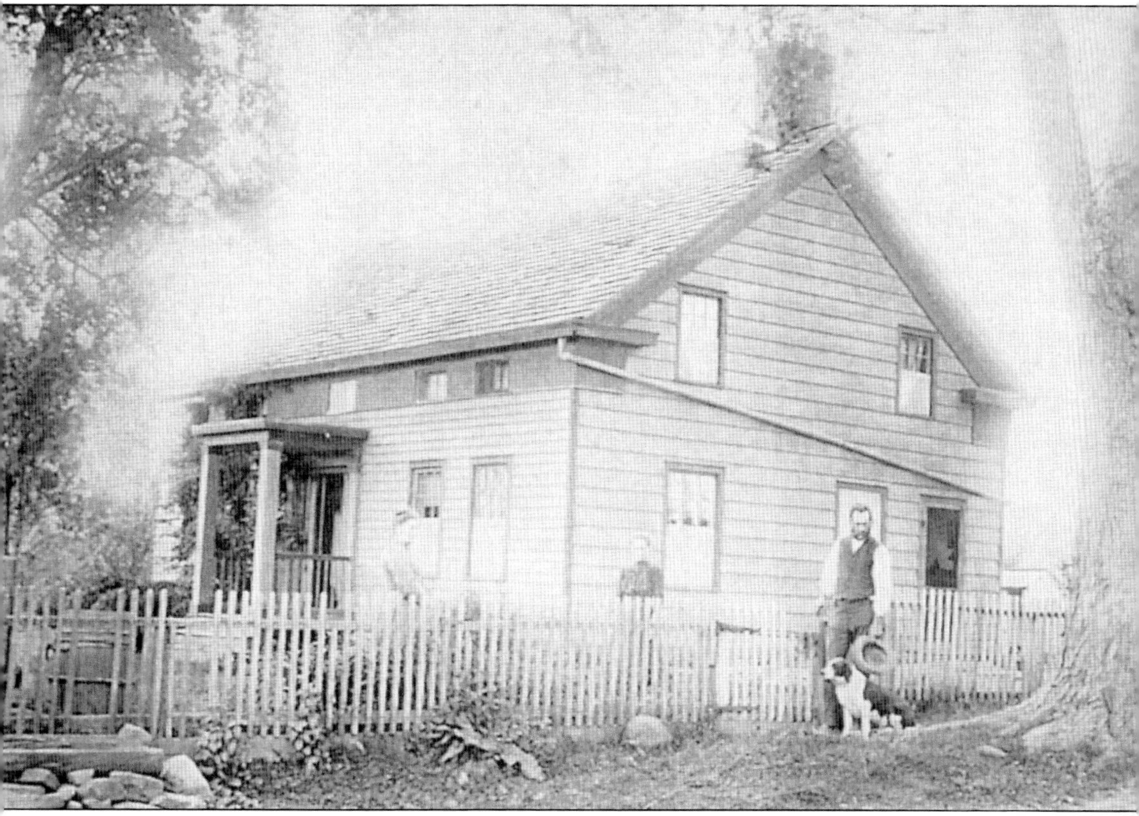

The George Bowlsby (or Bowlby)-DeGelleke House, built *c.* 1790. This home was built by George Bowlsby, a wealthy landowner, probably in two sections. Tunis Cobb purchased the home and 70 acres of land in 1849 for $1,800 from the estate of George Bowlsby Jr. Other owners included Stephen H. Card (1885) and Isaac Baas (1910). Peter DeGelleke (architect of Central Middle School) and his wife, Alethea Baas, bought the house and the remaining 13.5 acres in 1922. The back parlor served as the "burying room." When a family member passed away, it was the custom for the deceased to be laid out at home. Alethea DeGelleke sold the house to the township in 1977. Located on Baldwin Road, off Route 46 West, it serves today as the Parsippany Historic Museum. (Fran Kaminski.)

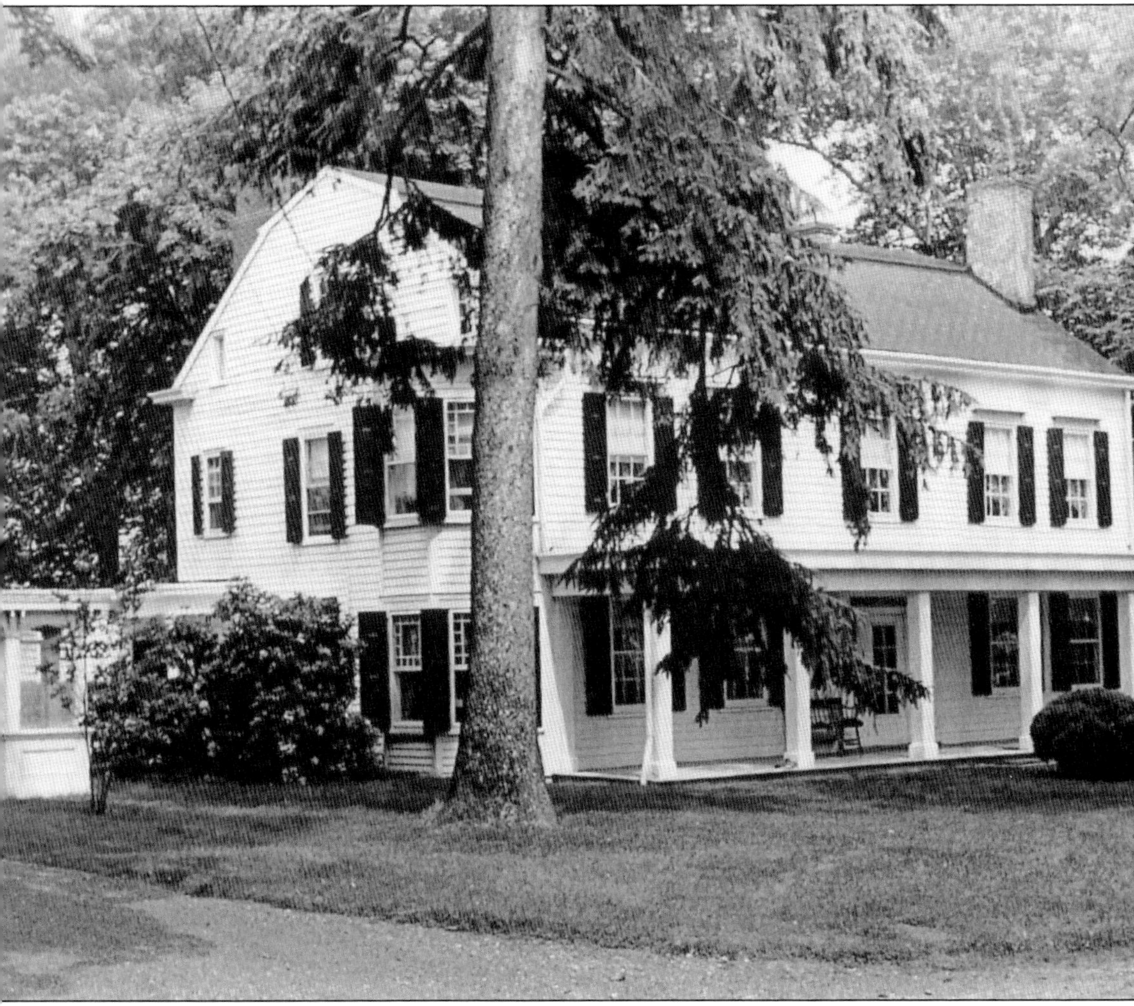

The Livingston-Benedict House at 25 Old Parsippany Road, built *c.* 1750. This Georgian/Victorian home was built with wooden pegs. The two-story bay windows were installed in the 1880s. Tradition says this house was originally erected as a tavern. It was later owned by Lemuel Bowers, a county judge. Governor William Livingston lived here from 1777 to 1780. The building is on the state and federal historic registers, and is presently owned by Mrs. Helen Benedict Dutton, who was very active in the civic affairs of the township for many years. (Fran Kaminski.)

A silhouette of William Livingston dated January 19, 1781. Livingston was the first governor of New Jersey under the new American nation. One of Governor Livingston's daughters, Sarah, married John Jay, first chief justice of the Supreme Court (1789–1795). (Joint Free Public Library of Morristown and Morris Township.)

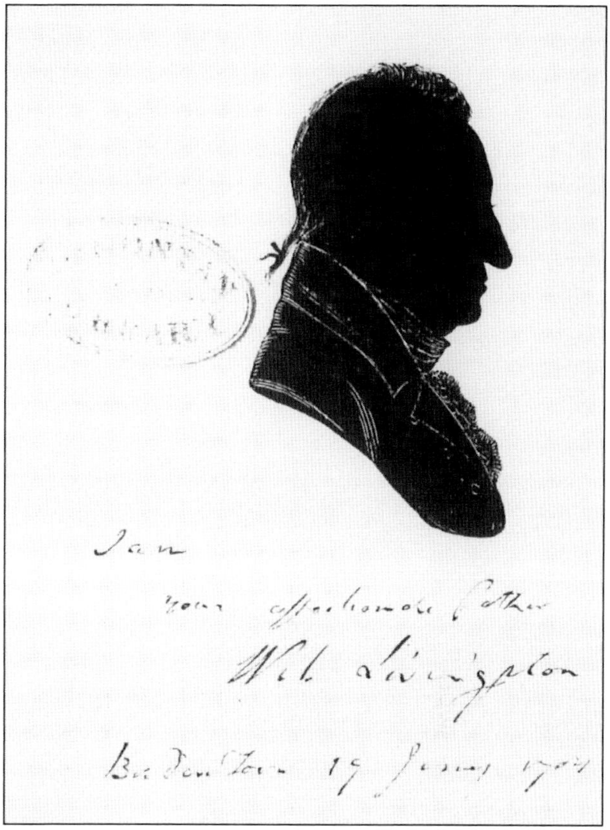

The Fairchild-Dawson House on Littleton and Parsippany Roads, built *c.* 1875. This home is reputed to have been owned by Drs. Stephen (1792–1872) and Richard Van Wyck (1819–1874) Fairchild, two locally prominent physicians of the nineteenth century. Richard Van Wyck Fairchild was the husband of Elizabeth Howell, a daughter of Benjamin Howell. The home was demolished when the Hills of Troy development was built in the 1960s. (Charles Bates.)

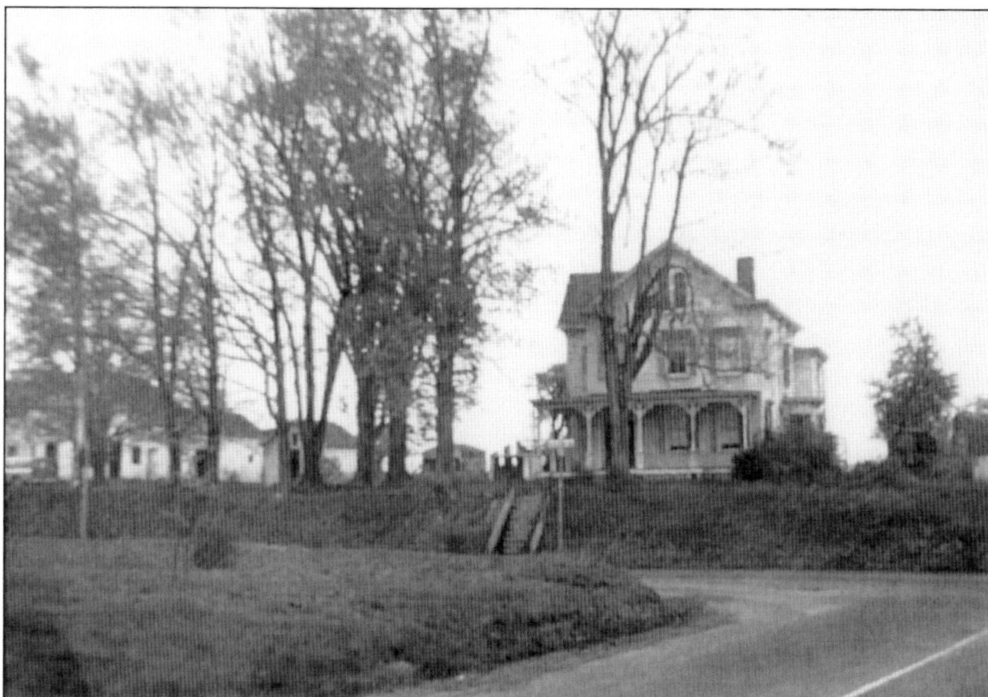

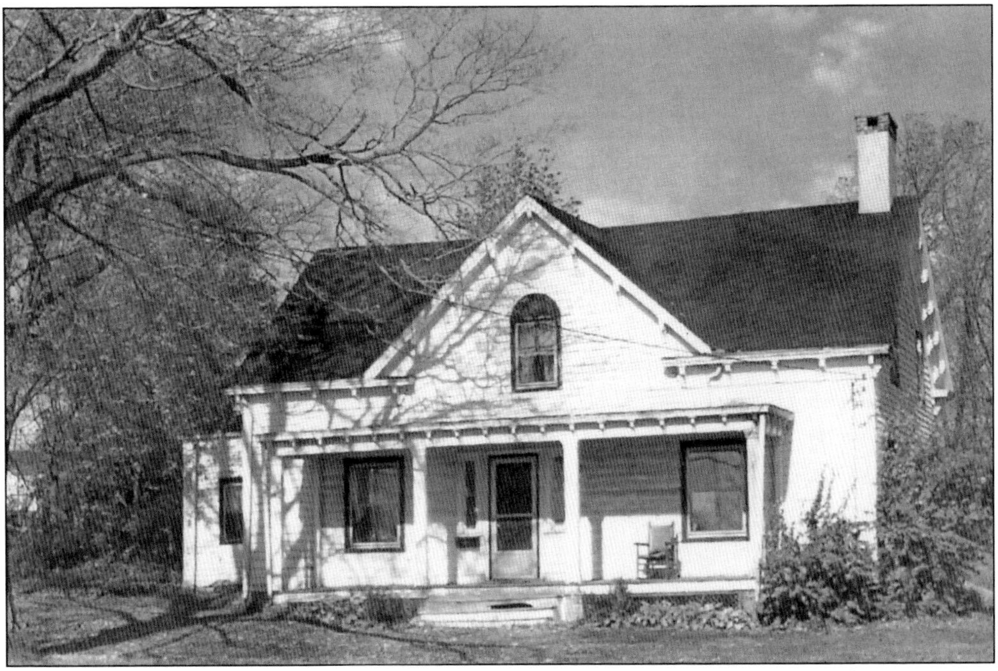

The Cory House on Littleton Road, built in 1841. This Greek Revival home has late Victorian additions. It was inhabited in 1916 by Elva Cory, a local schoolteacher, and was razed in 1990. (Fran Kaminski.)

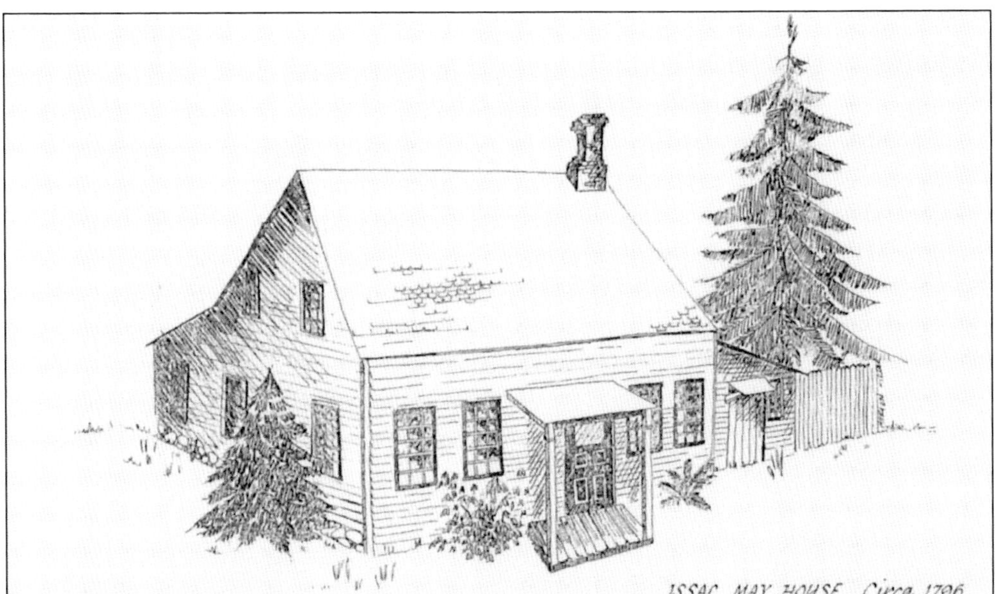

The Isaac May House on the northwest corner of Parsippany and Littleton Roads, built c. 1790. Isaac May (1771–1807) built this home on the 2 acres of improved land on which he had paid a tax of £1.10. He had three children by his wife, Theodocia, who inherited the property upon his death. The May House was the only saltbox construction left in Parsippany-Troy Hills until it was razed in 1990. (Marion Filler.)

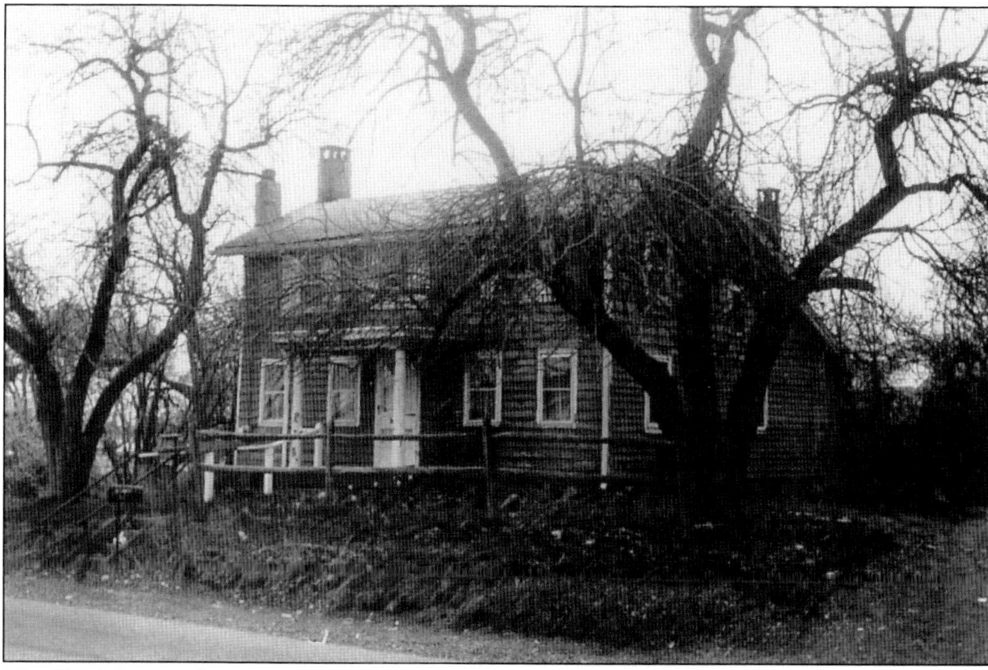

The W.H. Leonard House on Parsippany Road, built *c.* 1760. William Leonard was very active in raising funds for the Children's Home. The home was razed in 1990. (Fran Kaminski.)

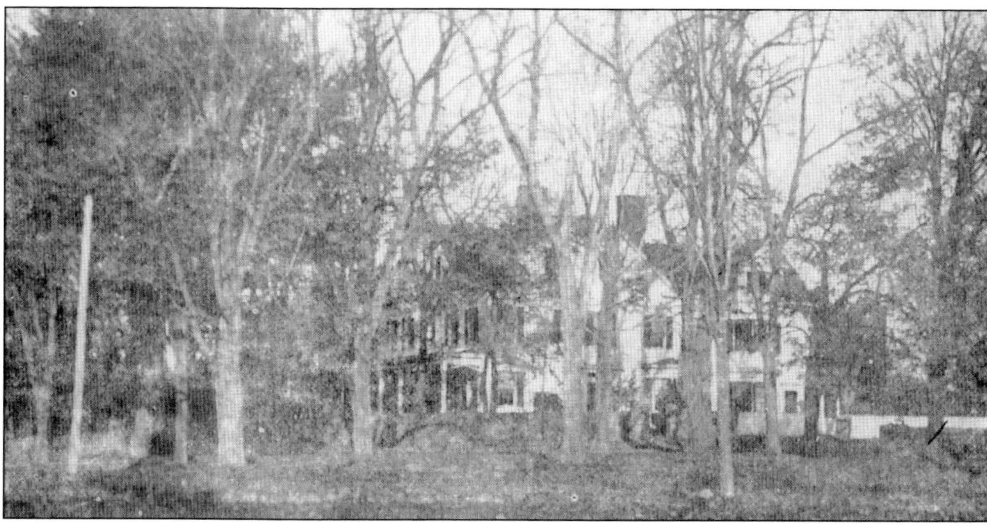

The Colonel Lemuel Cobb House on Parsippany Boulevard and Route 46 West, built *c.* 1795. This home was built by Colonel Cobb (1762–1831) and his second wife, Susan Farrand Cobb (1764–1816). Their son, Andrew B. Cobb (1804–1873), inherited the house and property of 10,000 acres. Andrew B. Cobb was a judge and a member of the General Assembly of Morris County. In later years the property was used as a boarding and breeding farm for horses. Mrs. Geraldine Dodge purchased the property, razed the Cobb Mansion (1918), and donated the land to the township. The township built a barn on this land, and used it as a summer theater until the early 1940s. The barn was taken down *c.* 1960 and the present municipal building erected. The original municipal building was located on Pumphouse Road. (Parsippany-Troy Hills Township.)

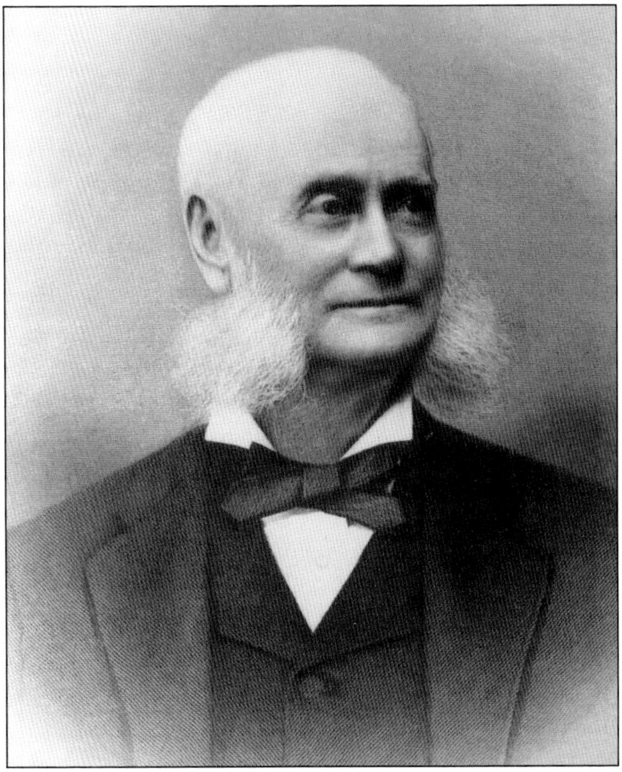

Peter Ballantine (1791–1883). Ballantine was a brewer who emigrated from Scotland when he was twenty-nine years old. In 1857, he formed the highly successful P. Ballantine & Sons in Newark with his three sons. He died of pneumonia at the venerable age of ninety-two. (Joint Free Public Library of Morristown and Morris Township.)

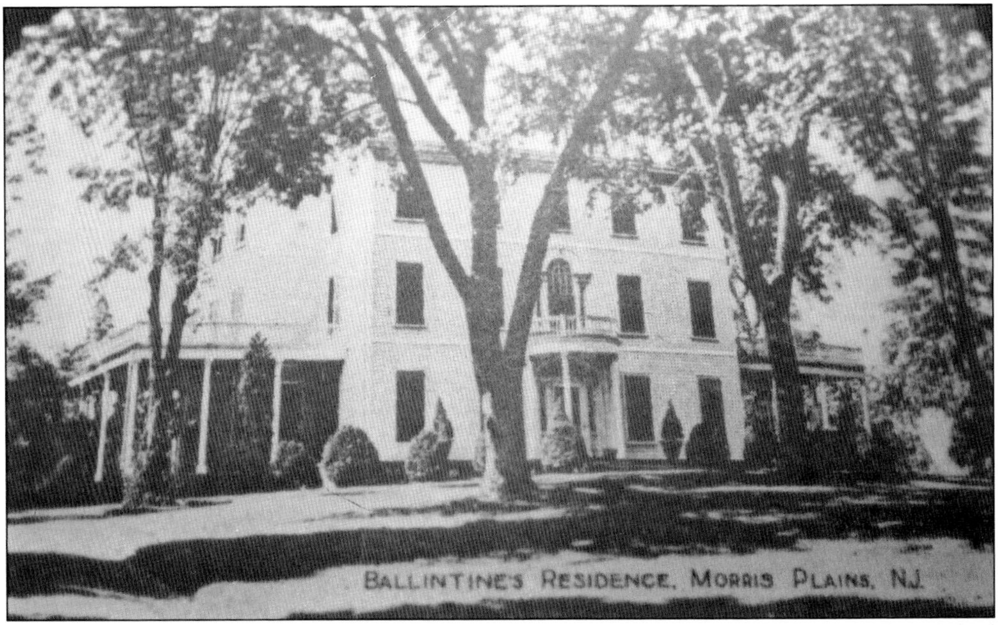

The Peter Ballantine residence at 500 Littleton Road, built in 1877. This home was demolished to make way for Beecham Products corporate headquarters, and part of the property was sold to the developers of the Sedgefield Houses (*c.* 1960). The architecture of the house was Georgian Revival, and the stable, barn, and gazebo are still standing. (Joint Free Public Library of Morristown and Morris Township.)

Three

Religion and Education

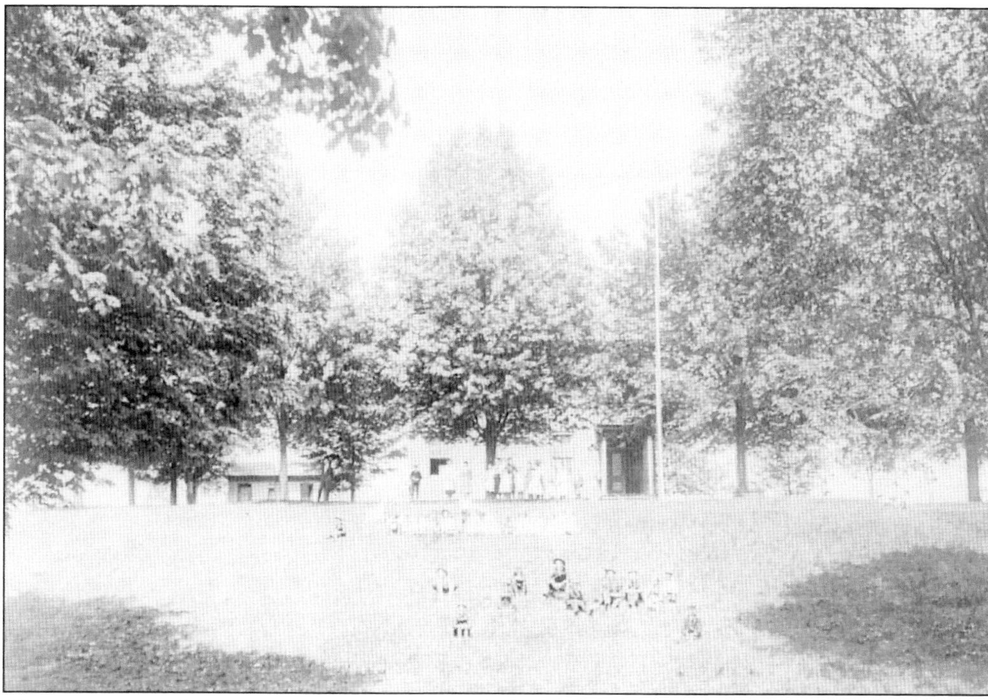

The Parsippany School in a photograph dated 1908. This privately funded academy may have been owned by Revolutionary War veteran Silas Condict. Located behind the present-day Morris Hills Shopping Center on Route 46 East, the school was built in 1859 and used until 1928. After being partially damaged by fire in 1949, it was converted into a private residence, and was subsequently razed to make way for the Tivoli Garden Apartments. (Joint Free Public Library of Morristown and Morris Township.)

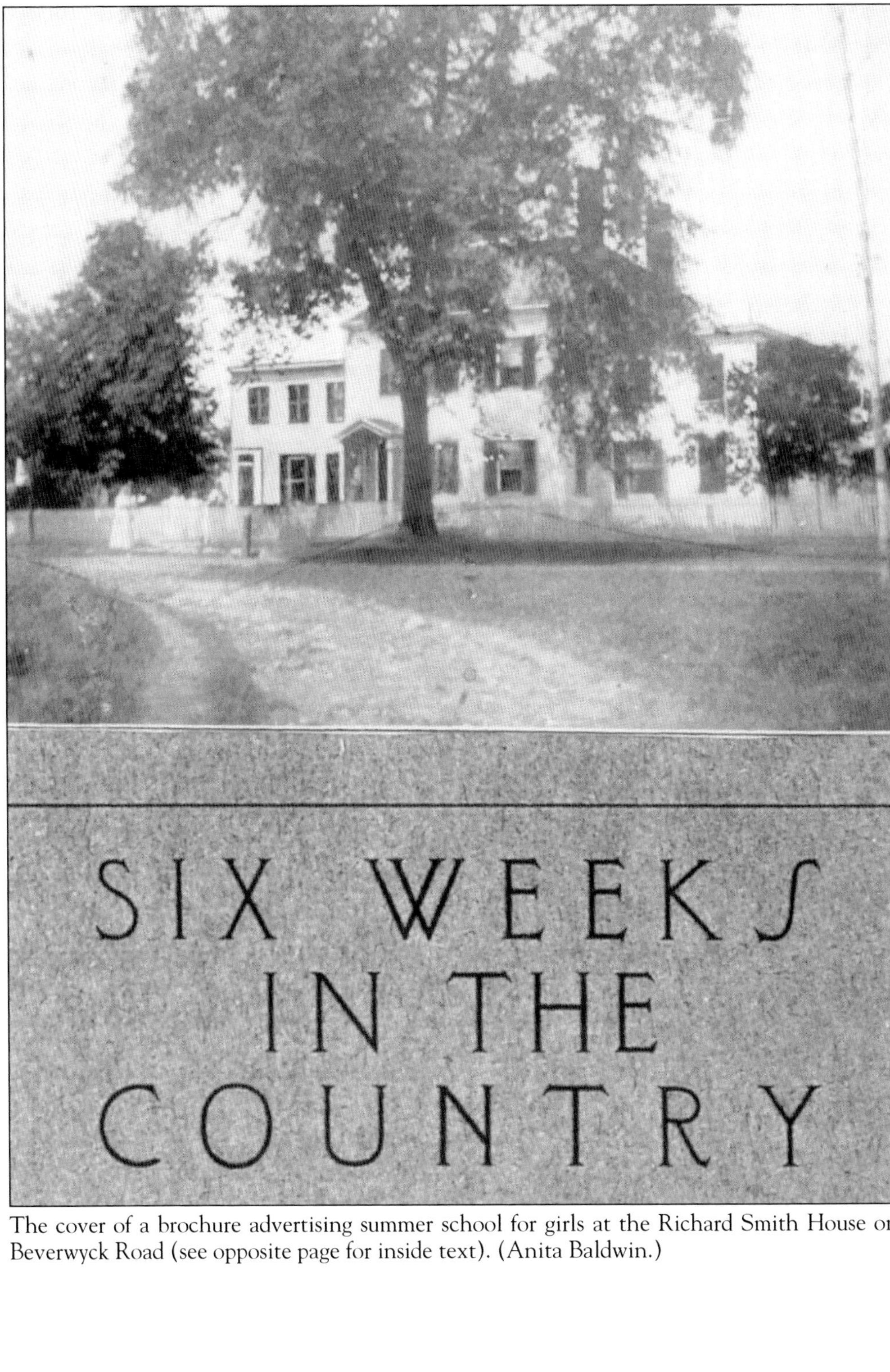

The cover of a brochure advertising summer school for girls at the Richard Smith House on Beverwyck Road (see opposite page for inside text). (Anita Baldwin.)

DURING the months of July and August Mrs. Richard Smith and Miss Smith will receive ten or twelve little girls into their country home among the hills of northern New Jersey. They will offer an opportunity for a healthful, simple life in attractive surroundings, and under intelligent and sympathetic supervision.

The homestead is situated at Troy Hills, between Morristown and Boonton, on a ridge overlooking the Orange Mountains, and is about an hour's ride from New York City.

There will be outdoor athletics, drives, picnics and walks through the woods nearby.

For those who care to join them, classes will be organized in botany, sketching, nature work, basketry and sewing. Morning hours may be arranged for those who desire special tutoring in the intermediate grades.

Parents may feel assured that an earnest effort will be made to give their children the same individual care which they would receive at home.

For information concerning terms and further details, address Miss Emily C. Smith, Detroit Home and Day School, Detroit, Michigan, and after June 1st, Troy Hills, N. J.

Promoting the activities of the summer school. (Anita Baldwin.)

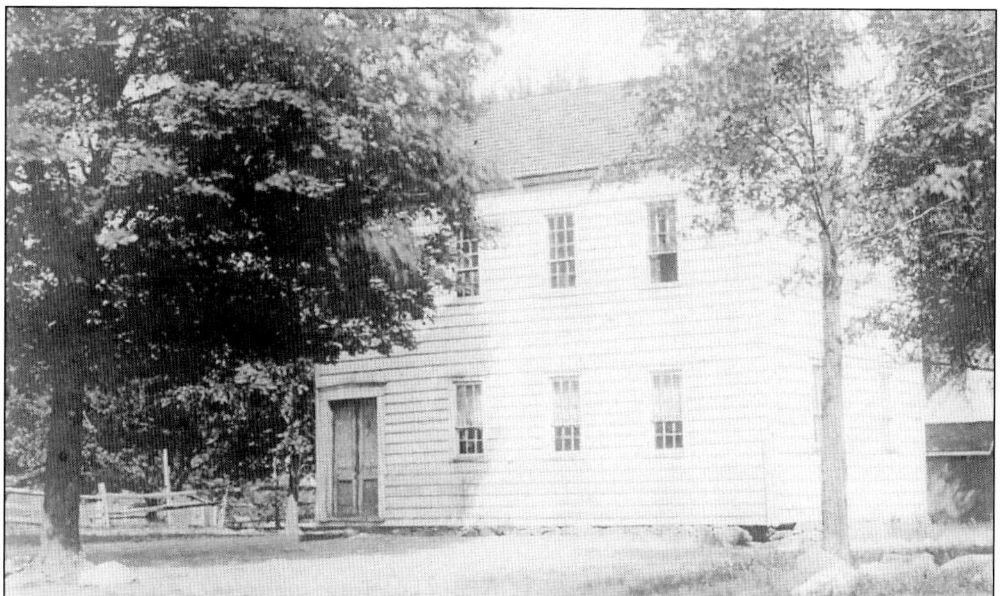

Troy Academy at 509 South Beverwyck Road, built in 1807. This private school was located on the present site of the Little Red Schoolhouse and was heated by wood provided by the pupils. In 1908, the building was moved to Troy Meadow Road, where it was used as a private home until being destroyed by fire in 1958. The last residents were John and Annie Miles. (Harold O. Farrand.)

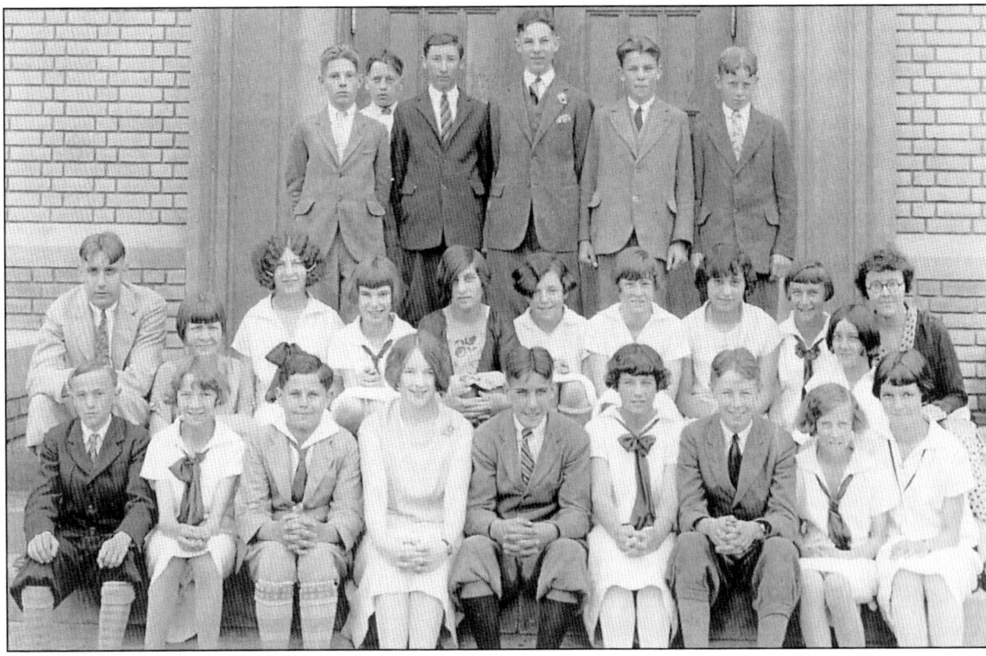

The Class of 1926 of the Morris Plains Grammar School, which was attended by Parsippany public school pupils. From left to right are as follows: (front row) William Decker, Jean Huber, Charles Burch, Marjorie Evans, Cip Lyon, Clara Wiedman, Don Kitchell, Muriel Rennie, and Mildred Walton; (middle row) Mr. Holcombe, Edna Mary Bardet, Henrietta Satoff, Anna Bladt, Louise Mount, Claris Camphle, Helen Mazzalo, Dorothy Willigus, Rose Chesney, and Miss Ayres; (back row) Judson Davies, Edward Crayon, Alben Rheinhart, Henry Bardet, Edgar Thurston, and George Van Winkle. (Parsippany-Troy Hills Public Library, Condit Room.)

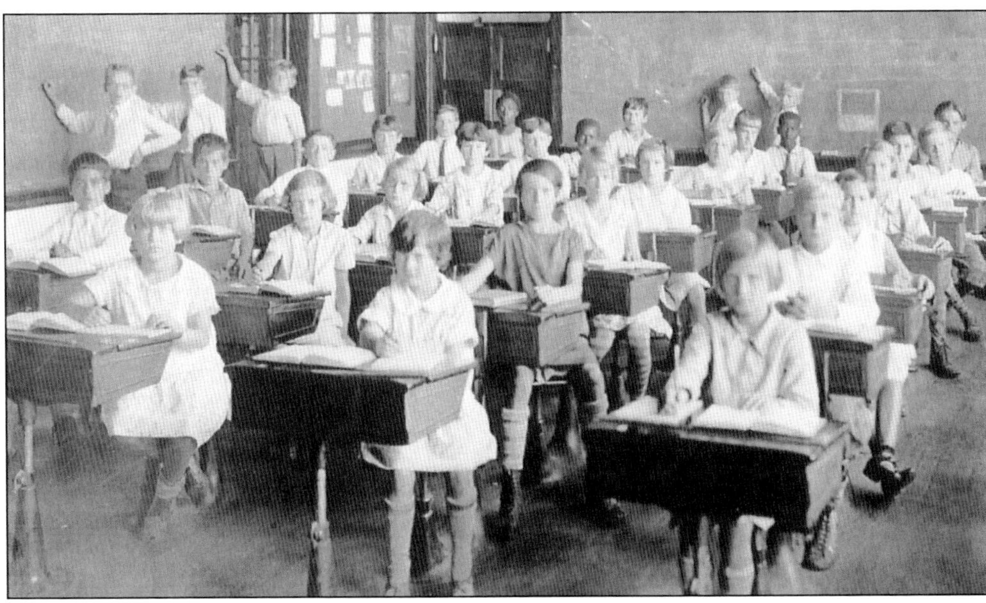

The Parsippany School fourth-grade class in 1930 at 509 South Beverwyck Road. At the blackboard are Willis Howell, Walter Losey, and Joseph Przyhocki. (Ann Przyhocki Morgenthien.)

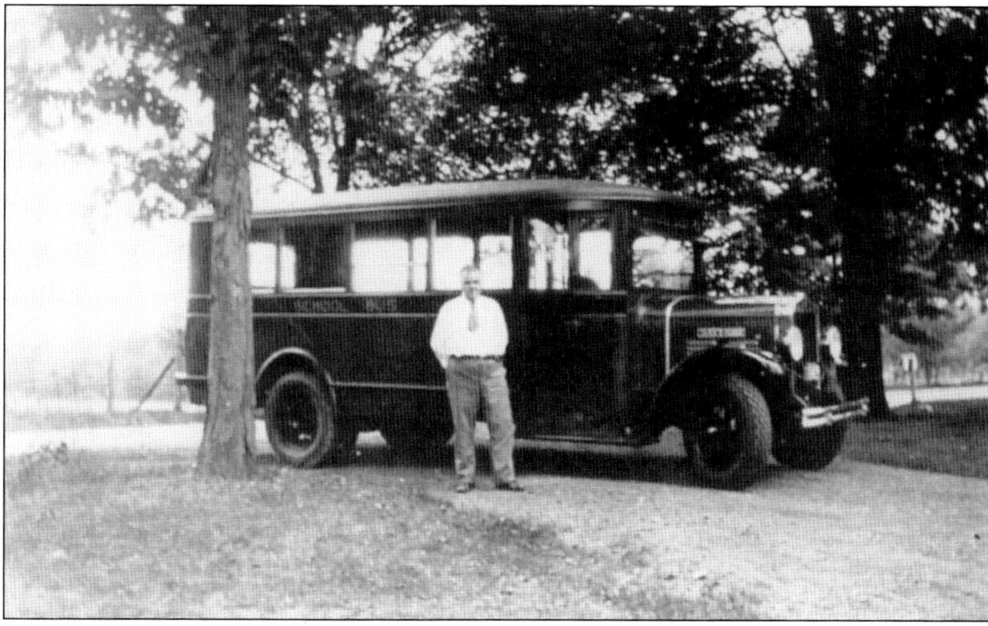

Jack Kitchell (a member of the locally prominent Kitchell family) and the earliest Parsippany-Troy Hills' school bus, *c.* 1930. (Harold O. Farrand.)

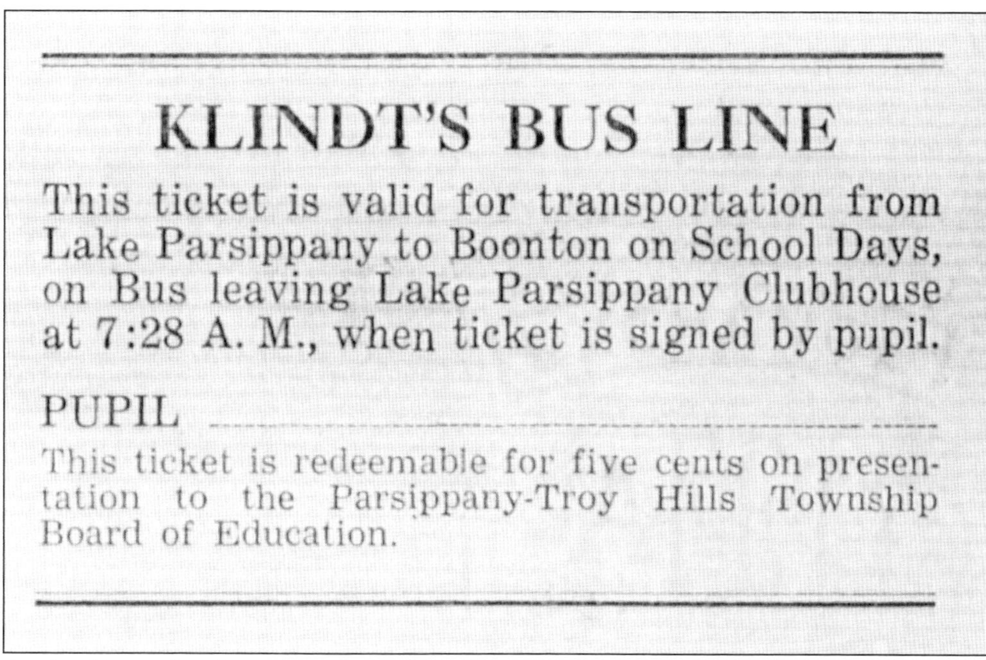

KLINDT'S BUS LINE

This ticket is valid for transportation from Lake Parsippany to Boonton on School Days, on Bus leaving Lake Parsippany Clubhouse at 7:28 A. M., when ticket is signed by pupil.

PUPIL ....

This ticket is redeemable for five cents on presentation to the Parsippany-Troy Hills Township Board of Education.

A school bus ticket for transportation from Lake Parsippany to Boonton. (Nick Cerbo.)

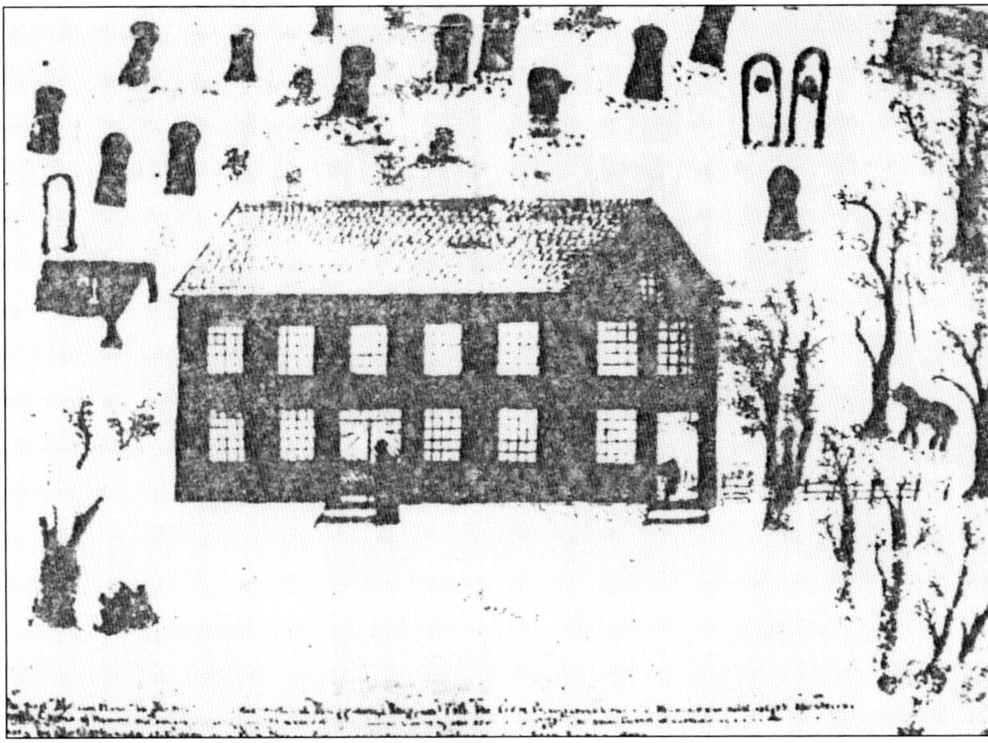

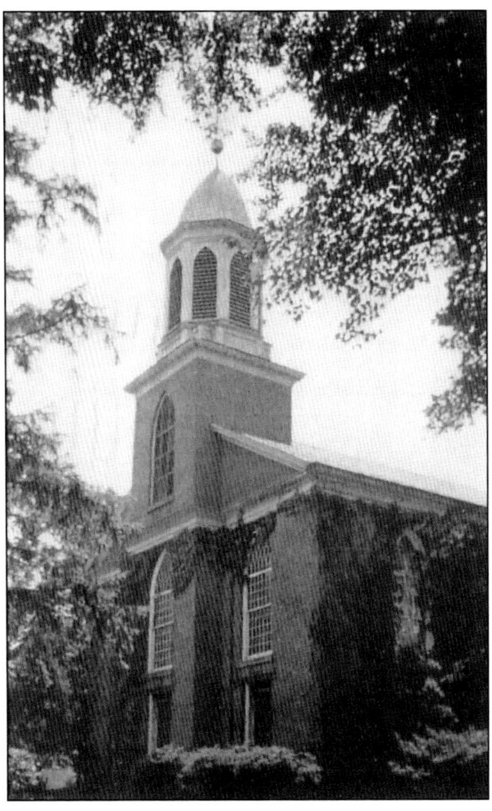

The second Presbyterian meetinghouse. Set on what is now the Presbyterian Cemetery at Vail Road and Route 46, this building was begun in 1770, but was not completed until 1790 due to the interruption of the Revolutionary War. It replaced the simple log structure built in 1755 on the same site. (Fran Kaminski.)

The Parsippany Presbyterian Church on Route 46 East. This church was built in 1828 on Paddleford Hill on land donated by the family of the same name. Reverend John Ford directed the construction and dedicated the new building. This was the third church for the congregation. The first two had been located across Route 6 on the Parsippany Presbyterian Cemetery grounds.(Parsippany-Troy Hills Public Library, Condit Room.)

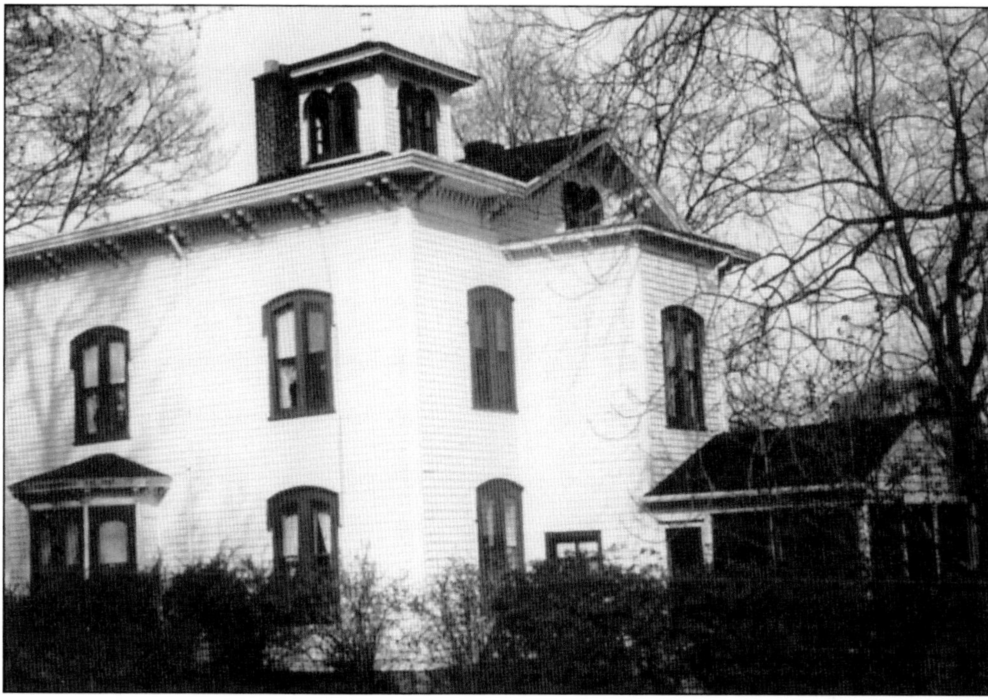

The Parsippany Presbyterian Church Manse (minister's residence), built in 1876. The manse was erected in the Italianate style of architecture for $4,000 on land donated by J. Condit Smith. (Fran Kaminski.)

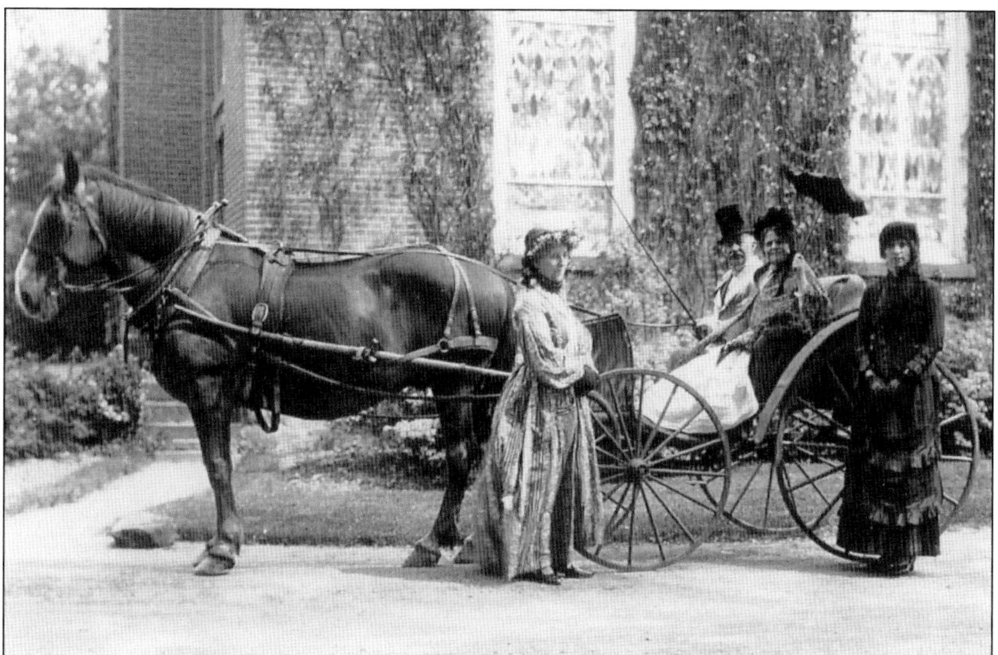

The centennial celebration of the building of the Presbyterian church, 1928. Standing are Helen Farrand and Mrs. Henry Dennis. In the carriage are Judd and Estelle Condit. (Parsippany-Troy Hills Public Library, Condit Room.)

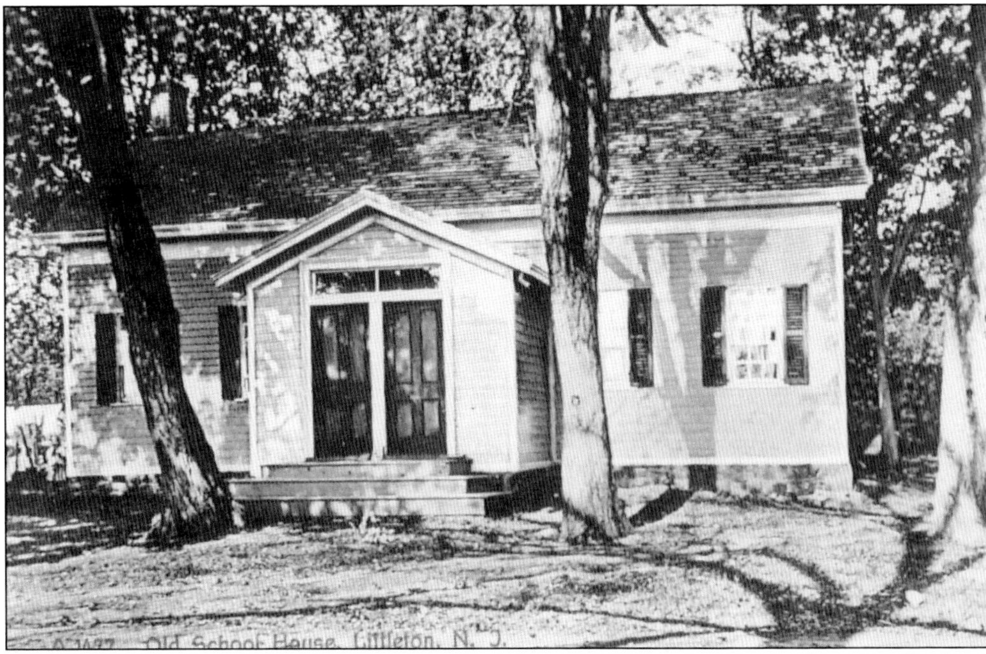

The Littleton School House at 1780 Littleton Road, built *c.* 1796. First used as a rural school, in 1810 this building housed an interdenominational Sunday school called the Union Bible School serving Baptists, Presbyterians, and Methodists. The Sunday school was started by Mrs. Silas Condict and Mrs. William Lee. A prize of a Bible was offered to any child who had read one thousand verses of scripture. Only two children ever won: Caroline Templeton and Mary Lee. The latter was the daughter of one of the founders, and later married Edward Howell. The building became a Hanover Township public school in 1872, and was sold to the Littleton Baptist Church in the early 1900s. (Robert D'Alessandro.)

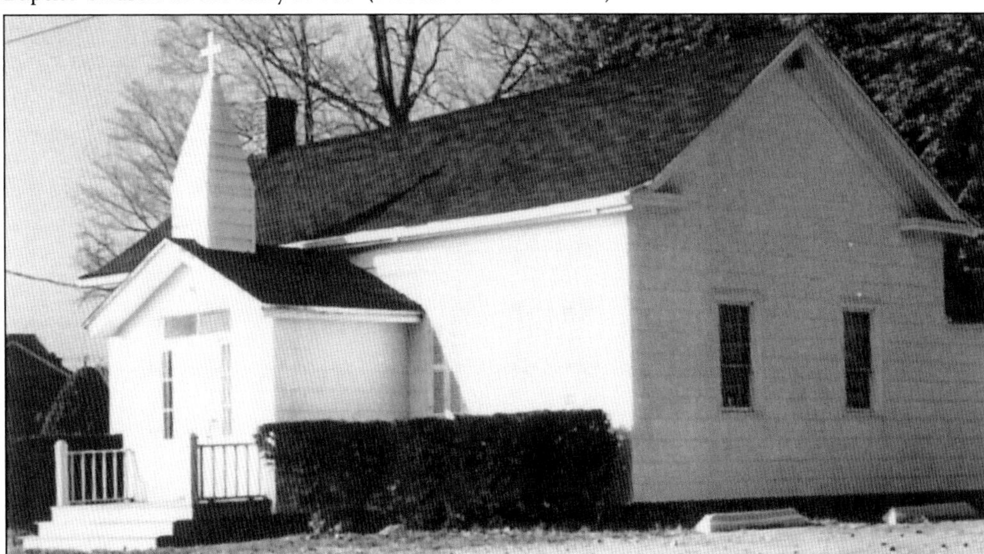

The Littleton School House, *c.* 1960. This building was once owned by Llewellyn Farms Restaurant, which used it for the storage of china. It was sold in 1996 and is presently threatened by development in the area. (Fran Kaminski.)

The Parsippany Methodist Church as seen from Route 46. Land was acquired in 1830, but lack of funding delayed the completion of the church until 1843. Remodeled in 1930, the church came to include a kitchen, stage, and folding doors. In 1947, Reverend Walton removed the stage to make room for a lavatory; the folding doors were replaced with a wall, and two schoolrooms were added. The building was demolished in the early 1960s for the construction of Route 287, and the new church was built on South Beverwyck Road in 1964. (Robert D'Alessandro.)

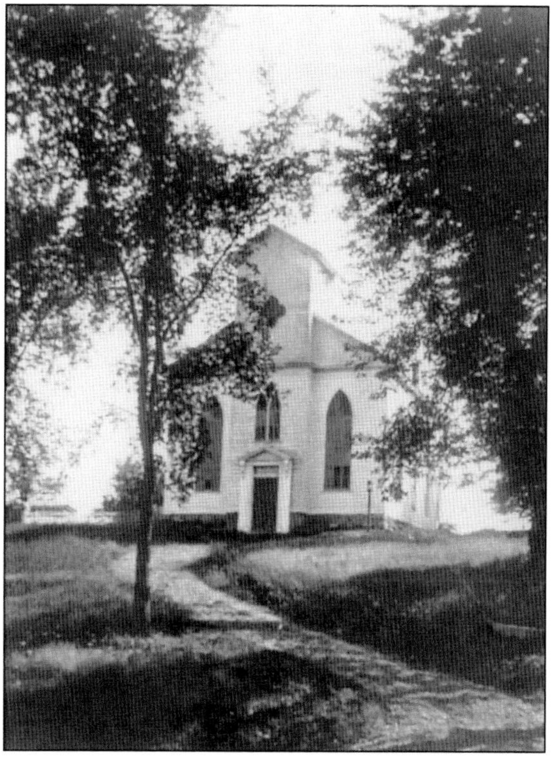

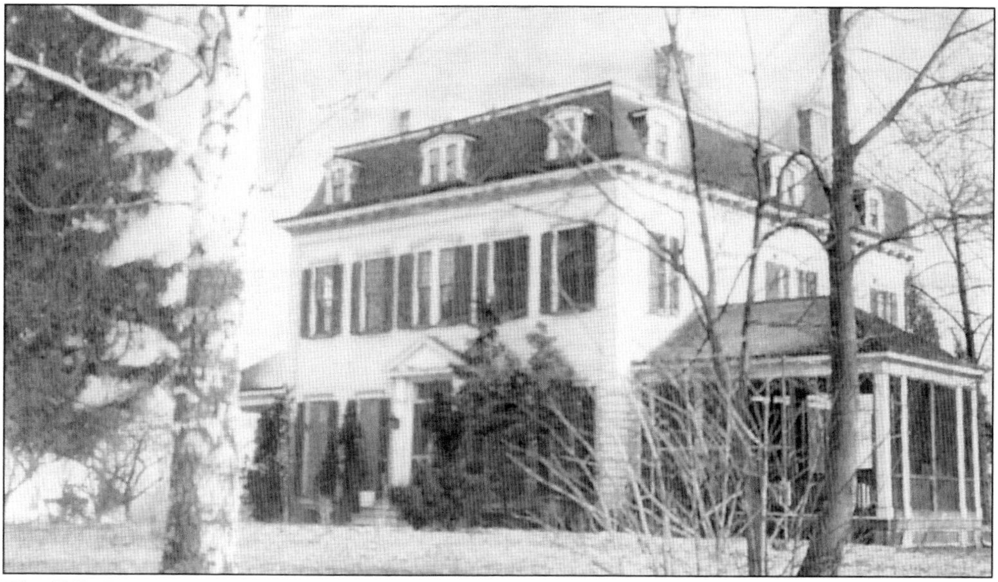

The E.B. Patten Mansion, located on Littleton Road at Camelot Way. The mansion became the Blue Swan Inn and later the old Saint Christopher's Church. Services were conducted on the first floor of the church and also in the basement for latecomers. In 1960, the church bought 23 acres from a farmer, A. Zoch, and relocated. The new church and parochial school were built further south on Littleton Road in 1963. The mansion was razed to make way for the Camelot Garden Apartments in the early 1960s. (Saint Christopher's Church.)

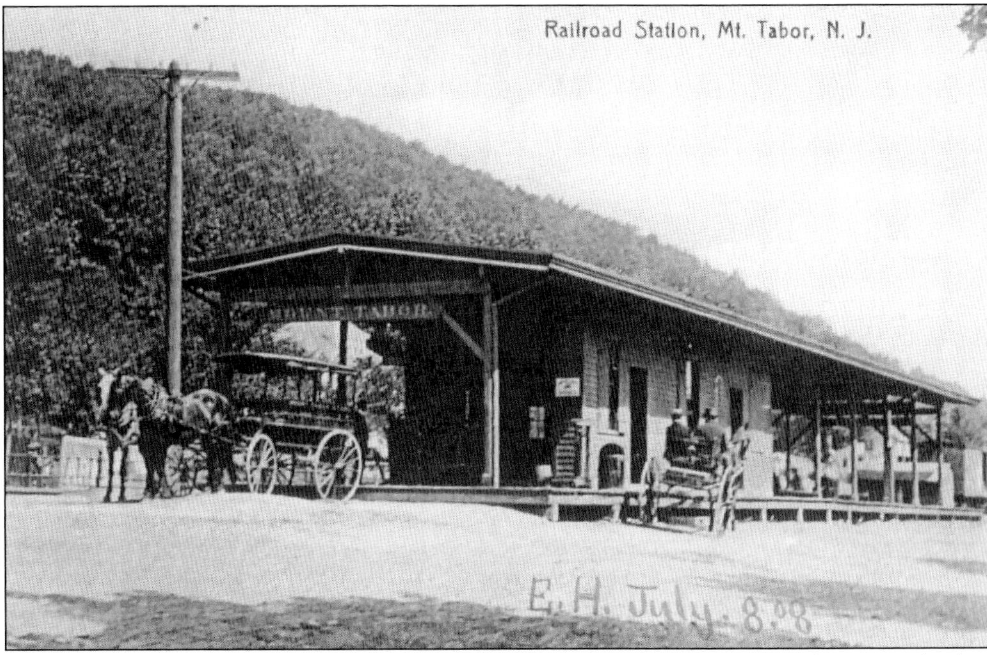

The railroad station at Mount Tabor in 1908. This station was built to bring Methodists from the large industrial cities in northern New Jersey to the annual camp meetings for enjoyment of the fresh air, cooler temperatures, beautiful countryside, and religious activities. (Robert D'Alessandro.)

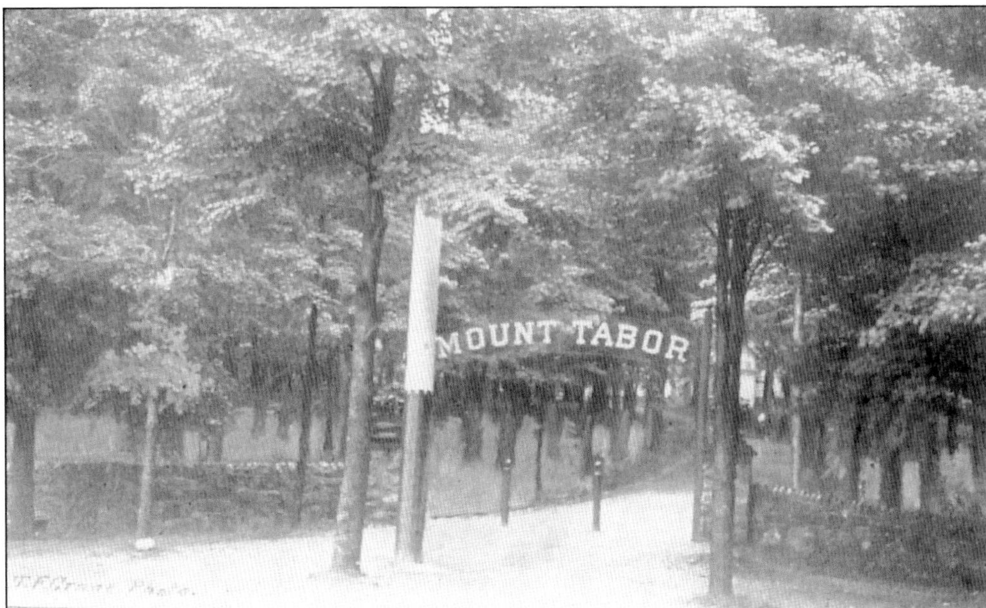

The entrance to Mount Tabor on Route 53. Mount Tabor was established on 31.5 acres of land purchased from the Dickersons in 1869; a 100-acre farm was acquired and added to the property in 1872. The first camp meeting was held from August through September in 1869. (Robert D'Alessandro.)

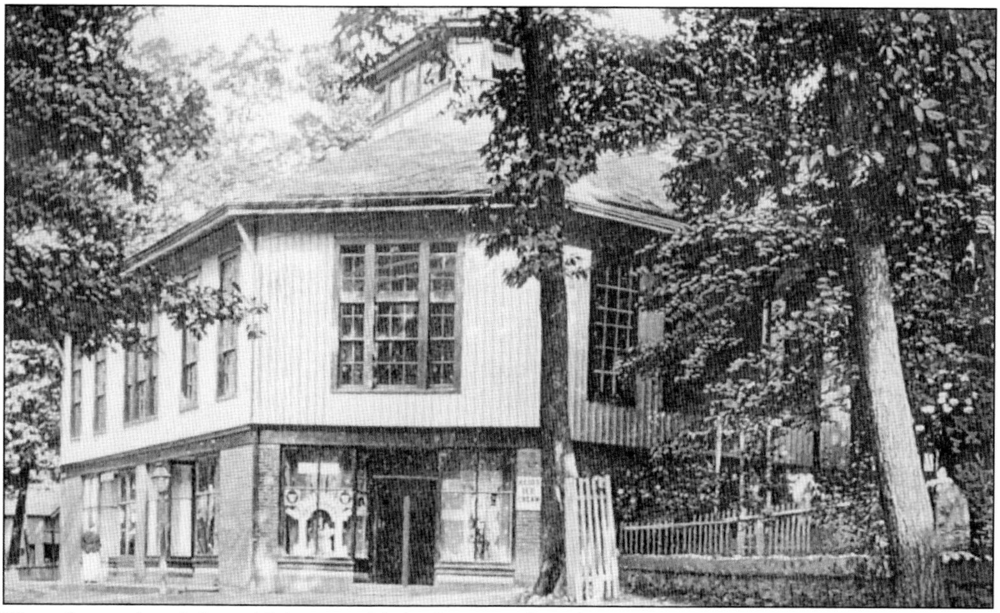

The tabernacle at Mount Tabor, established in 1869 for religious services. The altar dates from 1885. The tabernacle was not heated as the back was an open-air facility. (Robert D'Alessandro.)

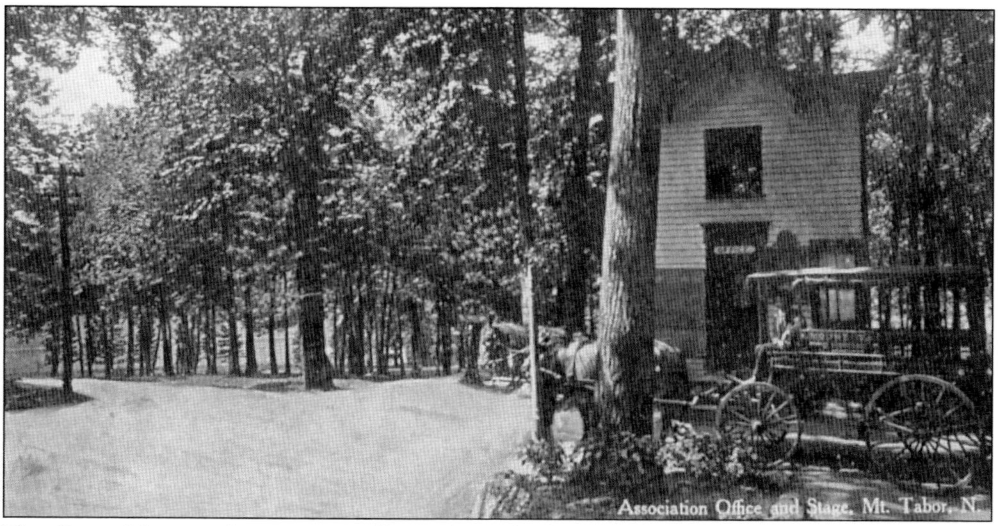

The Camp Meeting Association Office, where the board of trustees met. The board members were elected for a term of three years, and four trustees were elected annually. On March 17, 1869, the Camp Meeting Association of the Newark Conference of the Methodist Episcopal Church was organized. This religiously established community functioned as a municipality with its own police department and municipal court. Mount Tabor and Ocean Grove were the only two organizations of this type in New Jersey. However, in 1979, the New Jersey State Supreme Court held that it was unconstitutional for these communities to have secular governing powers. It ruled that the New Jersey State Legislature had violated the First Amendment of the Constitution (the separation of church and state) when it granted the Camp Meeting Association municipal powers. At this point, Mount Tabor became part of Parsippany-Troy Hills. (Robert D'Alessandro.)

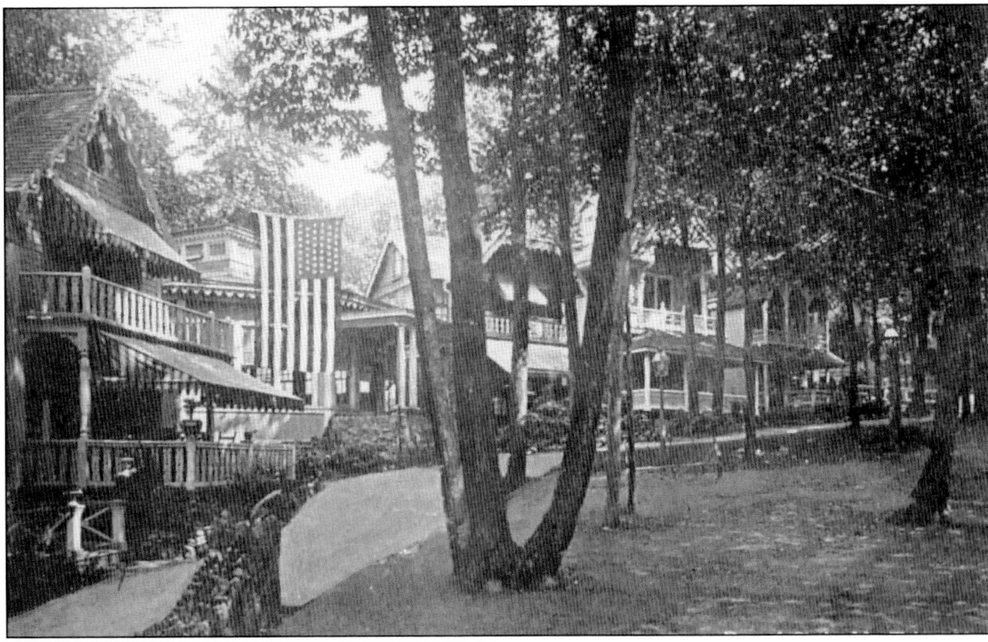

The Circle, showing the Victorian facades. Originally, 25-by-16-foot lots were rented to campers for tent sites at the cost of $25 and up. Many tent owners began to improve their tents by adding wooden floors, cabinets, etc. Eventually, these became year-round homes, still adhering to the initial dimensions of the tent sites. (Robert D'Alessandro.)

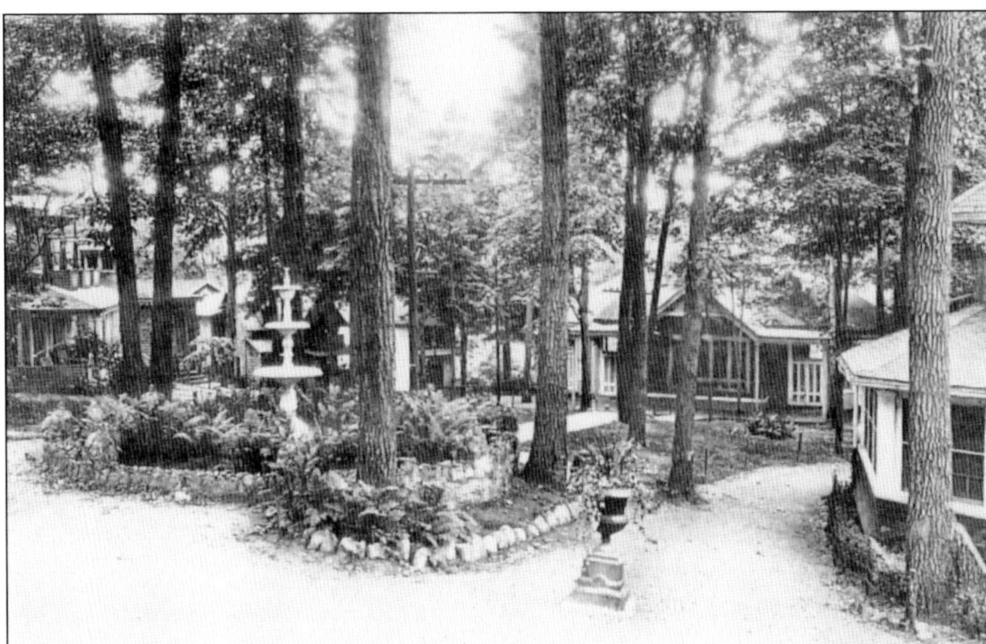

Trinity Park, Mount Tabor. The Mount Tabor Historic Society replaced the fountain in 1995. (Robert D'Alessandro.)

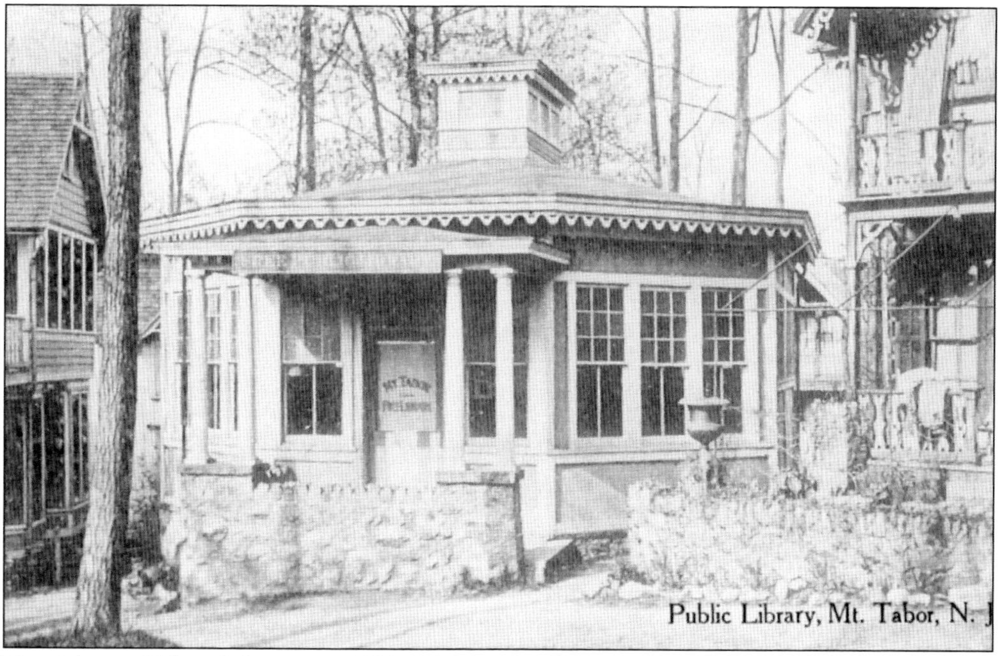

The Mount Tabor Library, *c.* 1920. Pharmacist Henry L. Coit founded the library with 150 books in 1889, charging a fee to borrow books. The library had canvas side flaps for walls until 1911 when a permanent structure was erected. Miss Charlotte Johns was appointed as the public librarian and she served in that capacity for forty years. The library is still in use. (Robert D'Alessandro.)

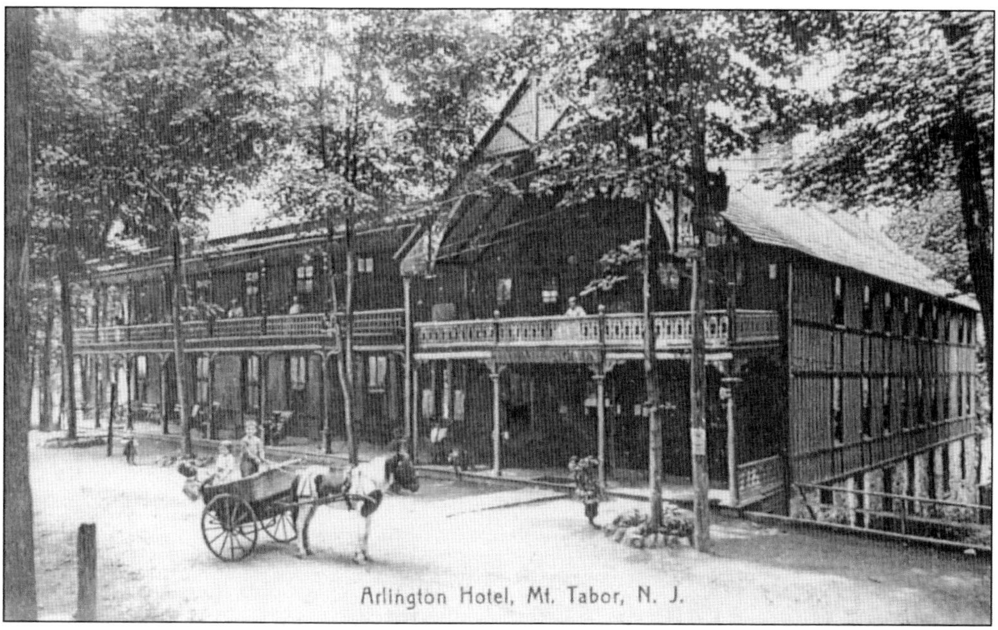

Some campers who did not care to "rough it" in tents took rooms at the new Arlington Hotel, located down the block across from the tabernacle. The hotel was built and funded by a member of the Camp Meeting Association. Only the foundation of the Arlington still stands, serving as a retaining wall for Mount Tabor Park. (Robert D'Alessandro.)

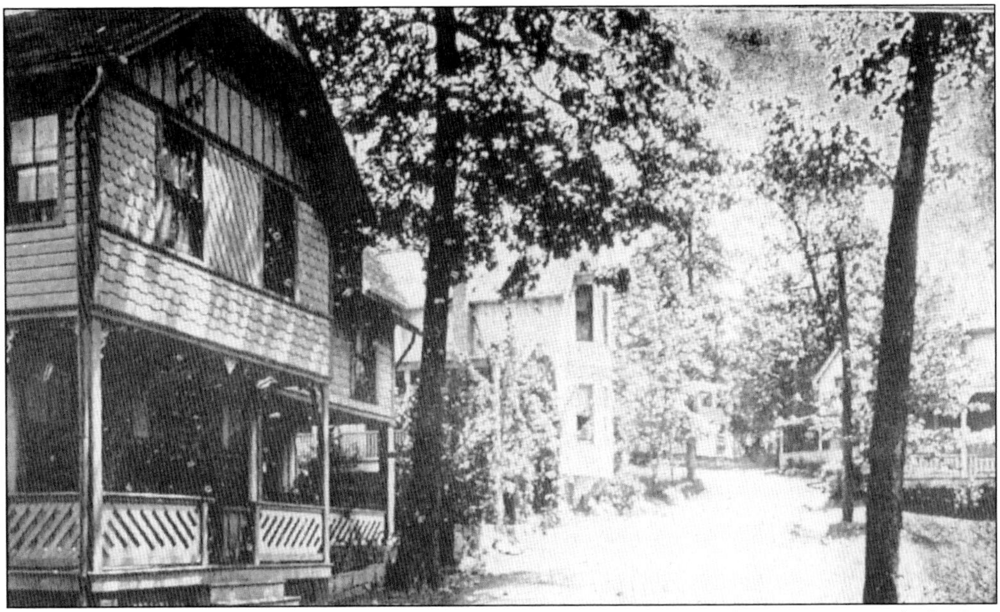

Asbury Place in Mount Tabor, *c.* 1910. The home at 25 Asbury Place is a particularly fine example of Queen Anne Victorian architecture since its restoration. (Muriel Berson.)

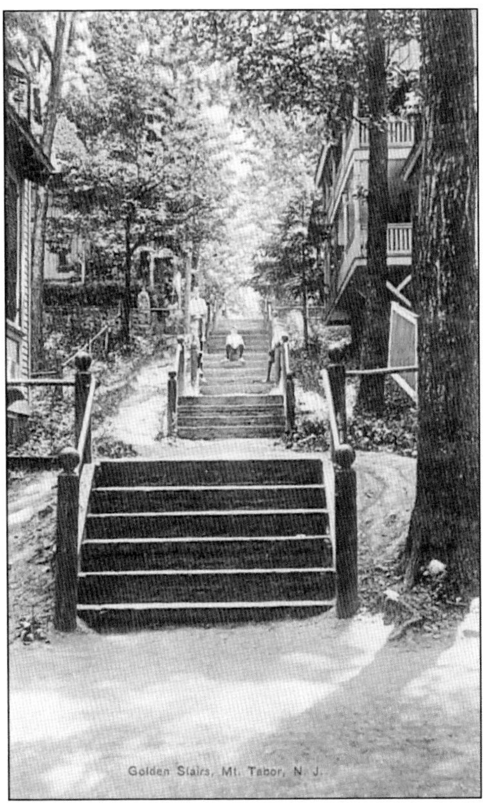

The Golden Stairs. The stairs were built by Victorian gentlemen of Mount Tabor for the ladies as a precautionary measure against accidents. The stairs erected on Searing Place enabled them to negotiate the hilly area with ease. (Robert D'Alessandro.)

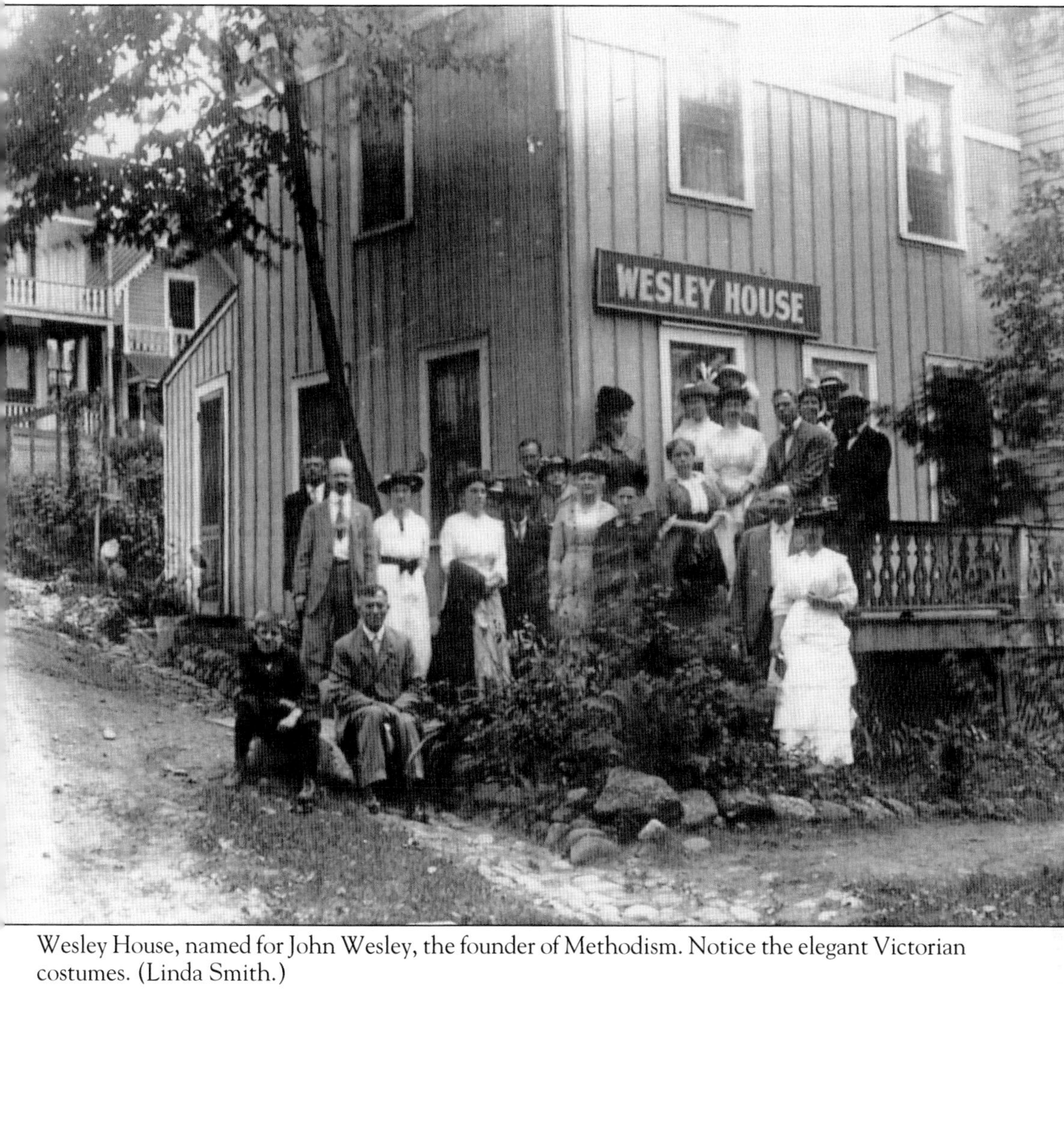

Wesley House, named for John Wesley, the founder of Methodism. Notice the elegant Victorian costumes. (Linda Smith.)

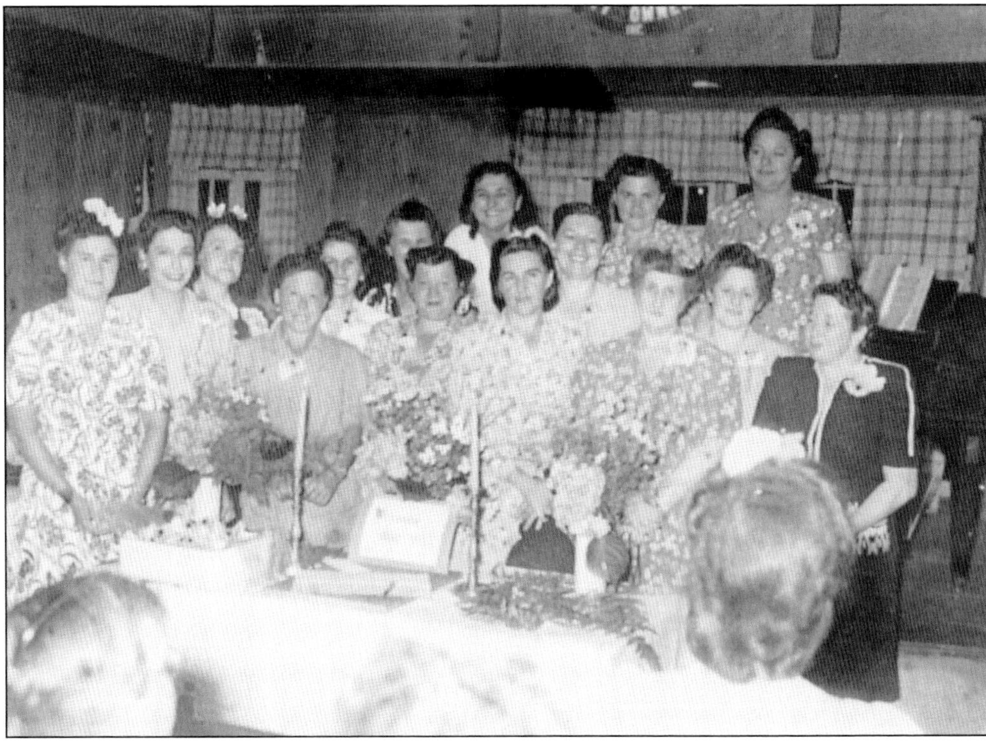

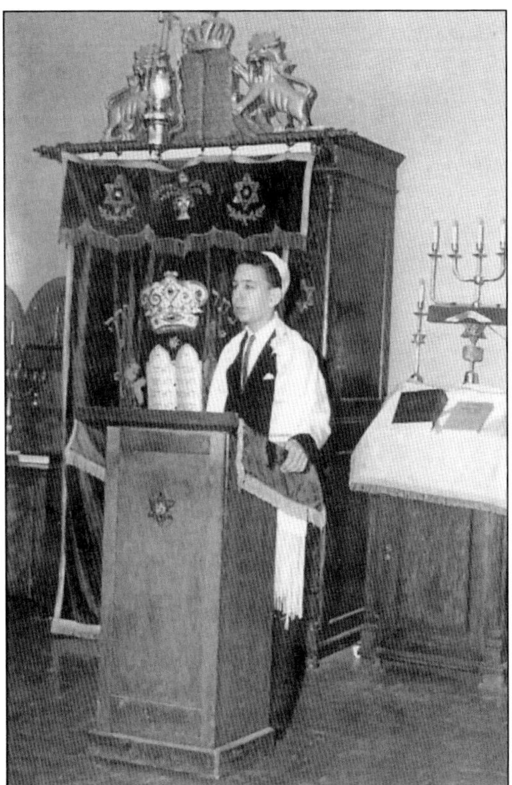

The installation of Mrs. Sam Levitt as president of the Lake Hiawatha Branch of Hadassah, *c.* 1942. Mrs. Levitt was instrumental in founding this local chapter. (Sam Levitt.)

The bar mitzvah of Will and Miriam Cohen's son Matthew at the first Lake Hiawatha Jewish Center. From 1942 until 1945, religious services were conducted by Rabbi Joseph Schreiber in his home at 156 North Beverwyck Road. In 1945, the first Lake Hiawatha Jewish Center opened on the corner of Nokomis Avenue and Lake Hiawatha Boulevard, and Rabbi Sam Mendelowitz became the first full-time rabbi of the congregation. In 1964, a new synagogue was erected on Lincoln Avenue. The congregation disbanded in September 1995, according to Sadie Wishnick, the oldest remaining member, and became part of the Pine Brook Synagogue. The site is now home to the Haridham Temple. (Will and Miriam Cohen.)

Four

Farm Life

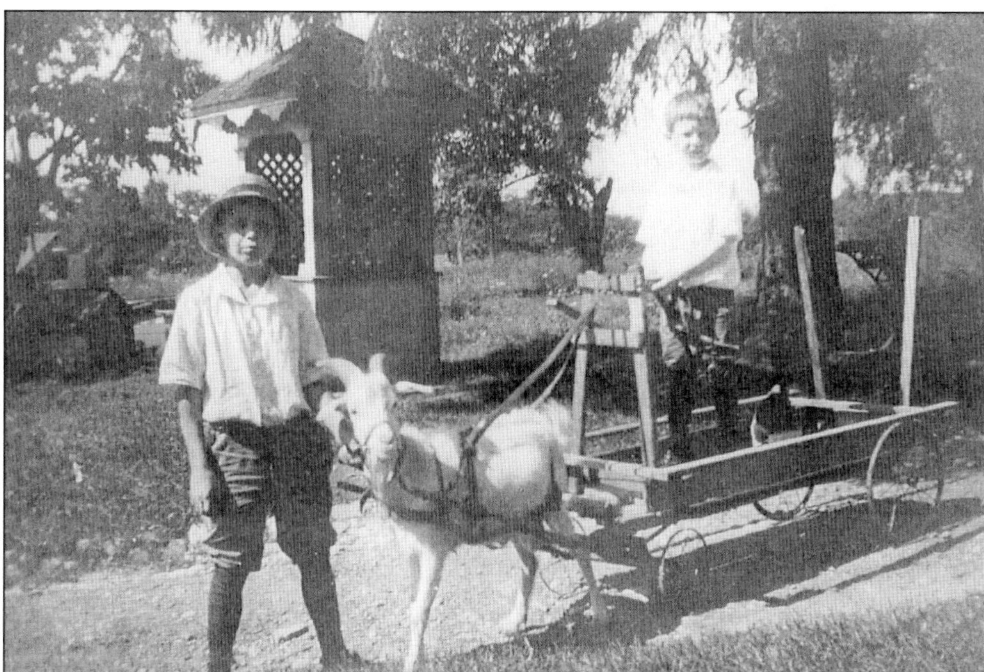

Stephen and Paul Condit (grandsons of Stephen Hobart Condit), with their pet goat Pete, at 41 North Beverwyck Road, *c.* 1918. The well is still standing on the family farm. A poem on back of photograph reads: "A very good hitch / P.C. age 6 / Pete, goat very fine / Stephen just nine / Wagon built by S.H.C. / A good time for all three!" (Parsippany-Troy Hills Public Library, Condit Room.)

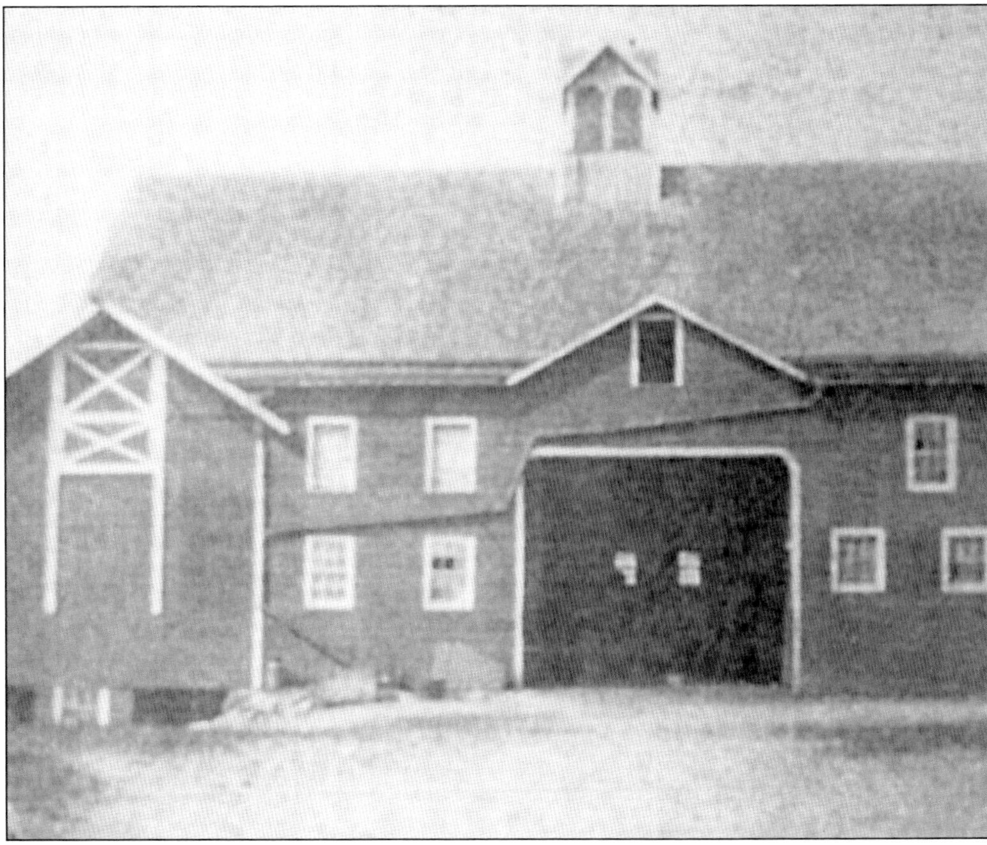

The dairy barn located on Route 202 off Cherry Hill Road. This barn was built by John Bates in 1846 and was later owned by his son Raymond. It was razed in the 1940s. (Charles Bates.)

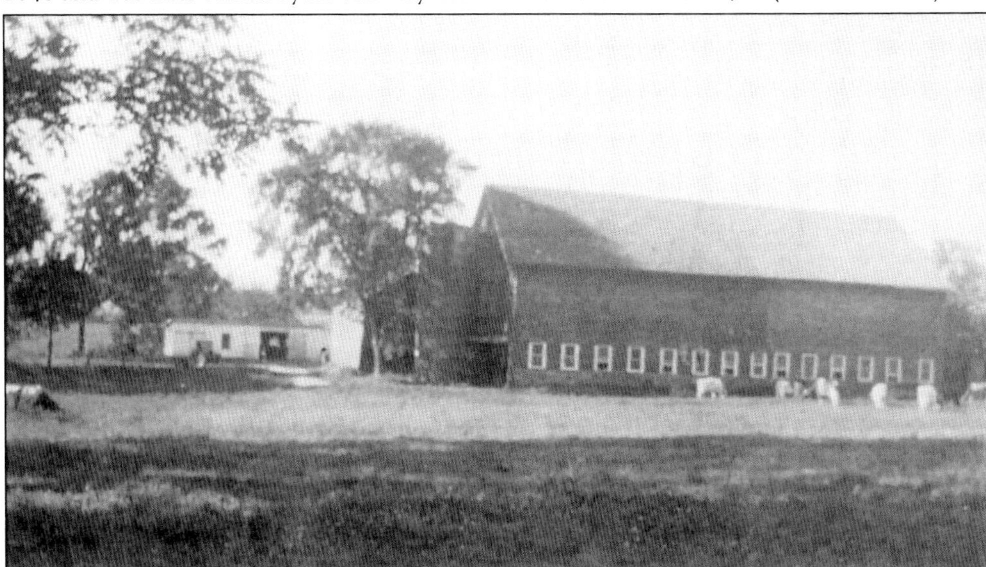

The Bates' Brook Farm dairy barn. This barn stood where Route 287 North and East Halsey Road now intersect. It was the largest barn in Morris County. (Charles Bates.)

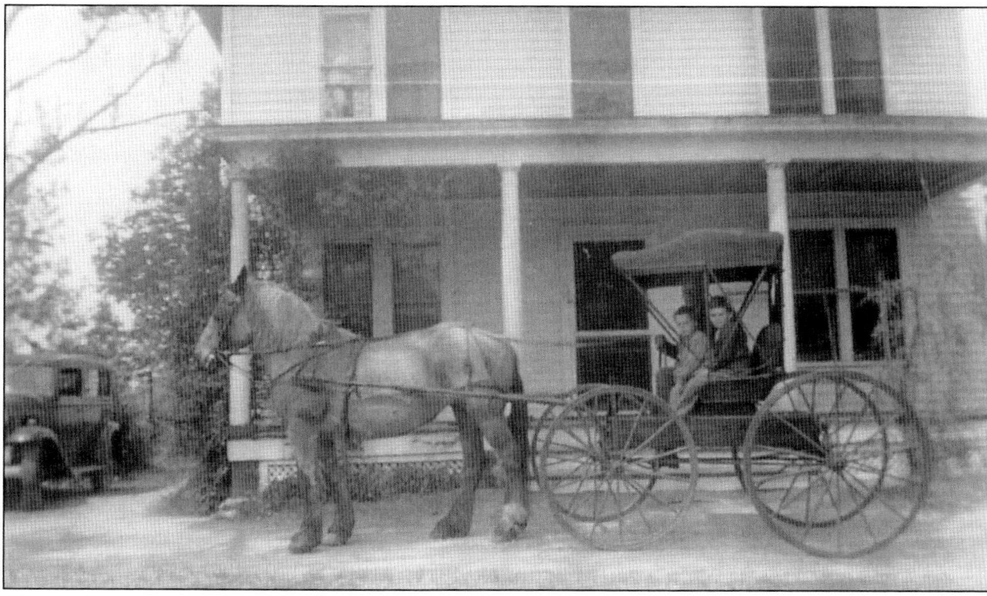

Charles Bates with sons Charlie and Dougie, being drawn by a roan mare, *c.* 1940. The three are in front of the family farmhouse. When the township changed the zoning in that area, the farmhouse was razed to make way for the office building that now stands next to the exit for Parsippany Road on Route 287. (Charles Bates.)

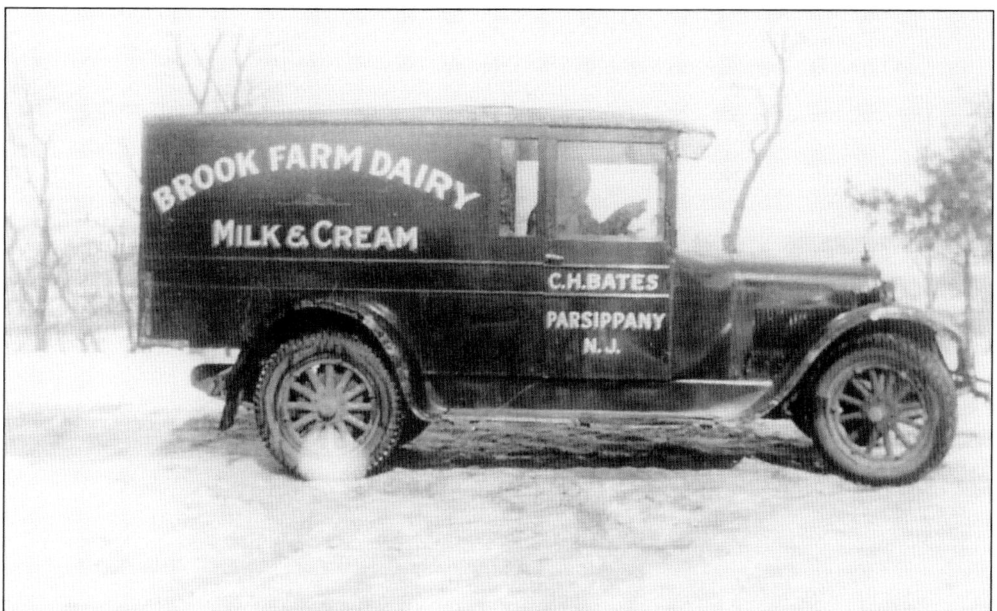

The 1927 Dodge delivery truck for the Bates' Brook Farm. Milk was sold wholesale from the farm until the operation went retail in the late 1920s. In 1954, the state purchased the farm to make way for Route 287. (Charles Bates.)

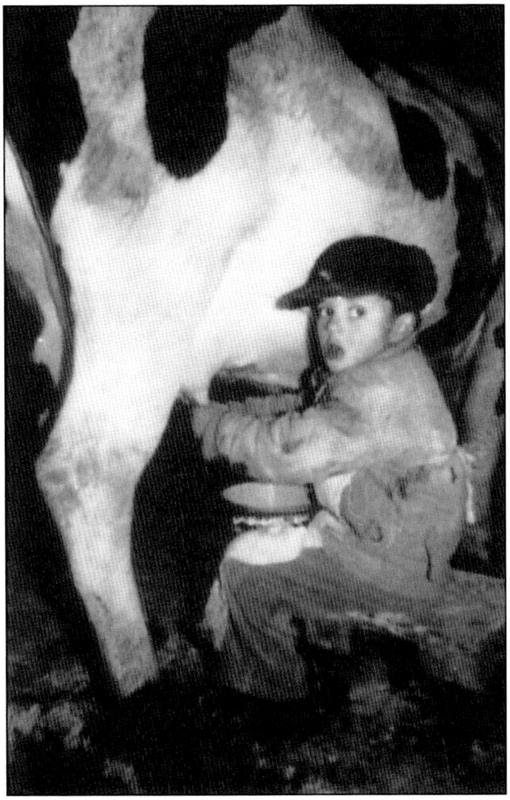

Charles Bates' son, three-year-old Charles Bates III, milking a cow, *c*. 1940. (Charles Bates.)

Beverwyck Dairy, the property of Charles DeHart Condit, on South Beverwyck Road and Route 46 East, *c*. 1920. The Lucas von Beverhoudt Mansion was located here. Called the Red Barracks during the Revolutionary War, it was the largest plantation with the greatest number of slaves in New Jersey. Beverwyck means "house of the beaver" in Dutch. *See Founding Families*. (Robert Benson.)

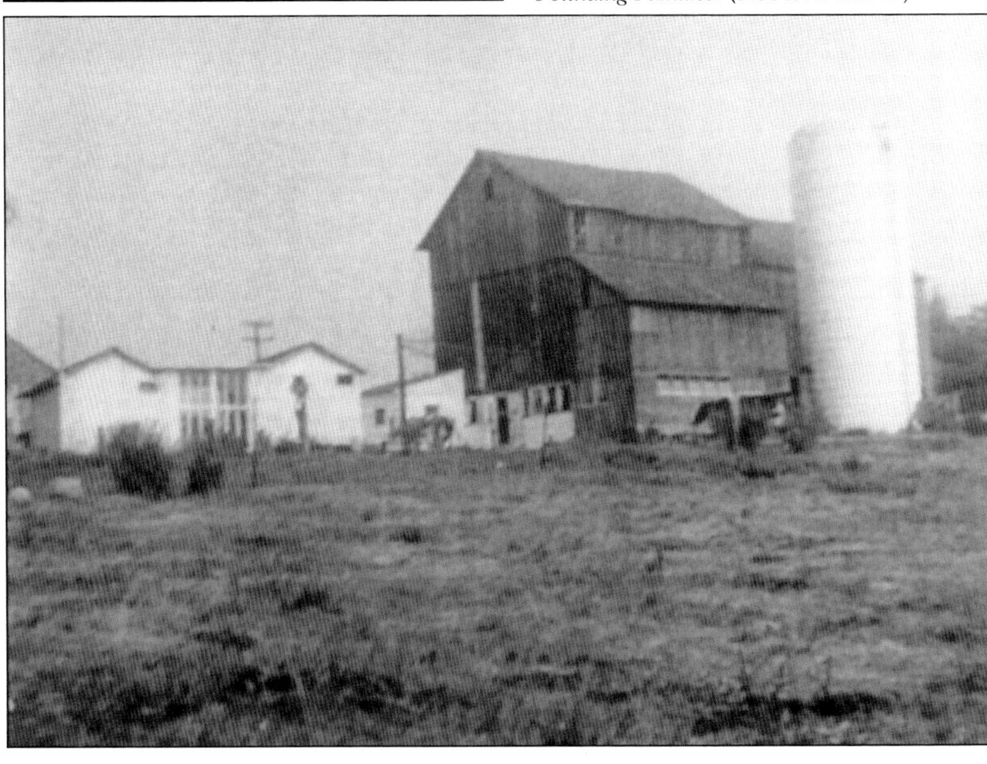

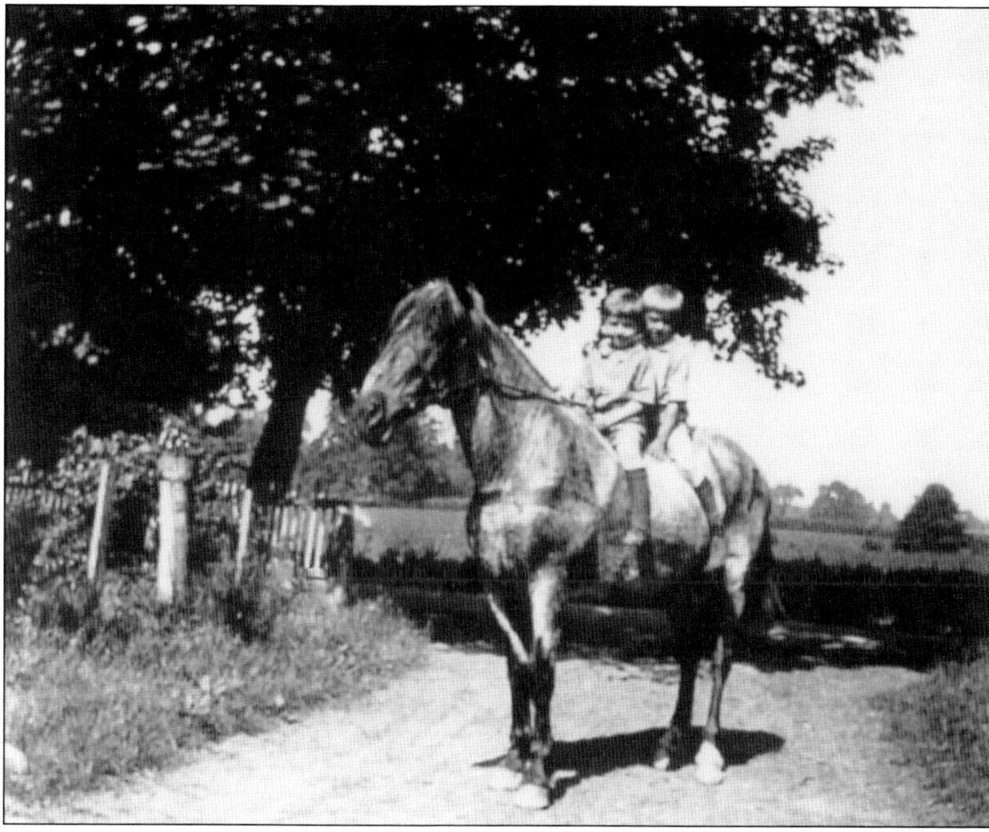

Harold and Edward Farrand on the Farrand Farm, 1923. (Harold O. Farrand.)

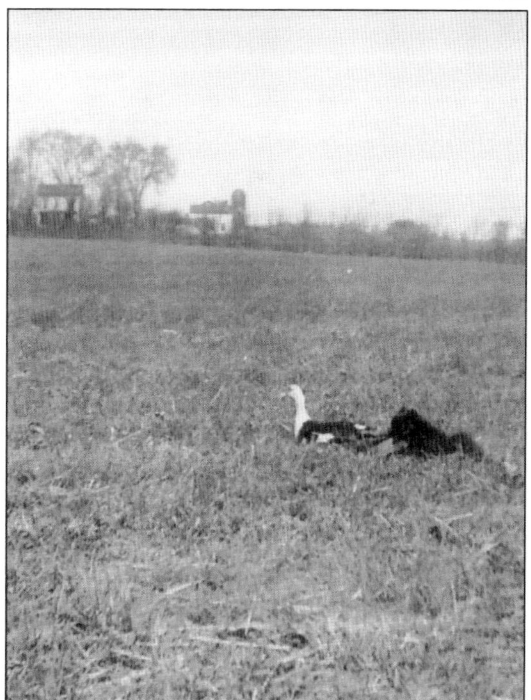

In the background is the Farrand-Wildeboer House on the northeast corner of Beverwyck and Vail Roads in 1938. This view is from the Farrand Farm, where the family dog is chasing a goose. (Harold O. Farrand.)

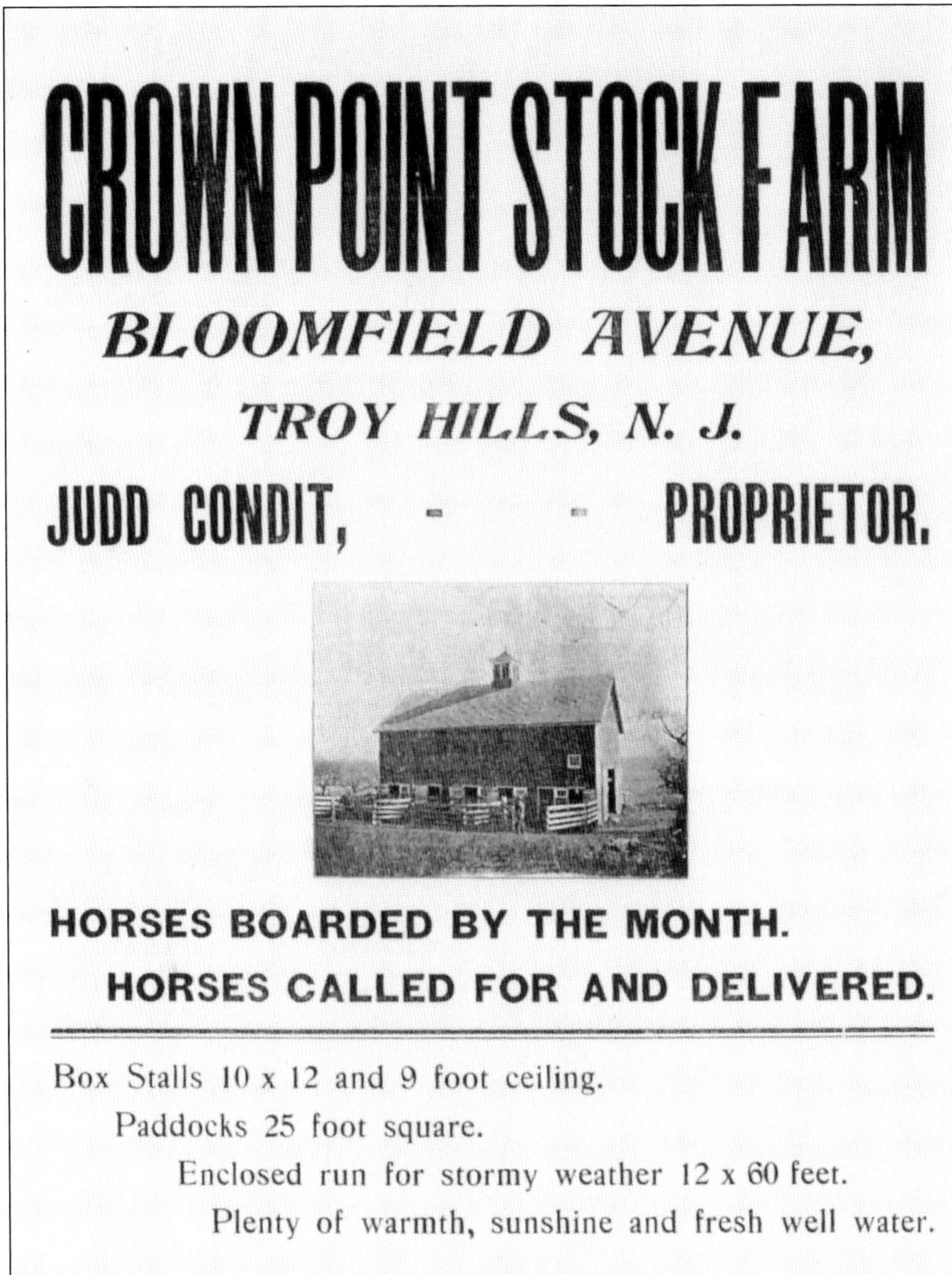

An advertisement for Crown Point Stock Farm, which was on the Condit property at 41 North Beverwyck Road and Route 46. The proprietor was Judd Condit. (Muriel Berson.)

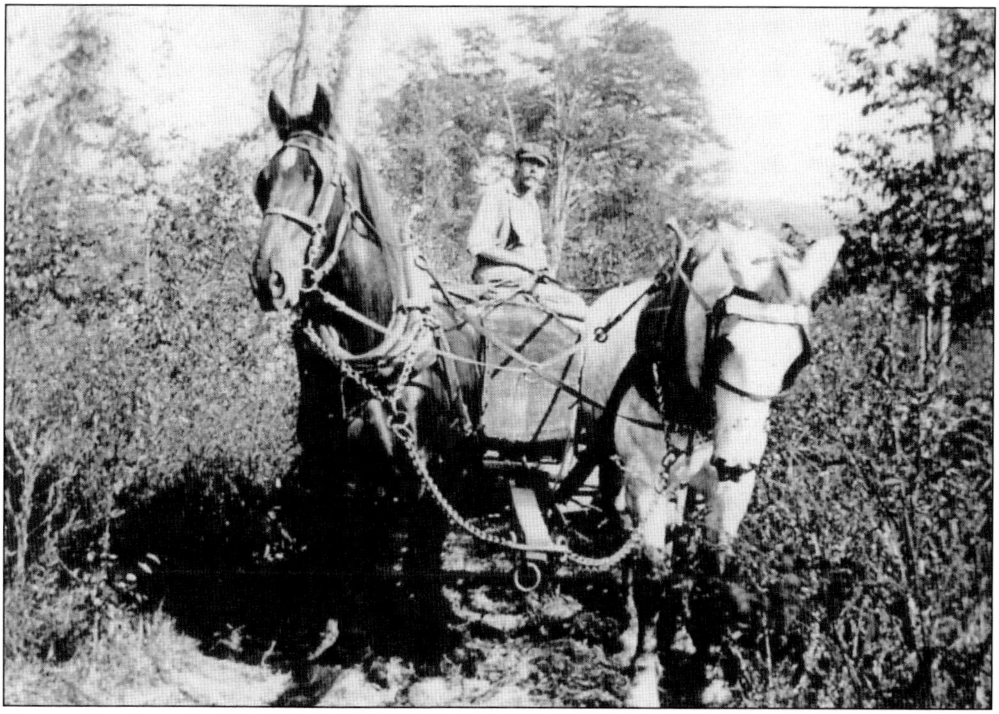

George Smith on his farm doing daily chores, *c.* 1920. (Muriel Berson.)

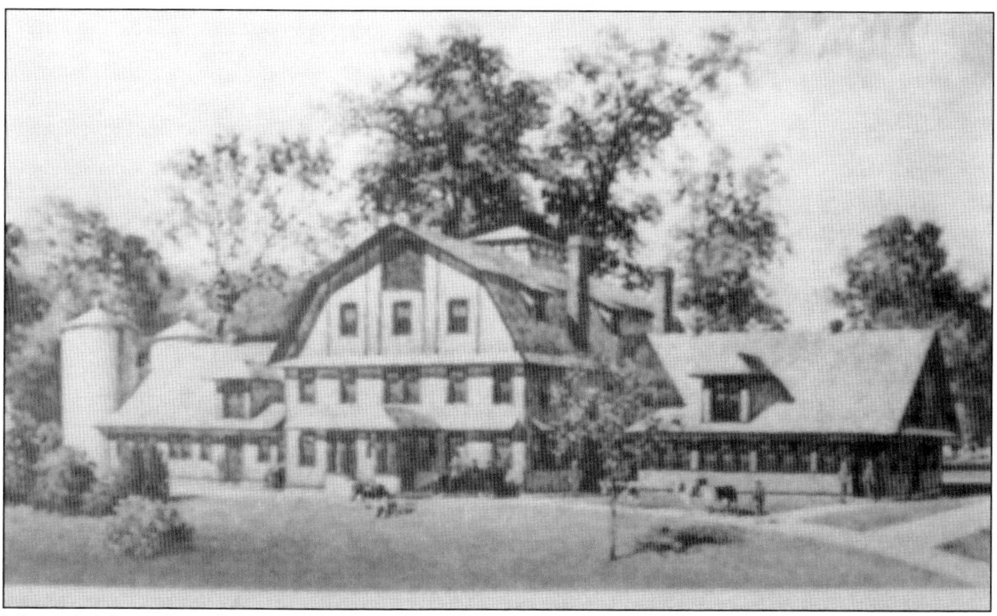

The McAlpin dairy barn on Littleton Road near Route 10, *c.* 1902. David Hunter McAlpin was a prominent businessman, owner of the Hotel McAlpin in New York City, trustee of the Children's Home, and brother-in-law of philanthropist Geraldine Rockefeller Dodge. (Joint Free Public Library of Morristown and Morris Township.)

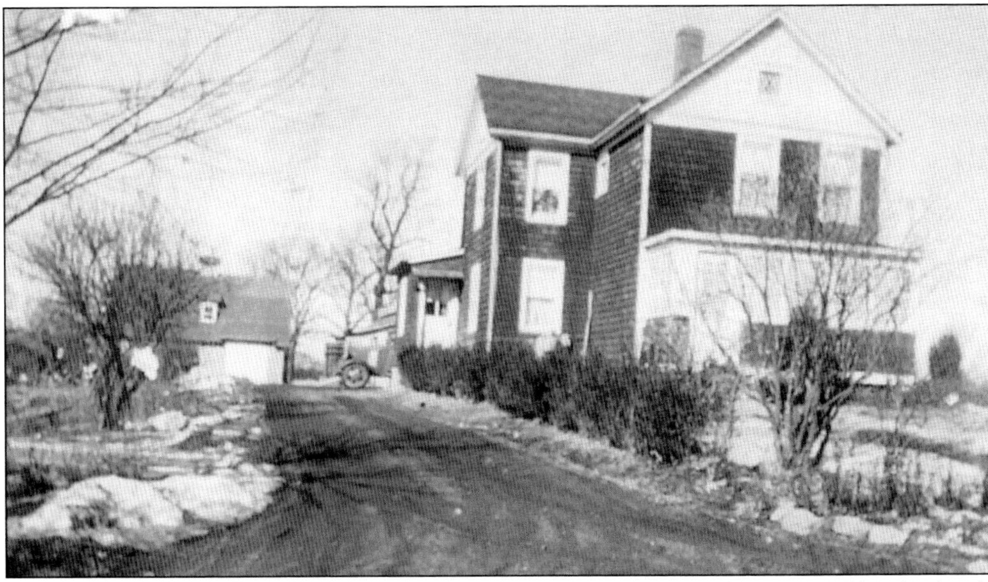

The Przyhocki home at 140 Reynolds Avenue, 1940. This home has been owned by the family since the 1920s. (Ann Przyhocki Morgenthien.)

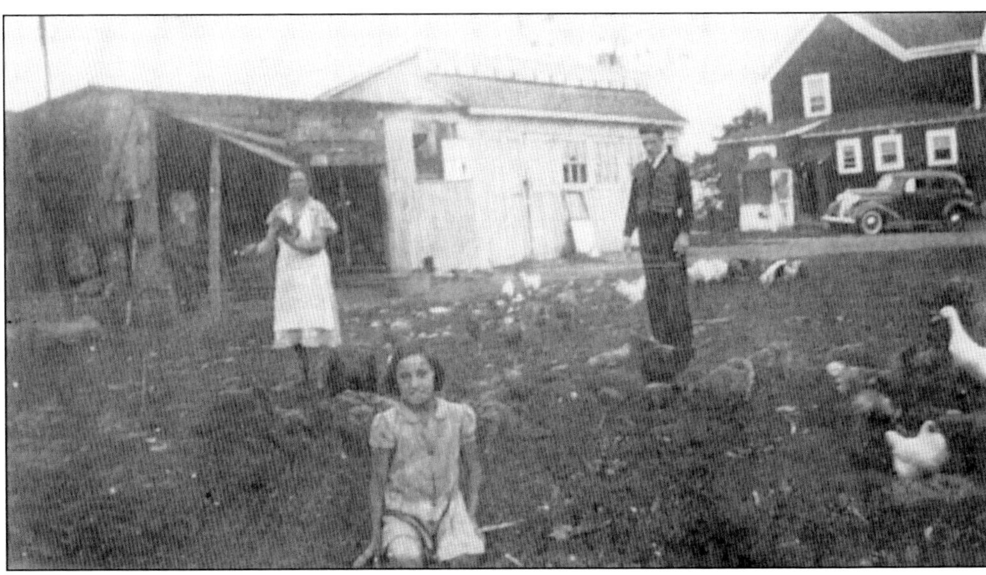

Mary Przyhocki feeding her chickens with daughter Ann and Paul Baransky, c. 1930. (Ann Przyhocki Morgenthien.)

The Levitt family, c.. 1932. From left to right are Sam, Carl, and Edna. The Levitts were one of the first Jewish families to settle in Parsippany-Troy Hills. (Sam Levitt.)

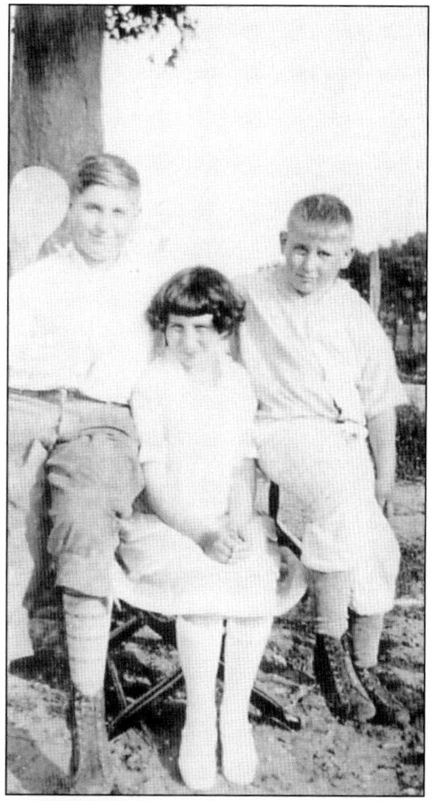

The Levitt Goose Farm at 621 Edwards Road. Geese are being fattened to be sold at market. Sam Levitt would purchase the geese out west and take them back here by train, traveling along with them in the boxcar. (Sam Levitt.)

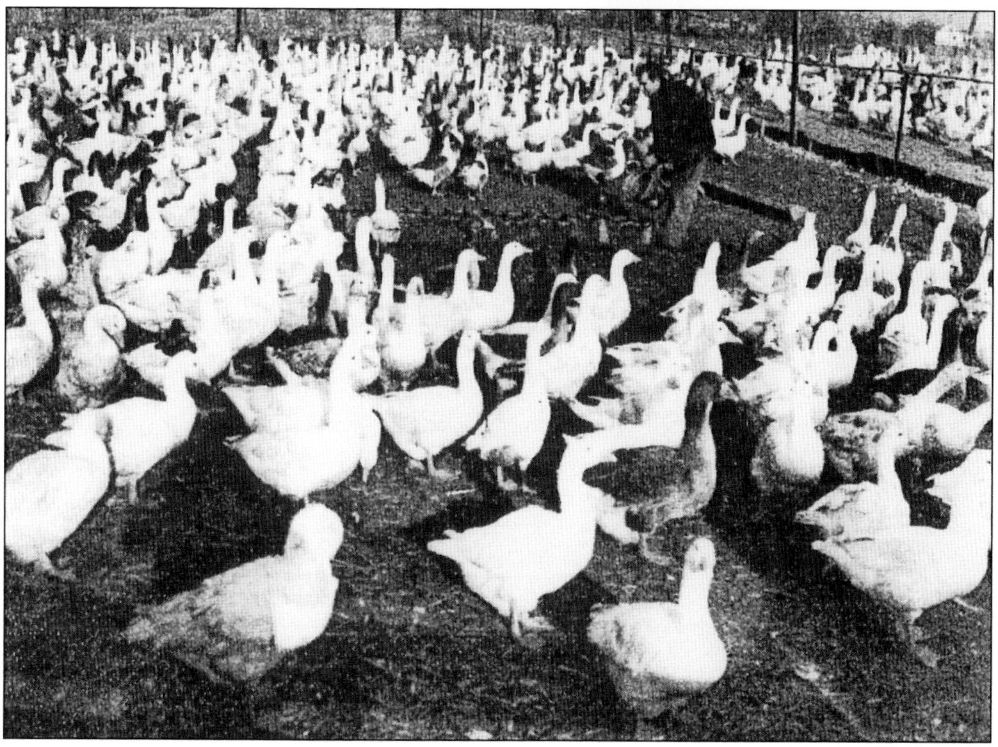

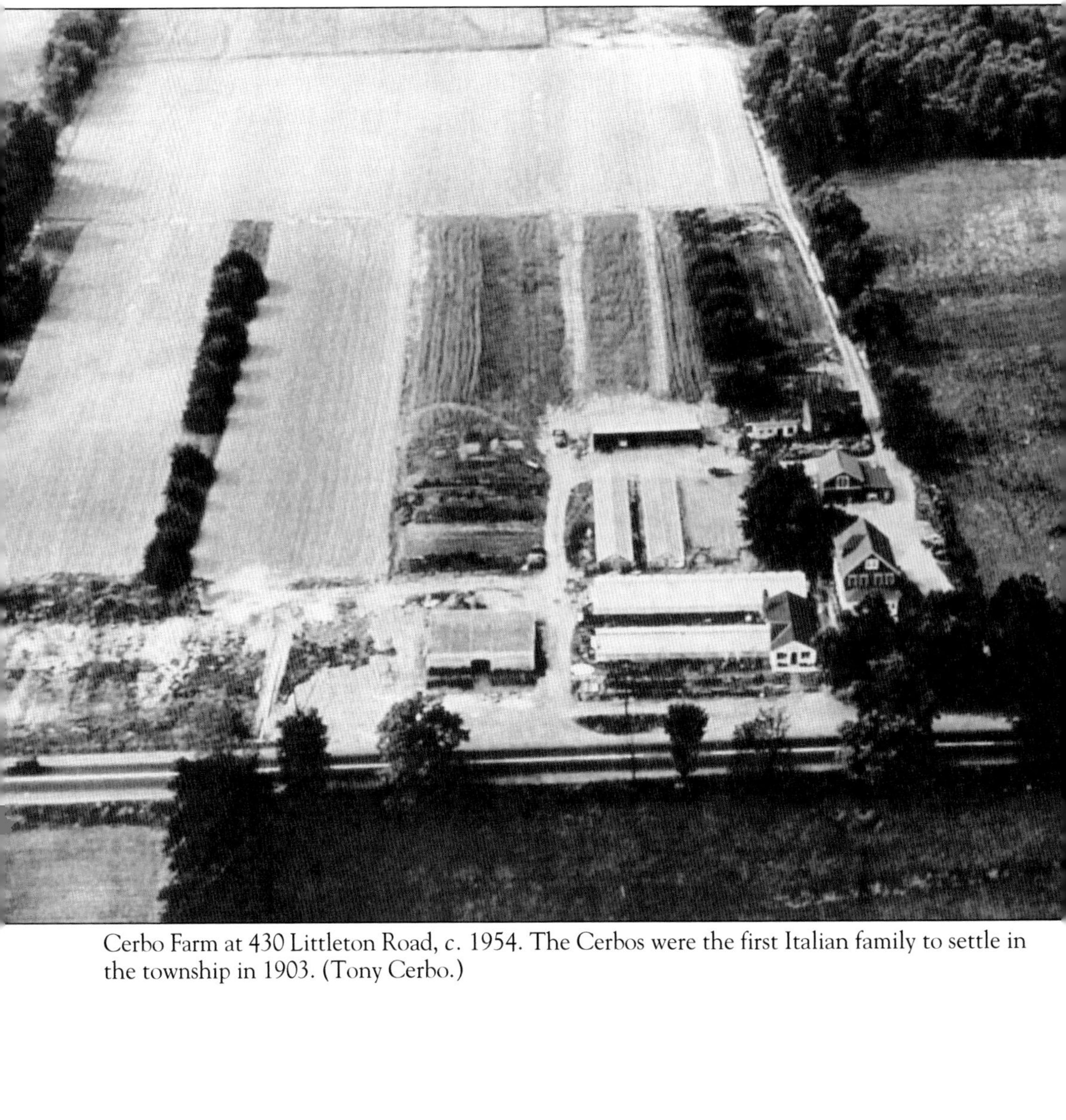

Cerbo Farm at 430 Littleton Road, c. 1954. The Cerbos were the first Italian family to settle in the township in 1903. (Tony Cerbo.)

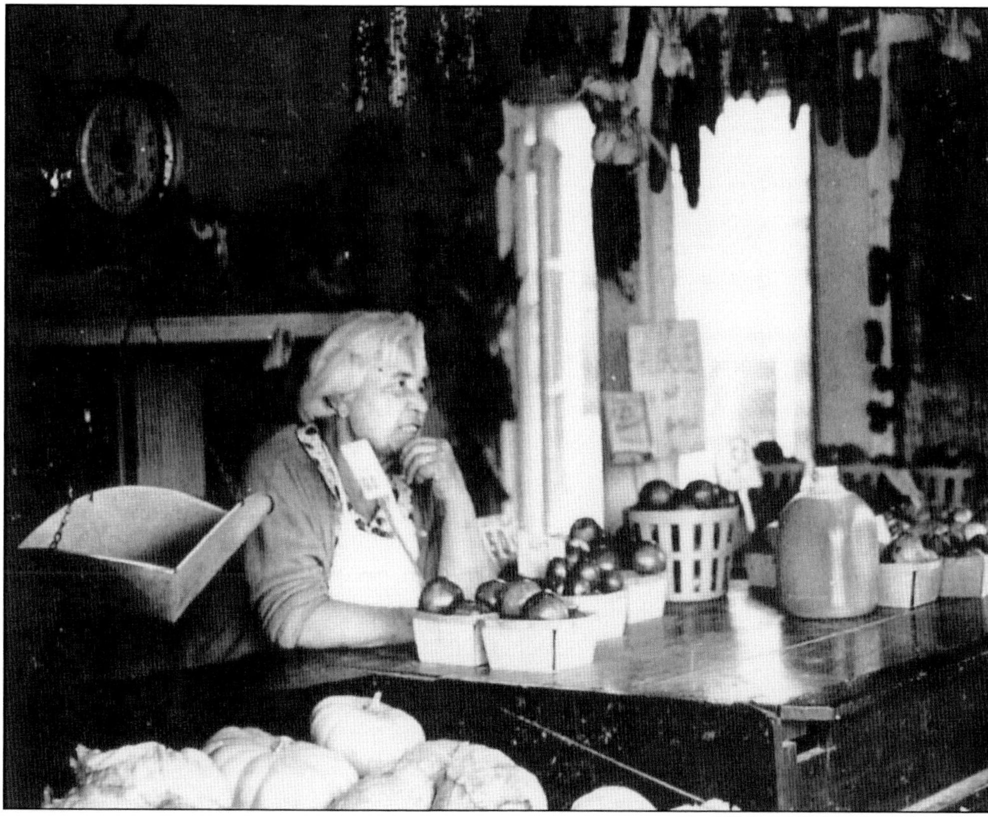

Cerbo Farm at 430 Littleton Road. Tony Cerbo's mother, Catherine, is at the vegetable stand. (Tony Cerbo.)

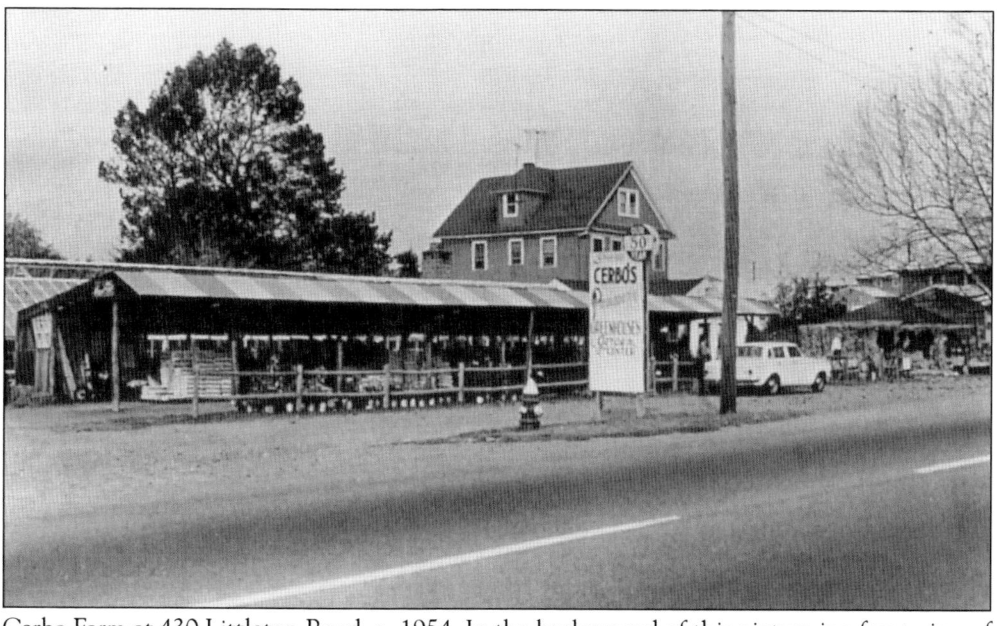

Cerbo Farm at 430 Littleton Road, c. 1954. In the background of this picture is a front view of the Cerbo home; in the foreground are farmstands. (Tony Cerbo.)

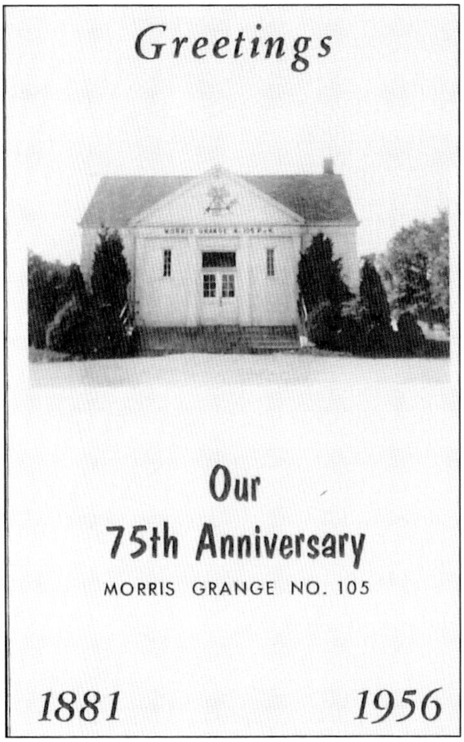

The grange at 232 South Beverwyck Road in 1956. The grange was a farmers' social and business organization. The site is presently home to the Chinese Christian Church of New Jersey. (Muriel Berson.)

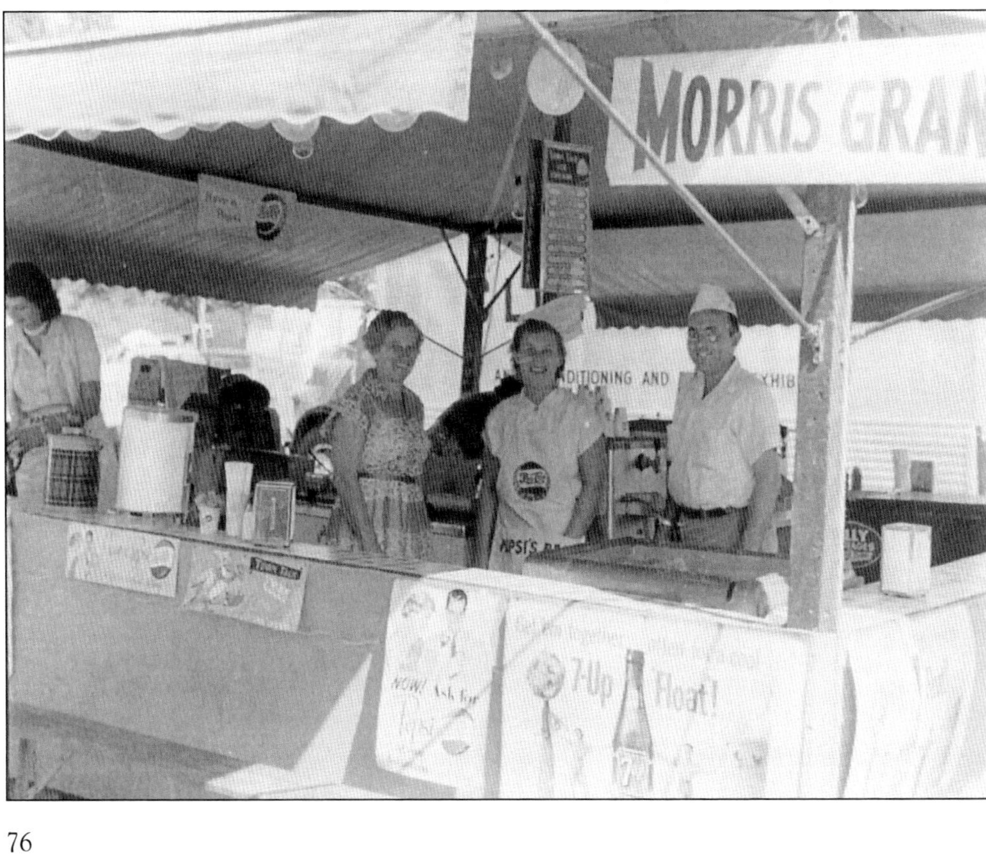

A day at the Morris County Grange Fair in 1956. From left to right are Ann Clifford, Gladys Bates, Helen Farrand, and Clarence Bates. (Muriel Berson.)

Five

Public Organizations

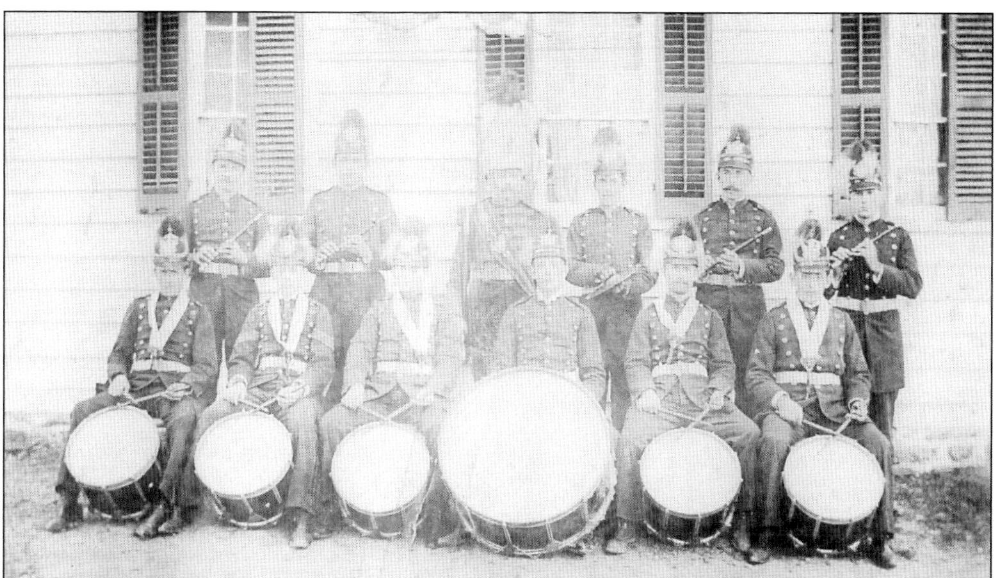

The Troy Hills Fife and Drum Corps, *c.* 1890. (Fran Kaminski.)

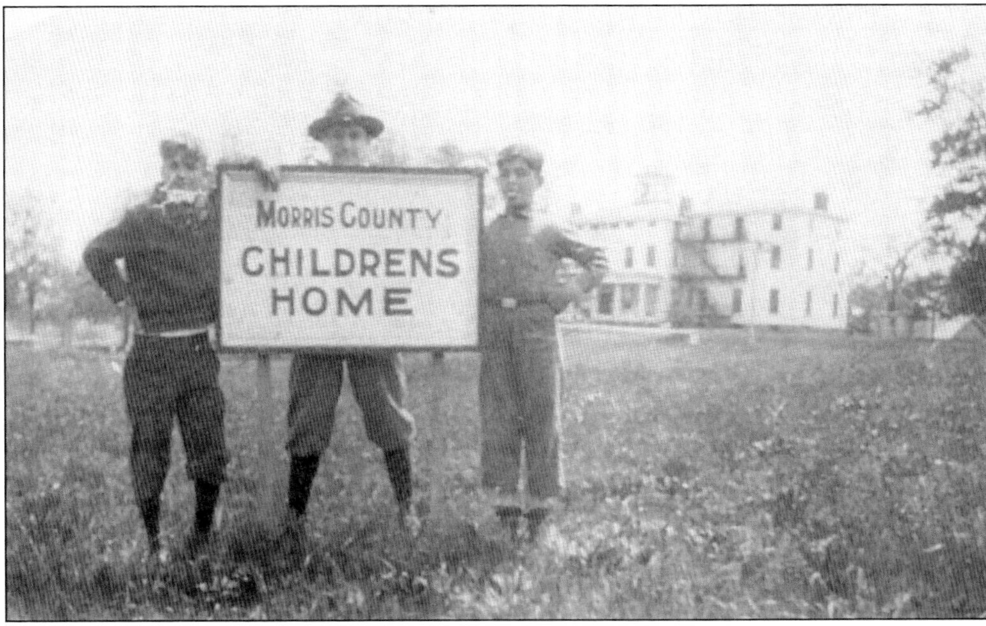

The Morris County Children's Home in a photograph dated 1930. The person in the center is Mike Stellate; the other people are unidentified. (Ann Egan.)

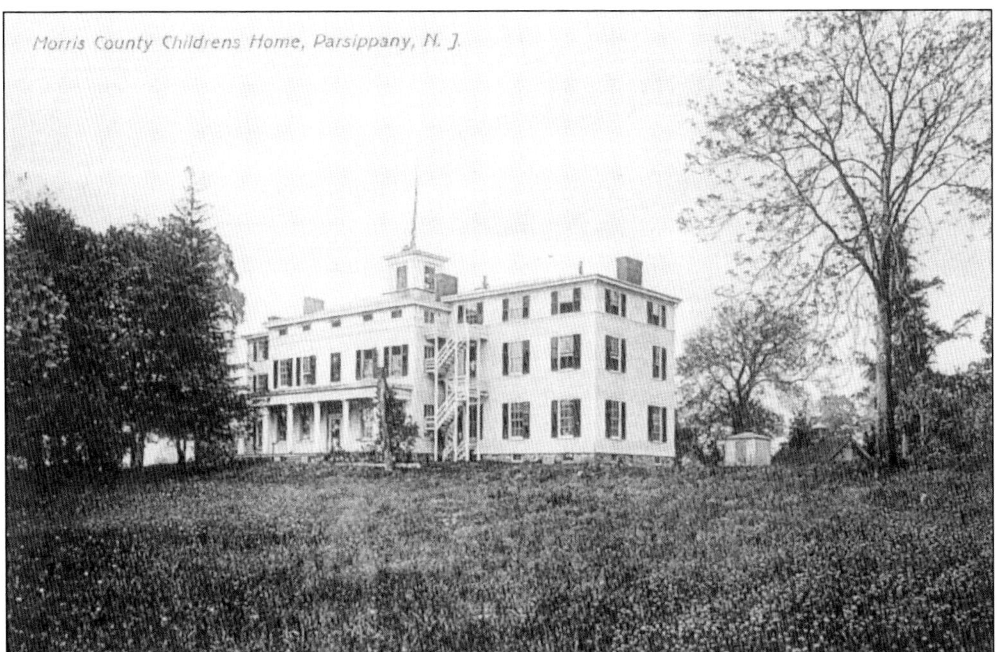

Another view of the Morris County Children's Home. Orphans were housed in the home from 1882 to 1929. Smith Ely, who was mayor of New York City from 1876 to 1880 and a descendant of distinguished local families, was active in supporting the Children's Home. In 1908, Mr. Ely matched the $25,000 raised by private contributions, and in his will he bequeathed a gift of $50,000 for the home's continued support. (Robert D'Alessandro.)

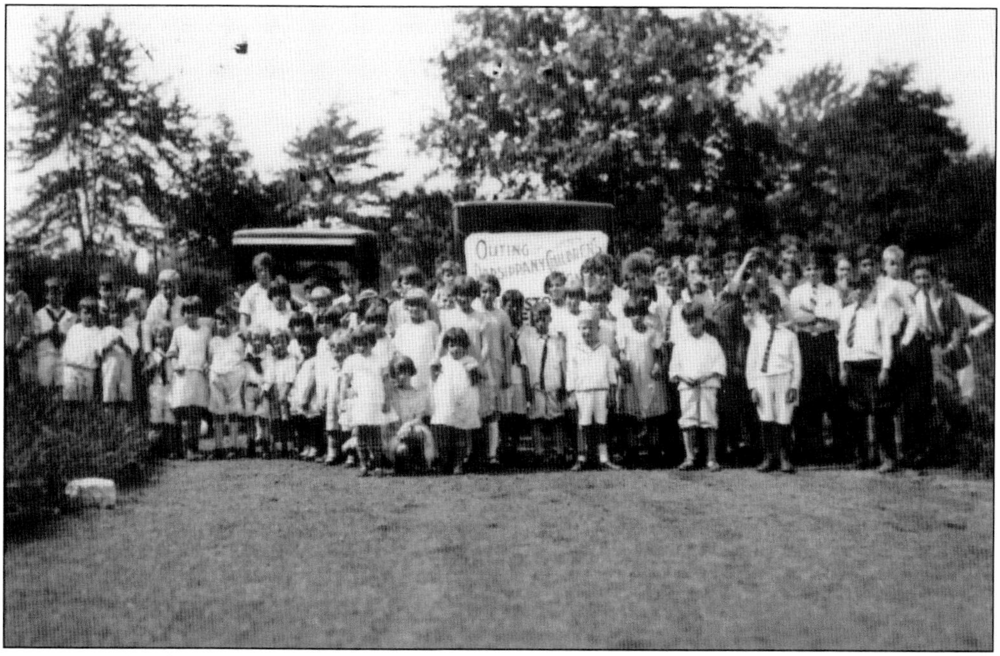

An outing for the children of the Morris County Children's Home, 1926. The home's motto was: "A model home is our goal." Both boys and girls wore checked uniforms and their hair was cropped very short up until 1916. When considered old enough, they were given employment as manual laborers or domestic workers. (Joint Free Public Library of Morristown and Morris Township.)

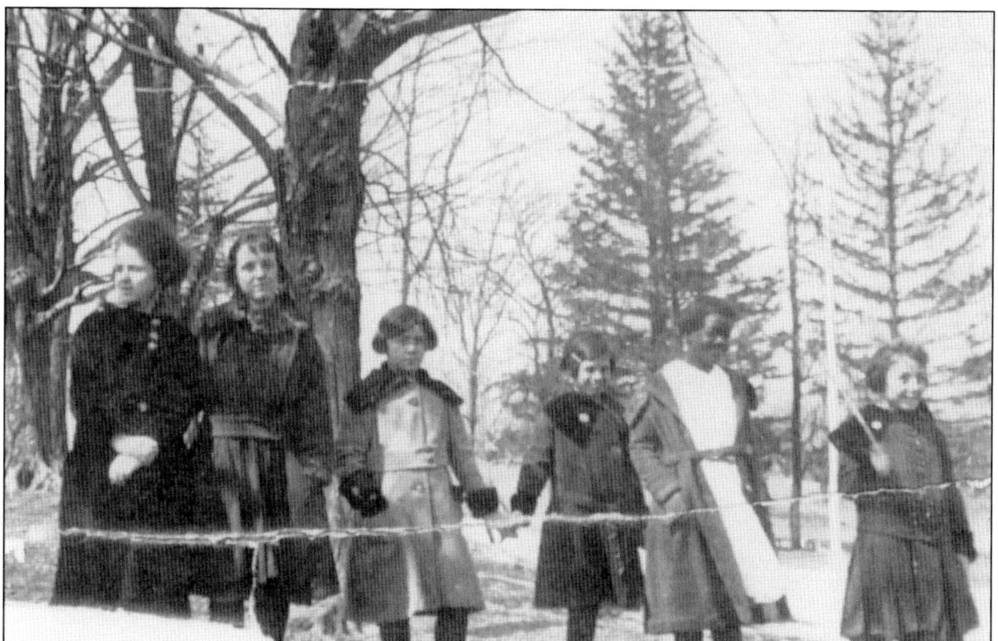

Children and workers at Ailanthus Hall. The Children's Home was purchased for $9,000 and was originally a mansion built by Richard Smith in 1738. Smith called it Ailanthus Hall for the many ailanthus trees that grew on his land. (Ann Egan.)

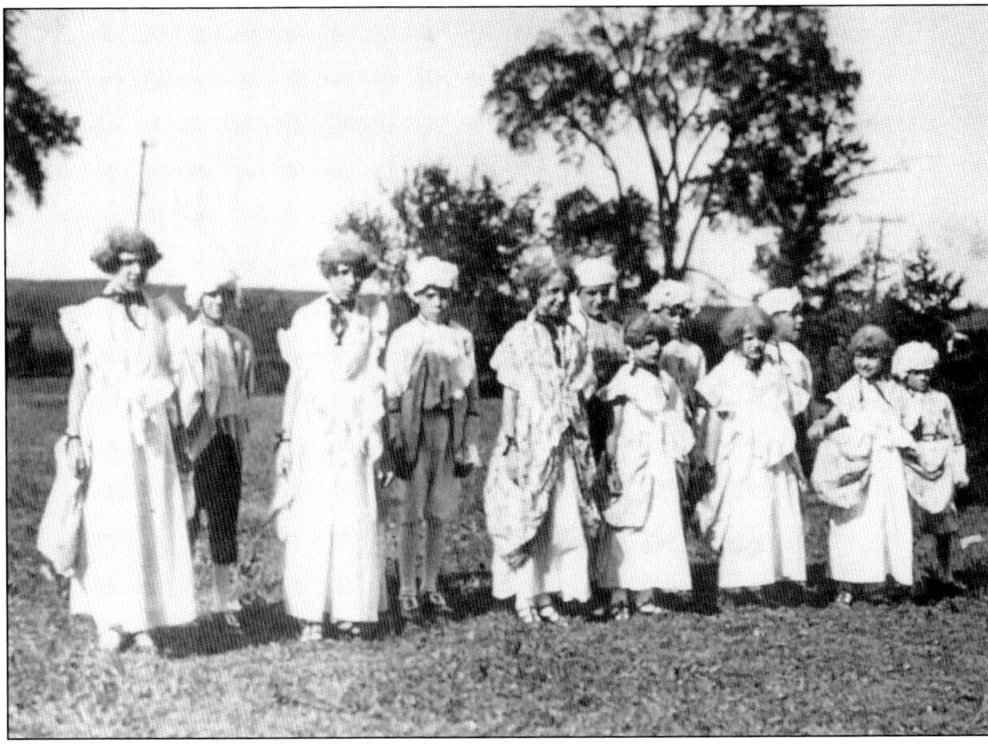

A Washington's birthday pageant held at the Children's Home. (Ann Egan.)

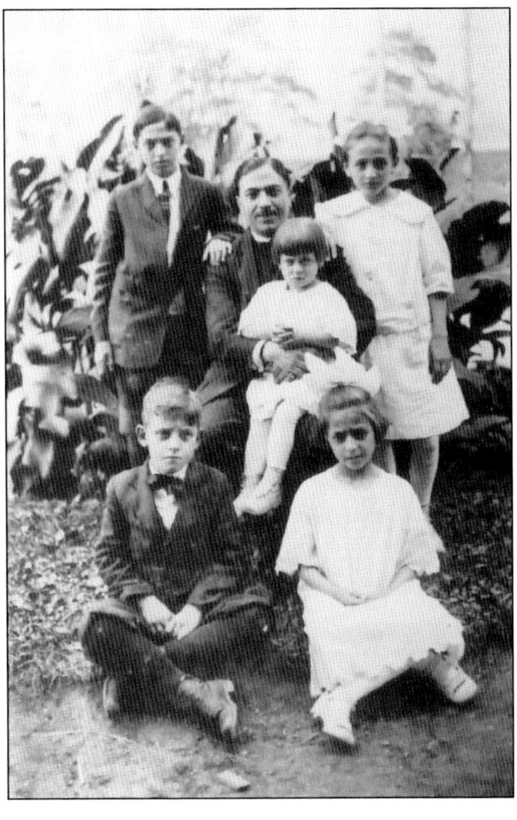

Joseph Lopifraro and his children at the Morris County Children's Home in a photograph dated October 6, 1918. (Joint Free Public Library of Morristown and Morris Township.)

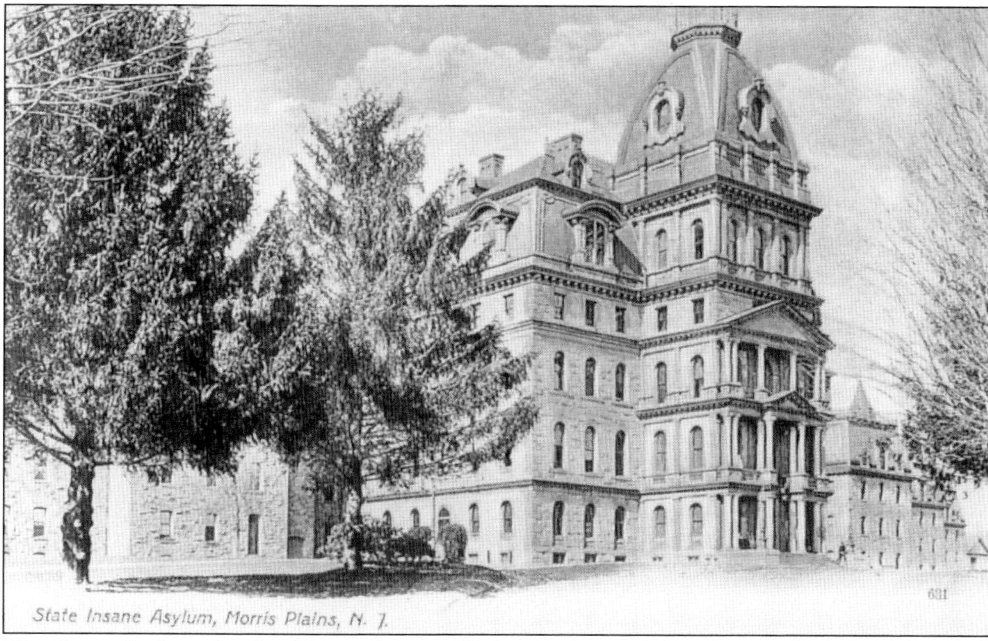

The State Asylum for the Insane (now called Greystone Park). The state asylum was built in 1876 at the cost of $2,500,000. Samuel Sloane (1815–1884) designed the institution in French Renaissance and Second Empire styles. Greystone was set on 450 acres of land, and had 600 beds for patients when first opened. The institution had a third-story embellishment and a mansard roof which was later removed in order to add a fifth floor. (Robert D'Alessandro.)

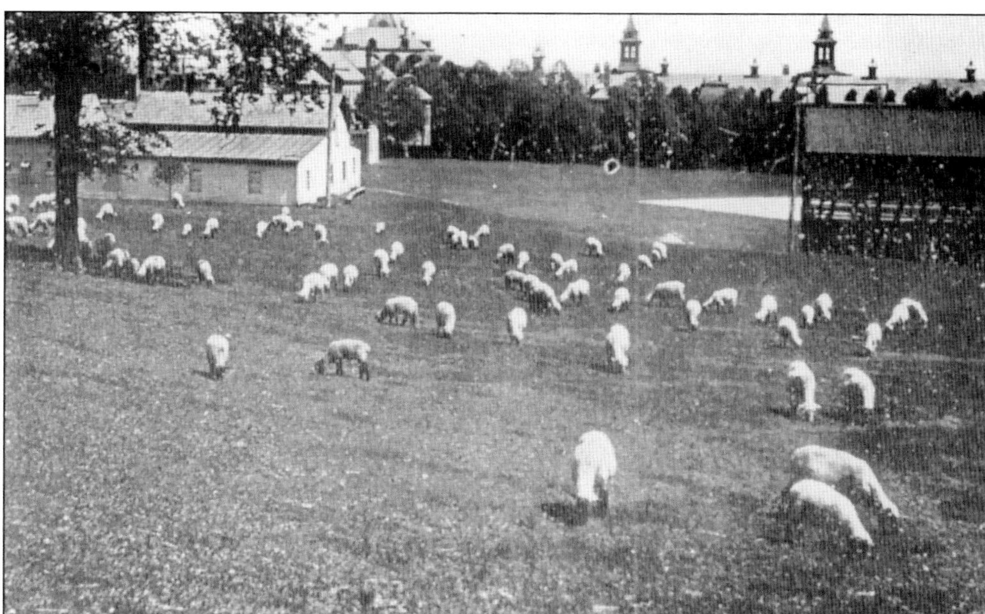

Sheep at pasture near the state hospital (Greystone). Patients tended the animals and grew their own produce. (Robert D'Alessandro.)

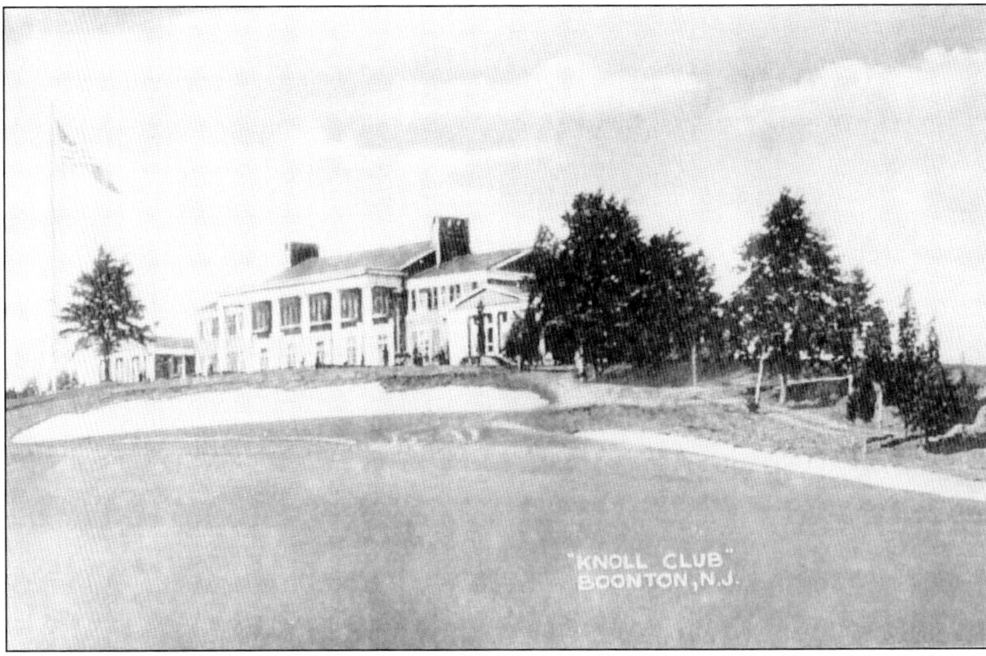

The Knoll Country Club, originally Peer property. The land was used as burial ground until 1906. A few years later, the headstones were removed and the graves plowed over. In 1929, twelve millionaires got together and had the country club built. In 1966, Bloomfield College acquired the property intending to build an annex, but they abandoned the project. The township purchased the holdings in 1976 with the help of Green Acres funds. Today, it is a public golf course. (Robert D'Alessandro.)

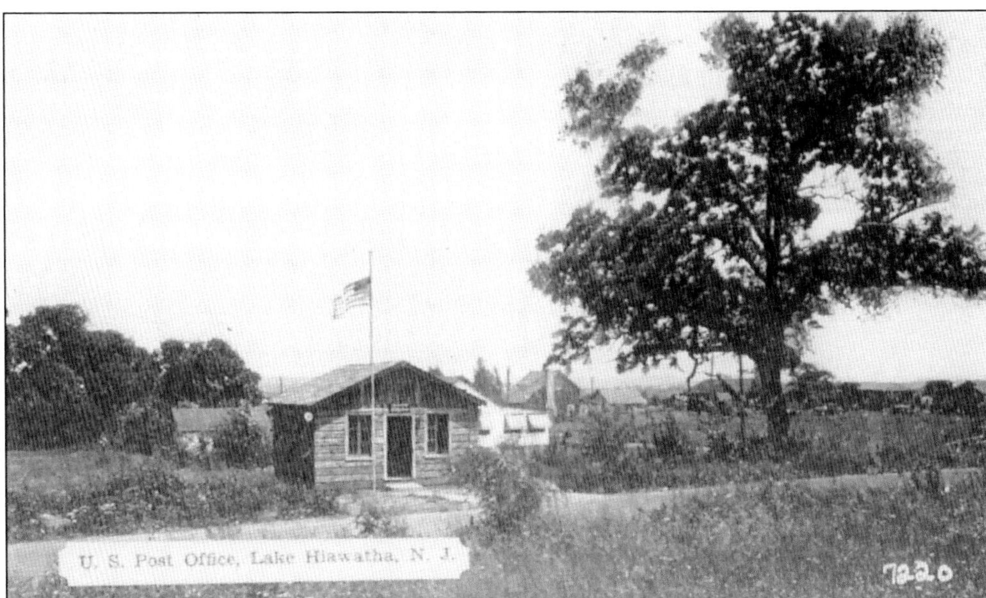

The United States Post Office in Lake Hiawatha. Mail was delivered without zip codes or computers. (Robert D'Alessandro.)

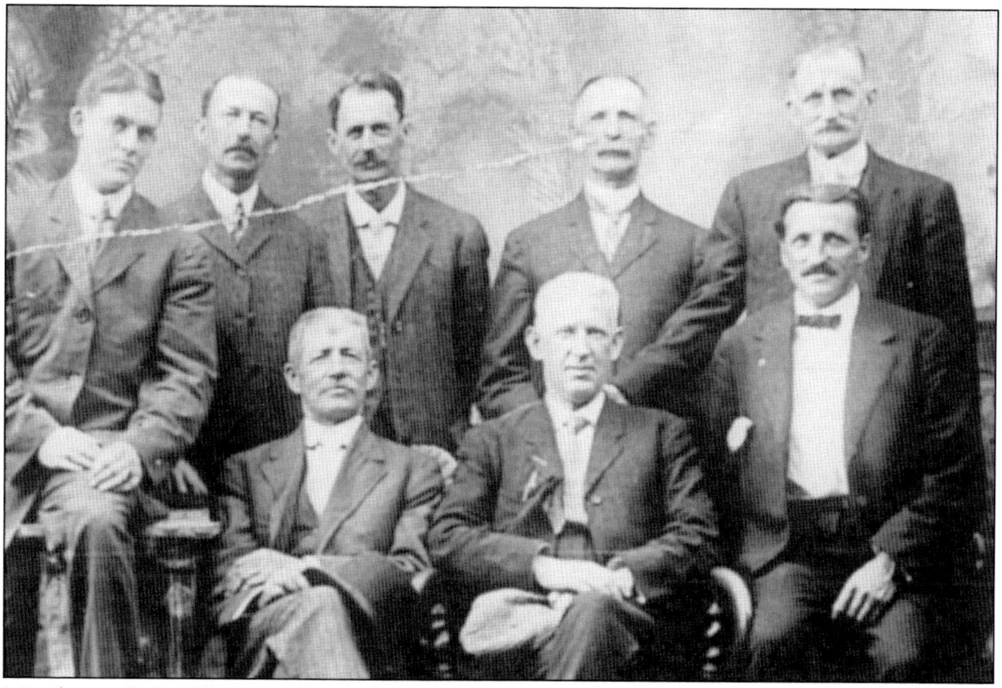

Members of the Hanover Township Committee. Many of these men later held elective office in the government of Parsippany-Troy Hills Township after it separated from Hanover Township in 1928. From left to right are as follows: (front row) Ed Connelly, Harry Mead, and Dr. Totten; (back row) Will Polhemus, Judd Condit (father of Stephen H. Condit), Will Davis, E. Halsey Ball, and Will Webb. *See Founding Families*. (Harold O. Farrand.)

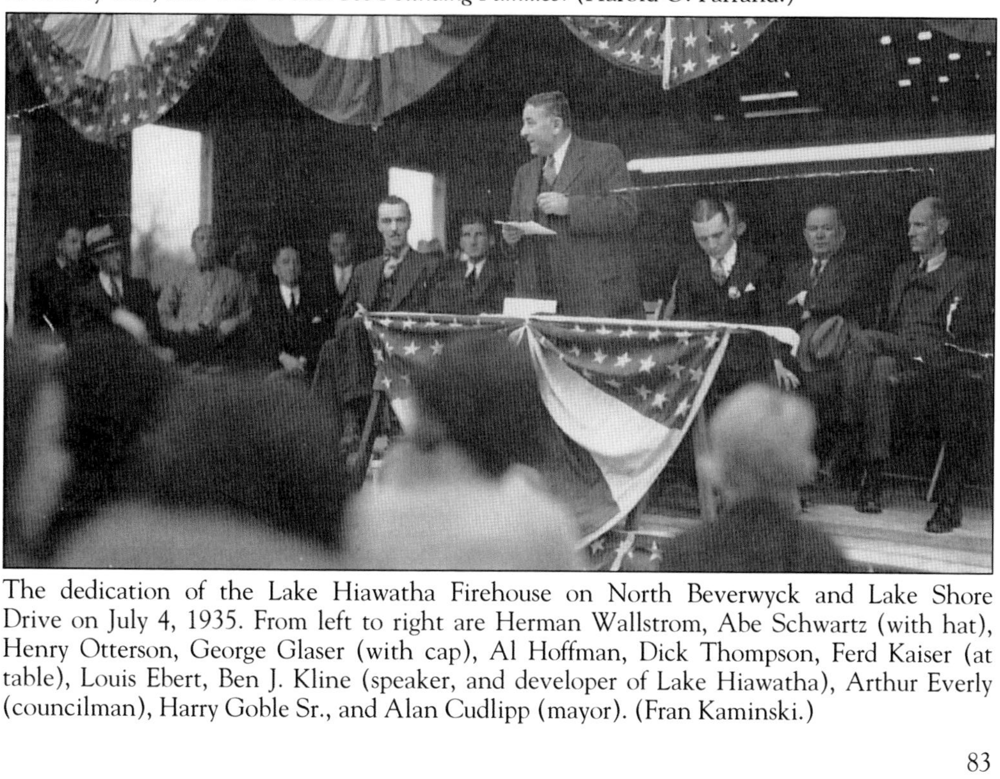

The dedication of the Lake Hiawatha Firehouse on North Beverwyck and Lake Shore Drive on July 4, 1935. From left to right are Herman Wallstrom, Abe Schwartz (with hat), Henry Otterson, George Glaser (with cap), Al Hoffman, Dick Thompson, Ferd Kaiser (at table), Louis Ebert, Ben J. Kline (speaker, and developer of Lake Hiawatha), Arthur Everly (councilman), Harry Goble Sr., and Alan Cudlipp (mayor). (Fran Kaminski.)

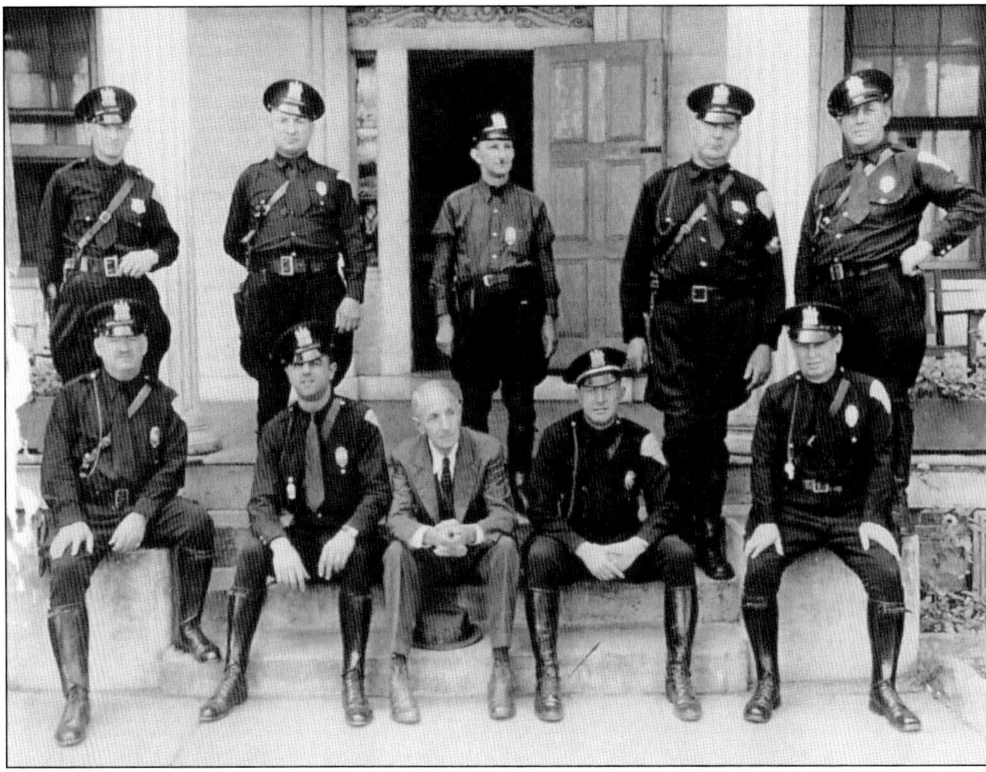

The Parsippany Police Department, *c.* 1930. The policemen are seated on steps of the Morris County Children's Home on Route 46. (Parsippany Historic Museum.)

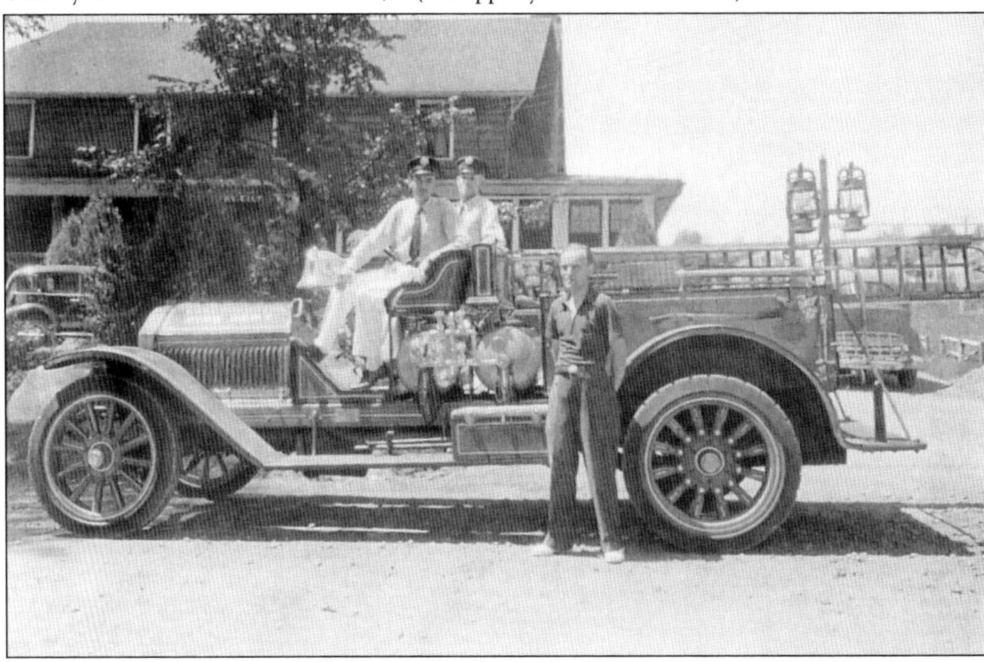

A fire truck and some members of the fire department in front of the Lake Hiawatha Rotary Clubhouse, *c.* 1930. (Parsippany Historic Museum.)

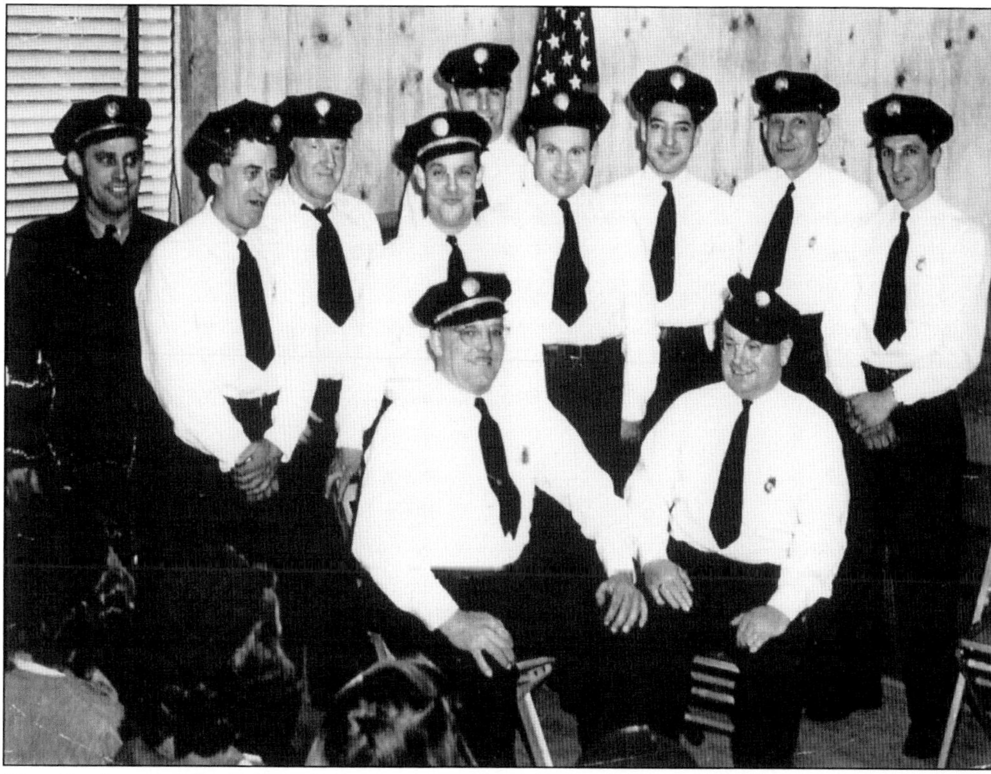

The Rockaway Neck Fire Company, *c.* 1940. From left to right are as follows: (front row) Richard Klepp and Former Mayor Francis X. Downey; (back row) Steve Giercyk, Ralph Stecker, Red Lands, Horace Green, Carl Levitt, Walter Coddington, Kent Dixon, and Charlie Coddington. Standing next to the flag is William Wood. (Fran Kaminski.)

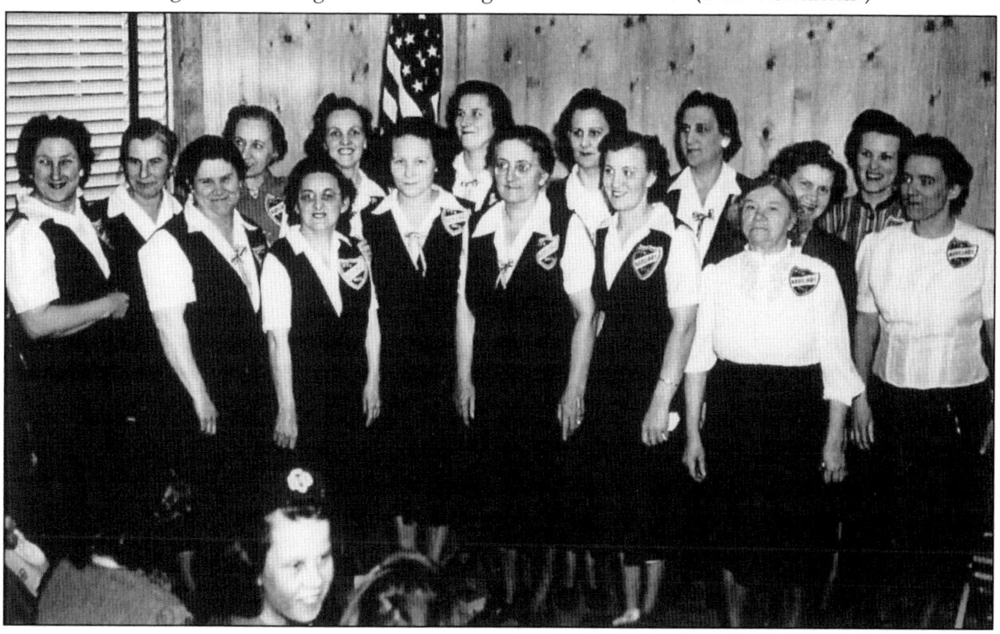

The Women's Auxiliary of the Rockaway Neck Fire Company, *c.* 1940. (Fran Kaminski.)

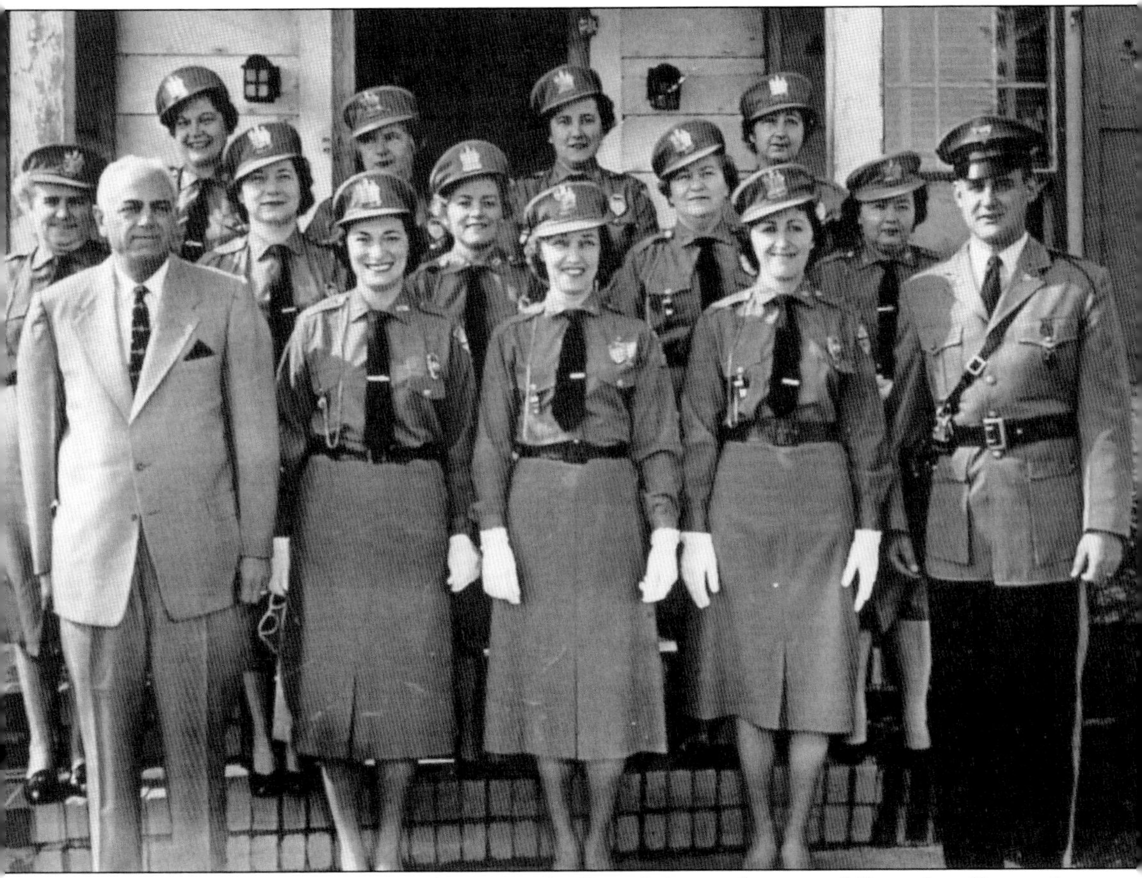

The Civil Defense Police Auxiliary in 1956. From left to right are as follows: Leo Dorsey (one of Parsippany-Troy Hills Township's first policemen), Gloria Sante, Grace Ur, Rose Czalo, and Frank Hopple; (middle row) unidentified, Tess Schaeffer, Helen Bach (wife of former owner of Bach's Tavern on North Beverwyck Road), ? Gosney, and Mike ?; (back row) unidentified, unidentified, Ann Morgenthien, and Marge Gravlek. (Ann Morgenthien.)

Six

Business and Industry

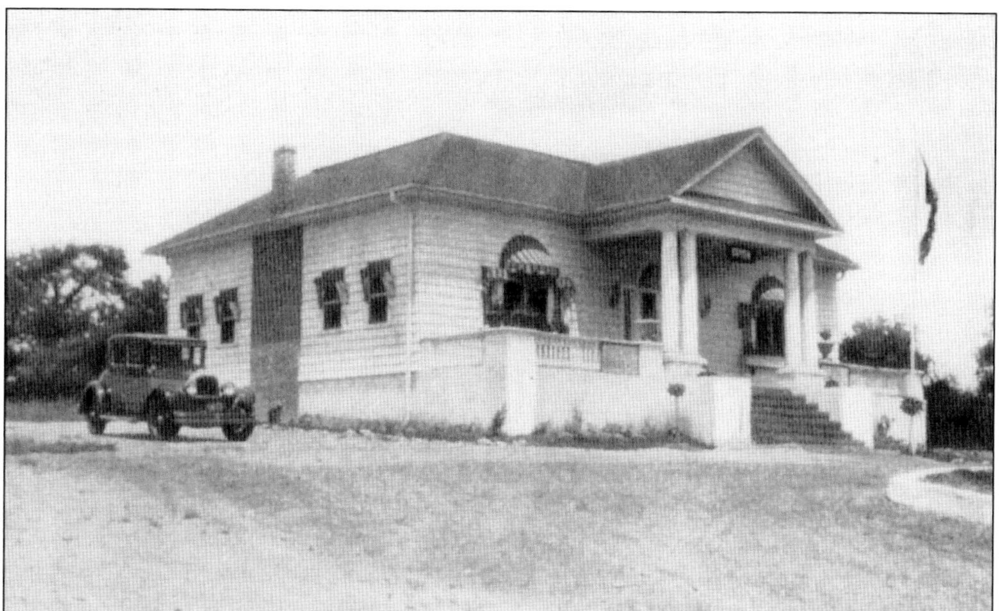

Ye Olde Mushroom Farm—a restaurant on the northwest corner of Route 46 and North Beverwyck Road—in a c. 1930 photograph. Mushrooms were actually grown in the cellar. The original restaurant, managed by French-Canadians, served a cuisine that included all types of wild game. Later the restaurant became Beatty's Roost, then the Rusty Nail, and is presently the Eccola Gastronomia. (Robert D'Alessandro.)

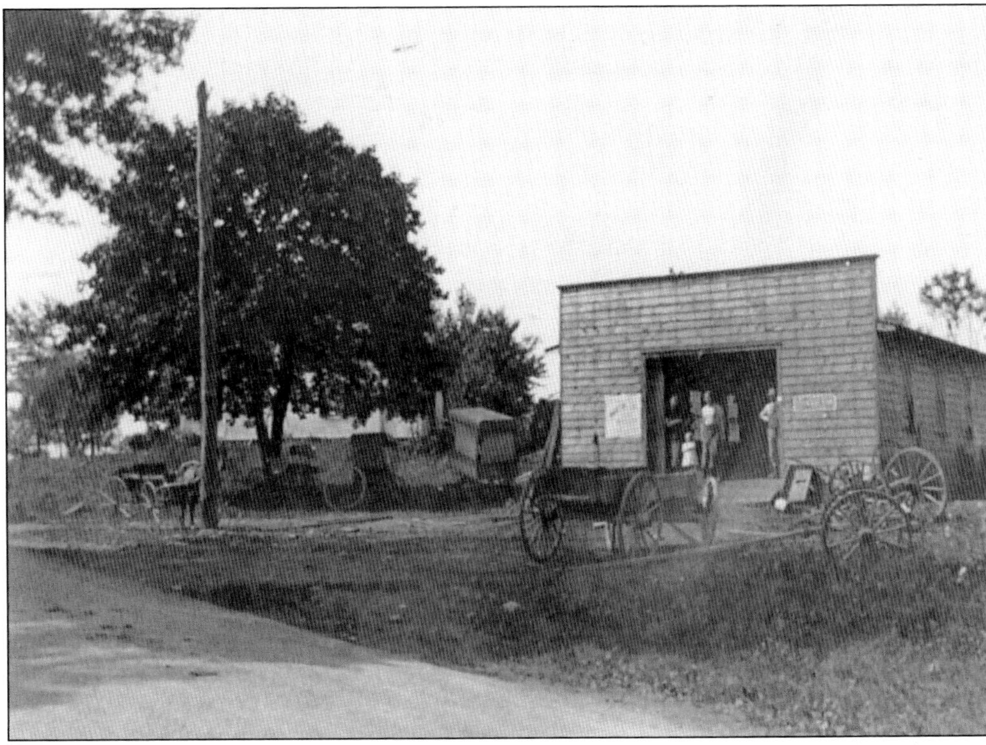

The Harry Moller Blacksmith Shop on the corner of Littleton Road and Littleton Road East, where Firehouse 6 is presently located. From left to right are an unidentified worker, Ruth (Wooton) Moller (1908–1981), Harry Moller (1881–1951), and an unidentified man. (Jack Wooton.)

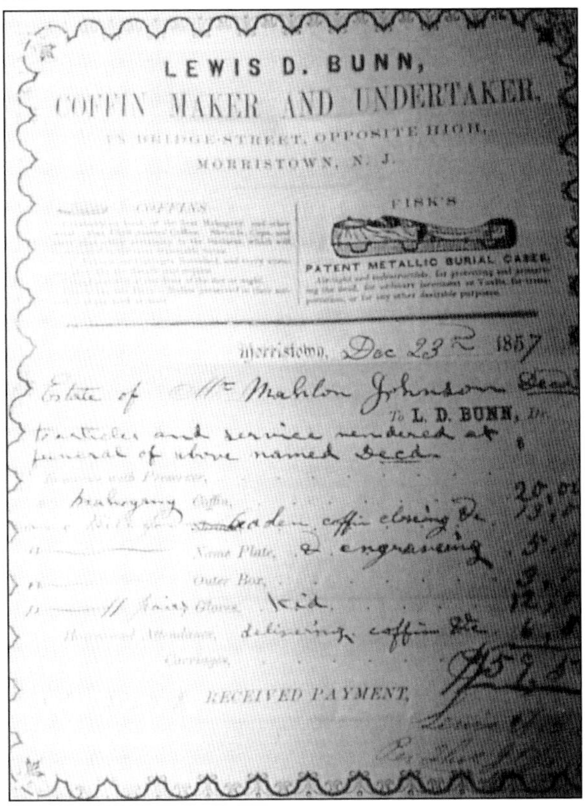

LEWIS D. BUNN,
COFFIN MAKER AND UNDERTAKER,
BRIDGE-STREET, OPPOSITE HIGH,
MORRISTOWN, N. J.

FISK'S
PATENT METALLIC BURIAL CASES

Morristown, Dec 23rd 1857

Estate of Mr Mahlon Johnson Decd
To L. D. BUNN, Dr.

to articles and service rendered at funeral of above named Decd.

Mahogany Coffin, 20.00
leaden coffin closing &c
Name Plate, & engraving
Outer Box,
Kid Gloves
delivering coffin &c

RECEIVED PAYMENT,

A receipt for the burial of Mahlon Johnson, dated December 23, 1857. The Johnson house was located on Route 10. It was approximately on the site of the present-day Parsippany Hilton Hotel. (Joint Free Public Library of Morristown and Morris Township.)

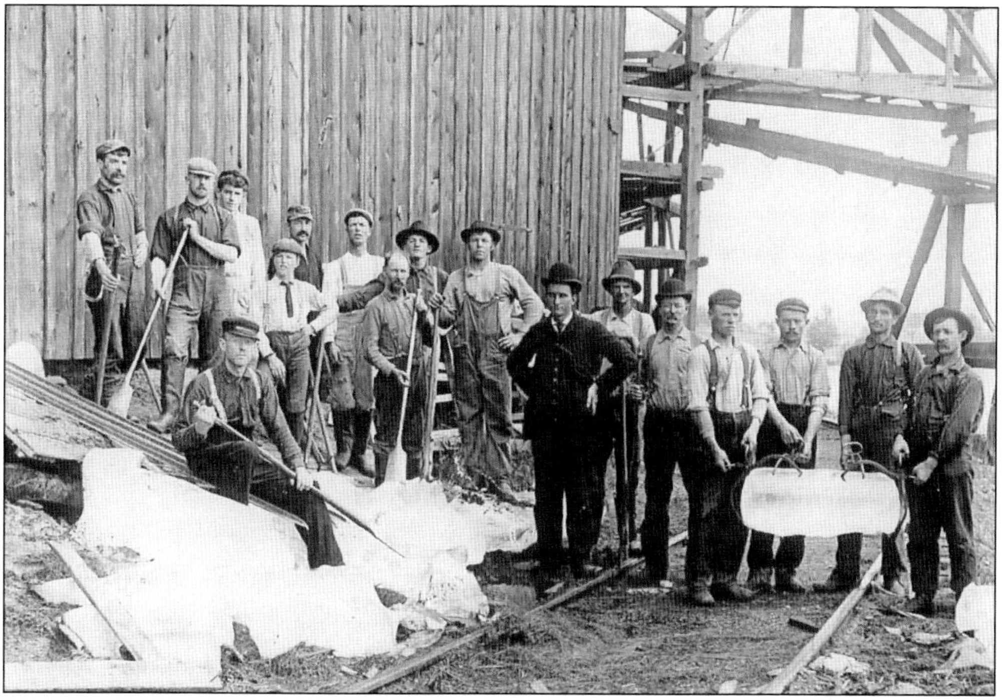

Ice-harvesting at Lake Hopatcong. Many of the men who lived in Parsippany-Troy Hills would travel to the lake during the winter to harvest blocks of ice, which would then be shipped to Newark and New York City by train and wagon. The man in the dark suit is a Farrand relative. (Harold O. Farrand.)

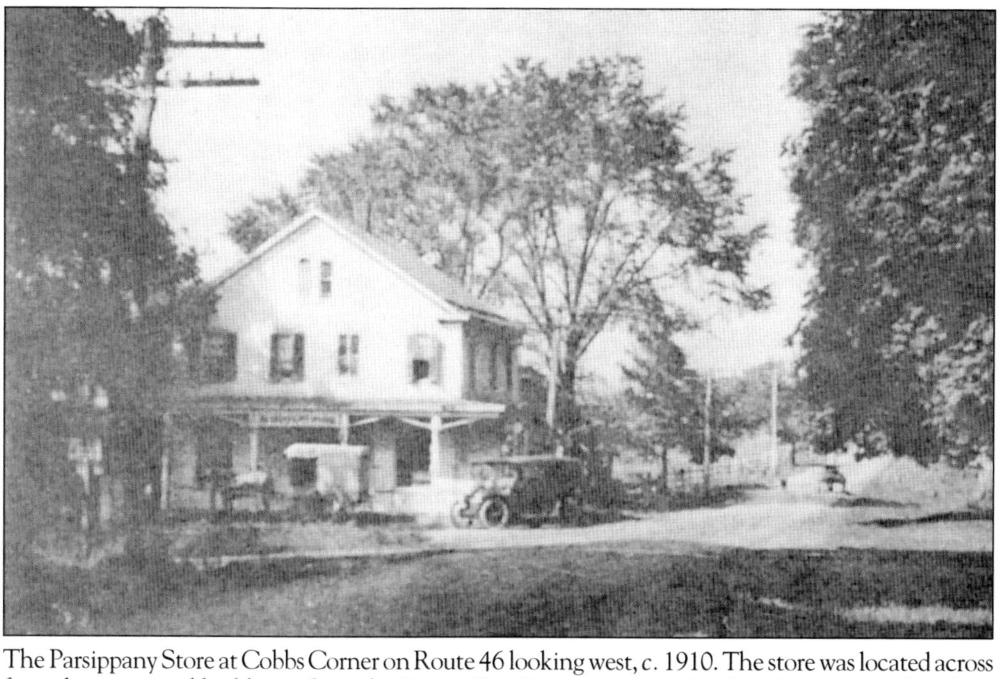

The Parsippany Store at Cobbs Corner on Route 46 looking west, *c.* 1910. The store was located across from the municipal building, where the Exxon Gas Station is situated today. (Howard Baldwin.)

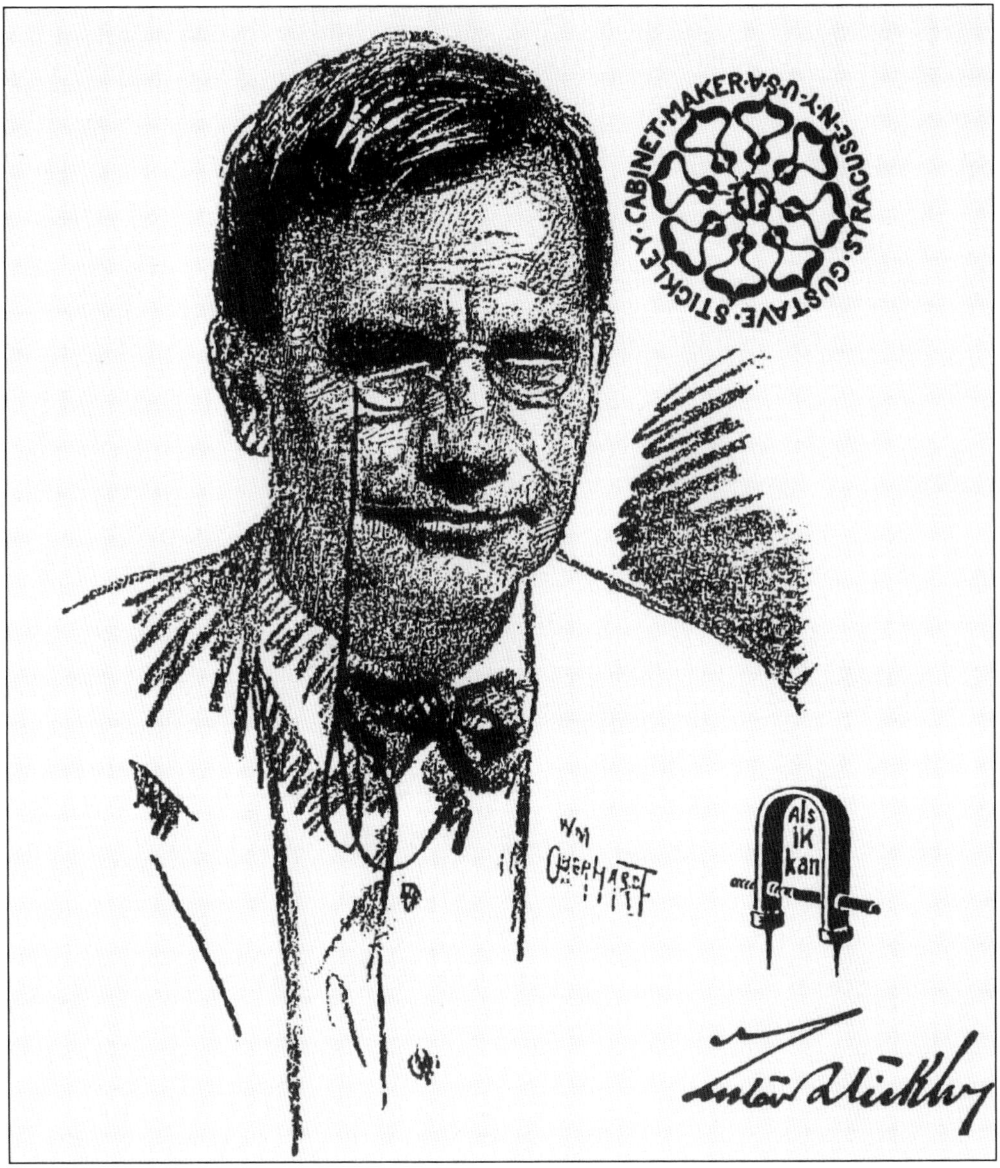

Gustav Stickley (1858–1942). Stickley was a famed turn-of-the-century designer and a spokesman for the arts and crafts movement. Living in Parsippany-Troy Hills, he commuted to his Manhattan furniture showroom and restaurant which were located in his twelve-story Craftsman Building just off Fifth Avenue at 6 East 39th Street. The two designs above were benchmarks for his "Mission"-style furniture. (Muriel Berson.)

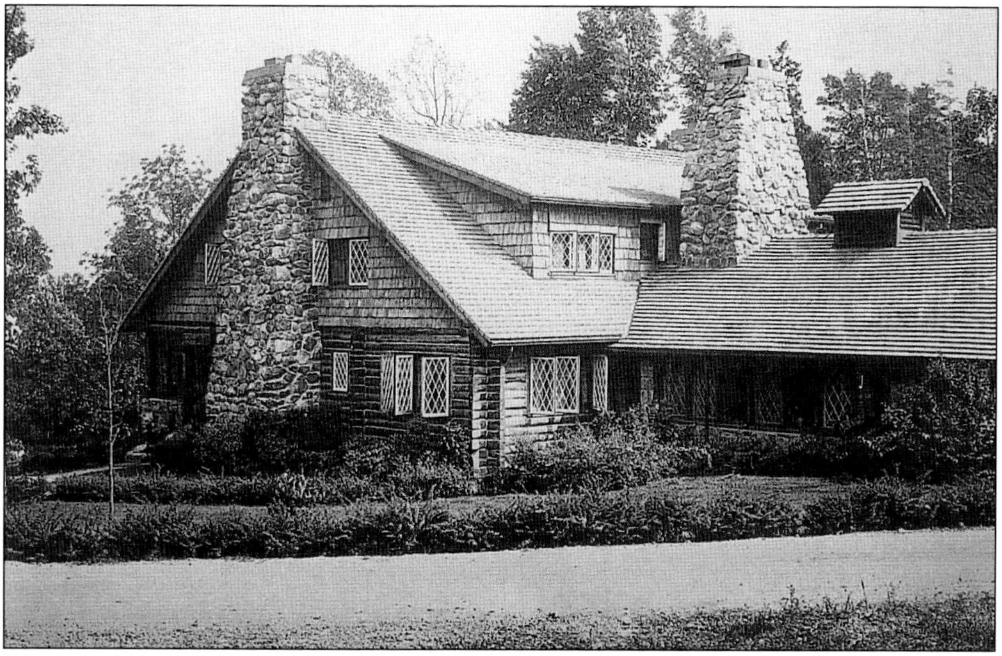

The main house at Craftsman Farms, *c.* 1915. In 1908, Gustav Stickley purchased 650 acres on the western edge of Parsippany-Troy Hills with the intention of creating a work-study school for boys in which they could learn farming and a trade. He designed this building as a clubhouse with large gathering rooms, a huge kitchen, and a porch opening out upon an expansive view of the farm and gardens. The school never got past the planning stage. (Robert D'Alessandro.)

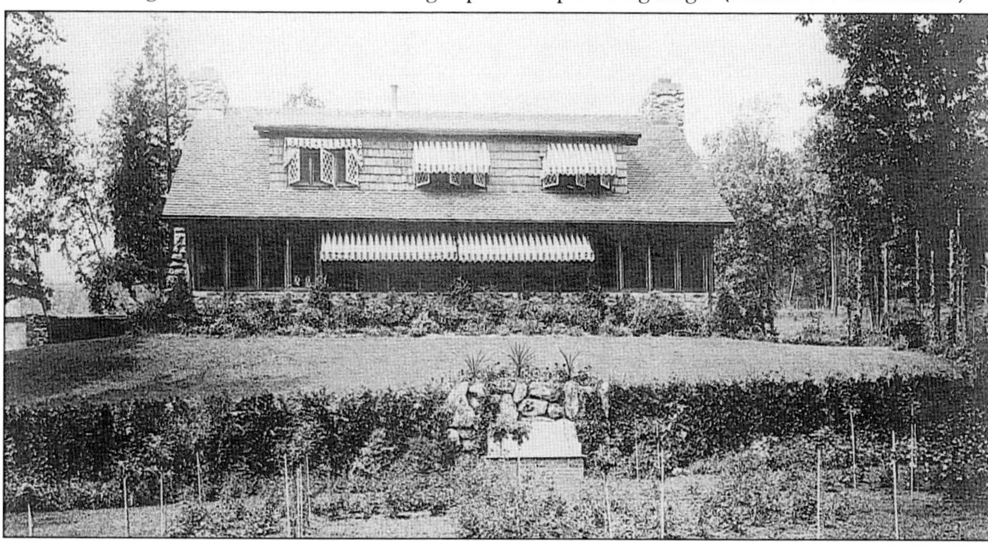

The main house at Craftsman Farms showing the porch (now enclosed). This view faces southeast. Gustav Stickley lived here from 1910 to 1917, but filed for bankruptcy in 1915. Major George Farny and his wife, Sylvia, a member of the Wurlitzer family (known for their pianos), purchased Craftsman Farms. In 1989, when the site was threatened with development, the township acquired the property by right of eminent domain. It is presently operated by the Craftsman Farms Foundation, which offers tours and exhibitions, and is listed as a national landmark. (Robert D'Alessandro.)

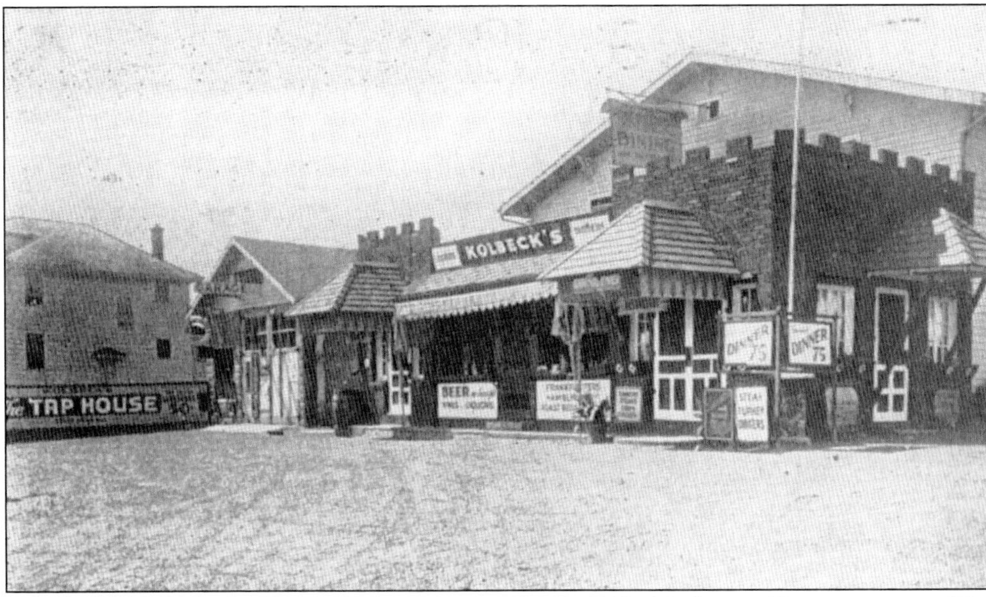

Kolbeck's Local Gin Mill on Route 46, next to the Ye Olde Mushroom Farm restaurant. The DeCroce House is on the far left. (Robert D'Alessandro.)

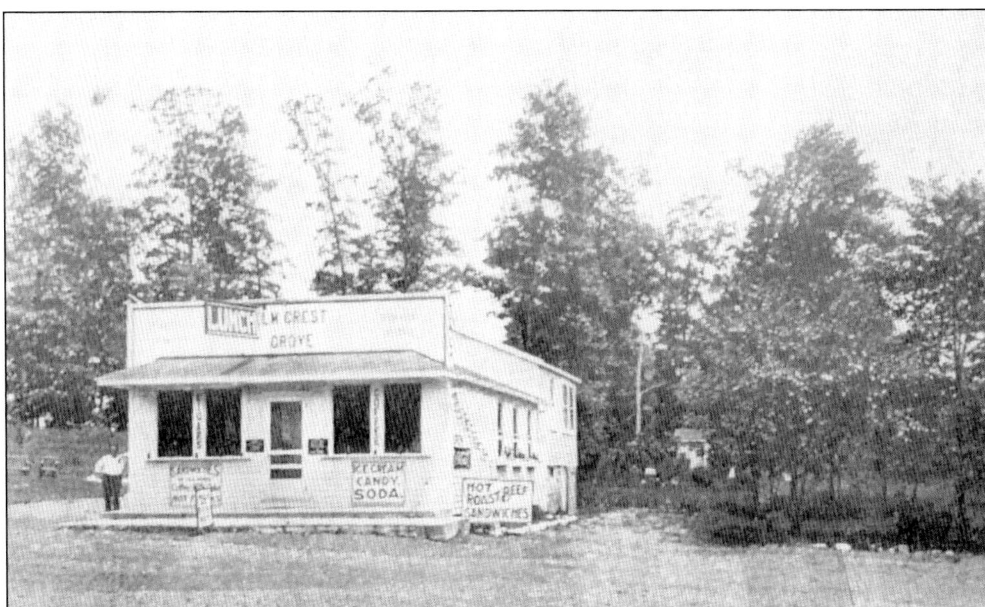

The Elm Crest on Route 46 East, just before the turn onto Edwards Road. This public establishment offered dining, dancing, refreshments, and picnic grounds. (Robert D'Alessandro.)

Beardsley's on Route 46 West, c. 1930. Beardsley's was located between Condit Avenue and Baldwin Road near Saint Peter's Church. (Robert D'Alessandro.)

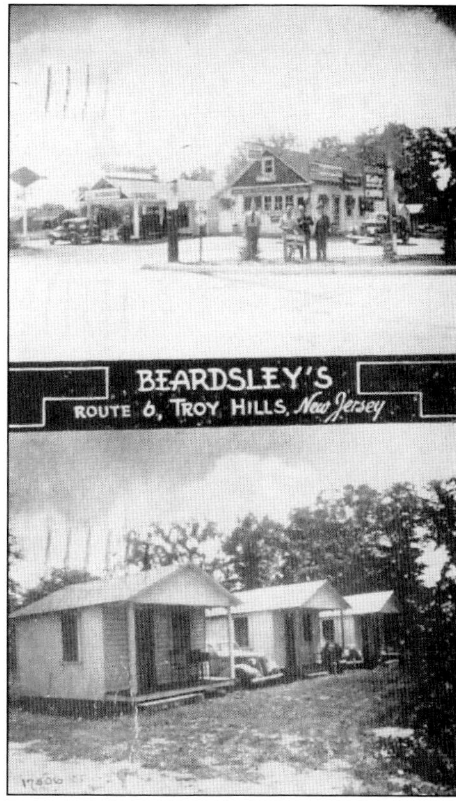

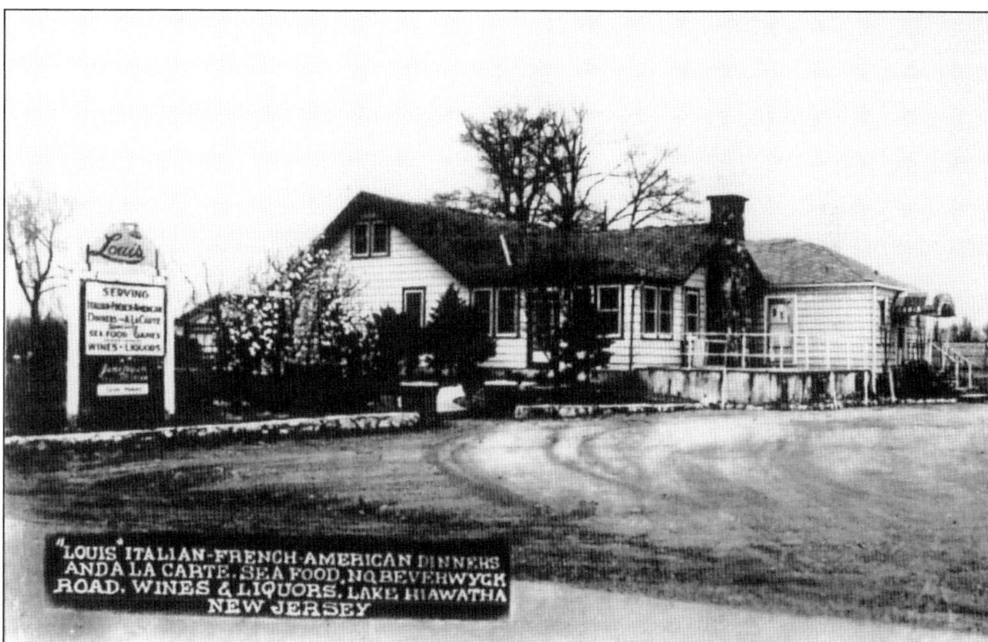

Louis' Italian-American Restaurant on North Beverwyck Road in Lake Hiawatha. The restaurant was demolished in 1996 to make way for a strip mall. (Robert D'Alessandro.)

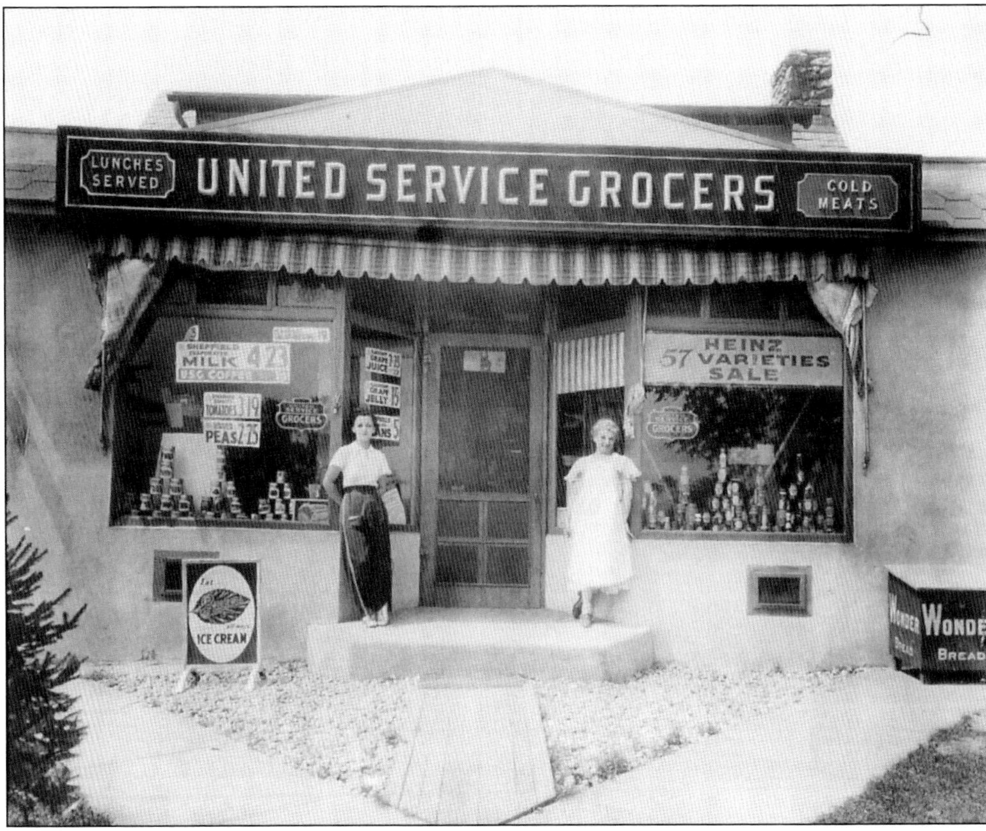

One of the original grocery stores in Lake Hiawatha, *c.* 1930. Notice that the cost of a pound of coffee was 25¢, and a can of beans was 5¢. (Fran Kaminski.)

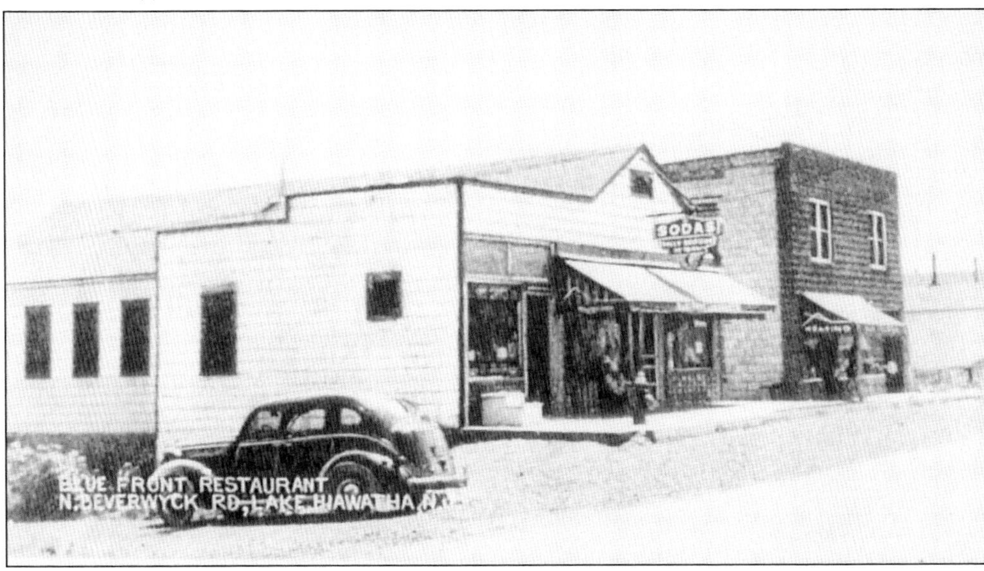

The Blue Front Restaurant on the corner of North Beverwyck Road and Hiawatha Boulevard, *c.* 1930. The restaurant was a popular meeting place for locals. These buildings are still standing. (Robert D'Alessandro.)

The Old Cross Roads Inn at Cobb's Corner on the northwest side of Route 46. The Old Cross Roads Inn was an antique store and dining establishment. (Robert D'Alessandro.)

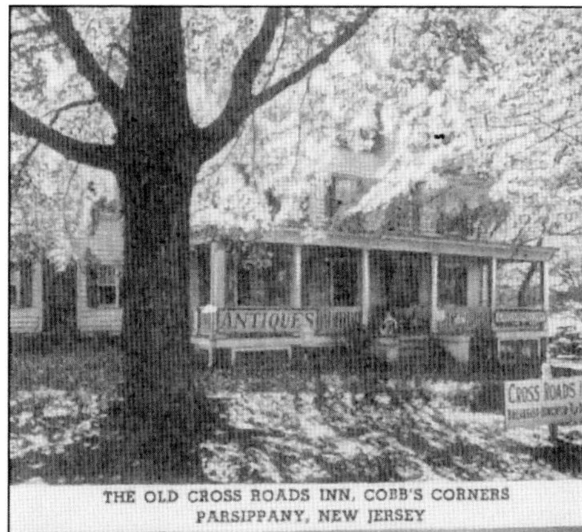

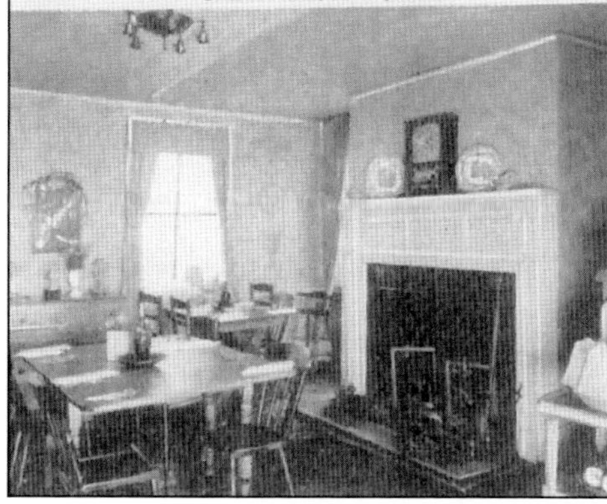

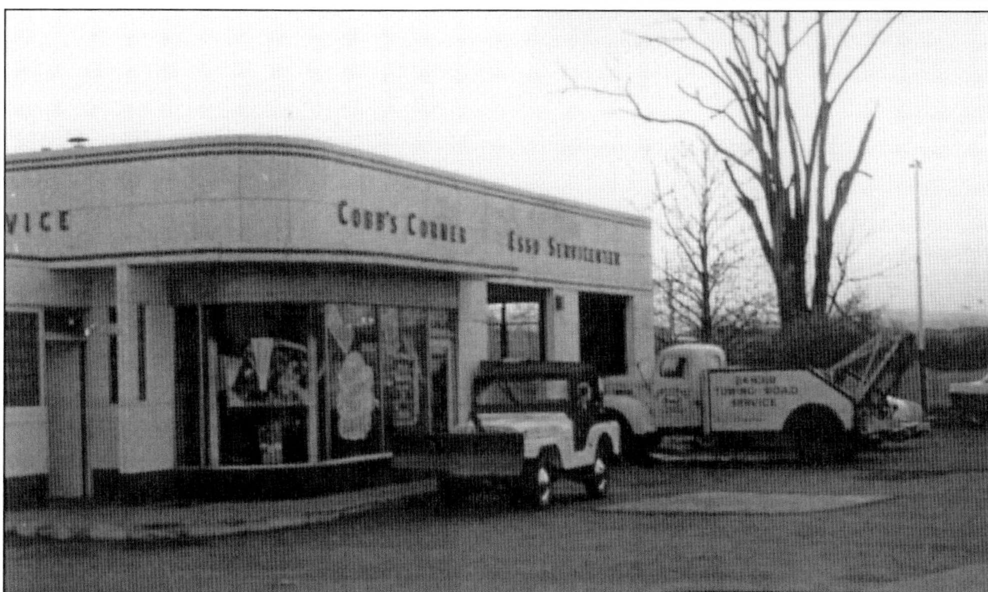

The Esso station located at the southeast side of Cobb's Corner. This station was owned by Charles Abbate in the 1950s and is presently the Exxon Gas Station. In the 1860s, the Parsippany Hotel occupied this part of Cobb's Corner; the proprietor of the hotel was Jacob Class. (Ann Egan.)

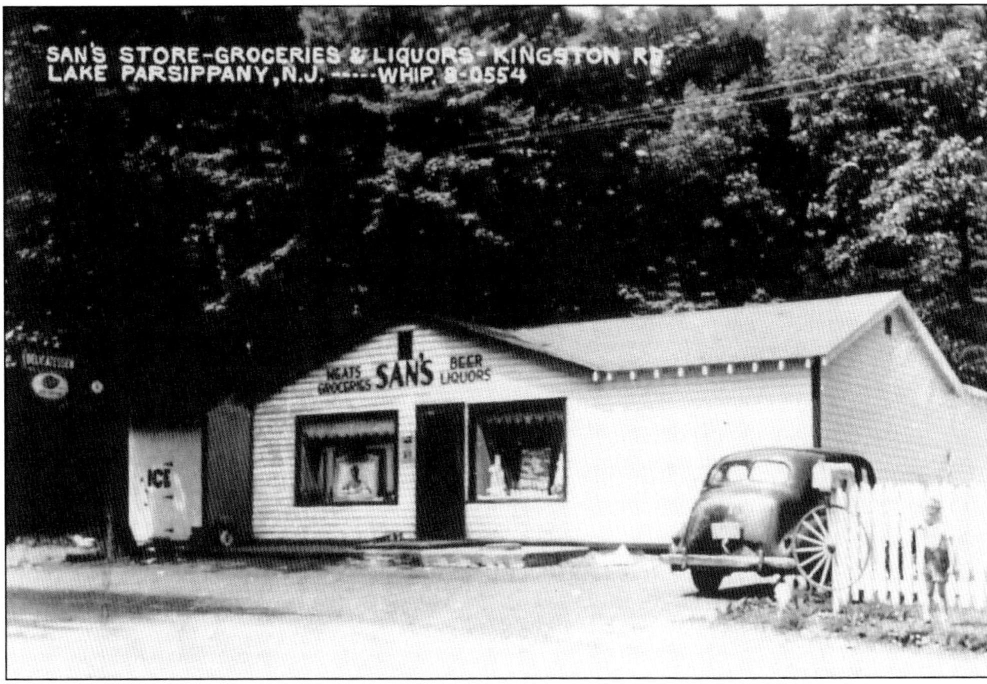

San's Store at 170 Kingston Road. The store was named for Santino DeCroce, the owner. It later became Dru's Grocery, then Dru's ShopRite Supermarket. It is now called the General Store. (Robert D'Alessandro.)

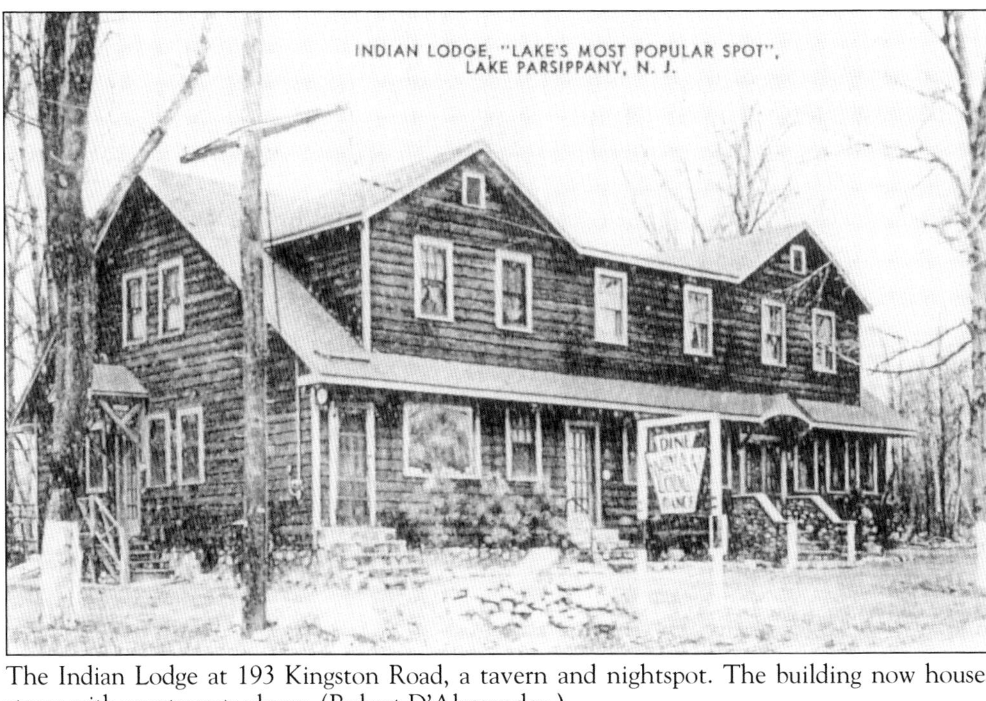

The Indian Lodge at 193 Kingston Road, a tavern and nightspot. The building now houses stores with apartments above. (Robert D'Alessandro.)

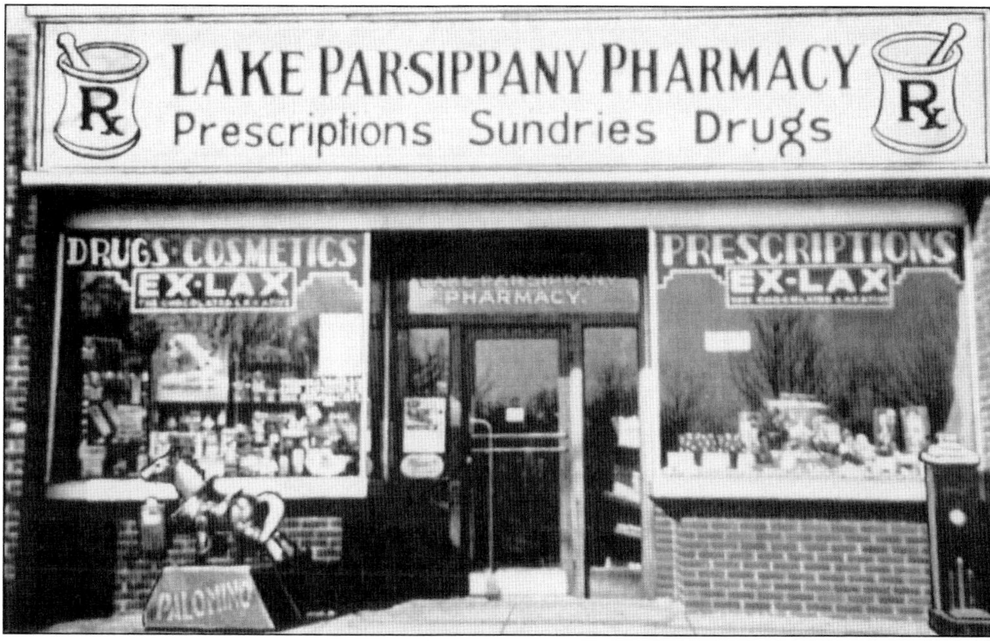

Lake Parsippany Pharmacy at 215 Kingston Road. The building is now a day-care center. (Robert D'Alessandro.)

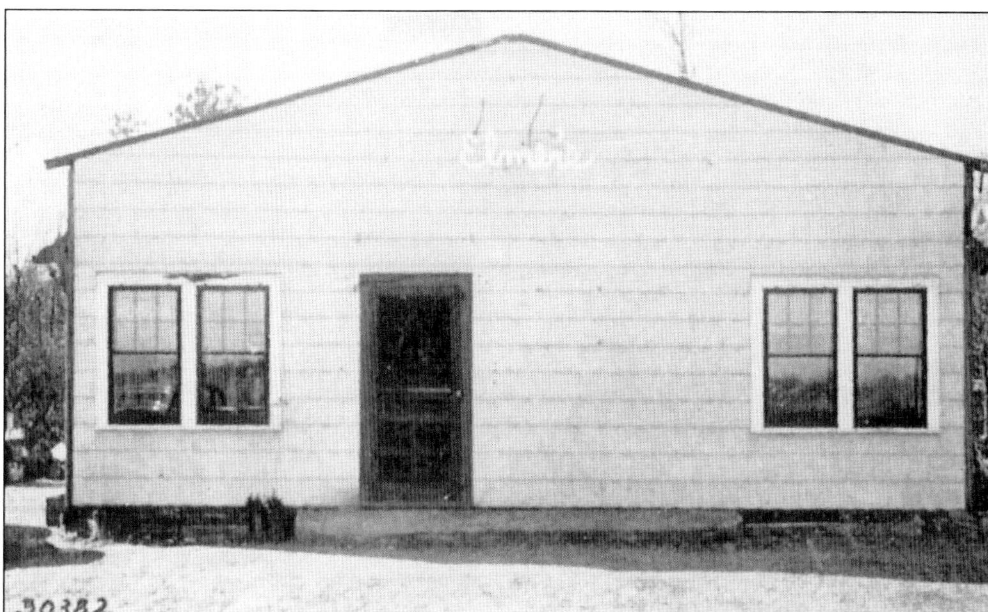

Elmer's Tavern on Halsey Road. Elmer's was one of eight gin mills available to patrons within a 2-mile radius during the 1930s and '40s. It is presently known as the Beach Pub at 701 Lake Shore Drive. The street names were changed by the township when Route 287 was built. (Robert D'Alessandro.)

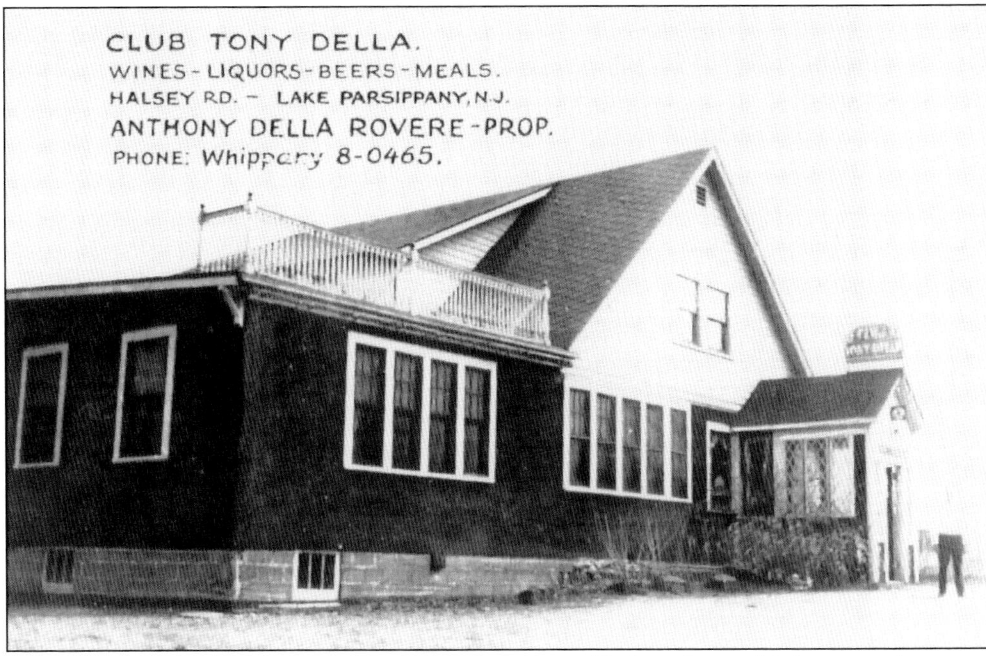

Club Tony Della on Halsey Road on Lake Parsippany. Today, the establishment is known as Bres' Corner and is located on 929 Lake Shore Drive, not Halsey Road, due to changes caused by the construction of Route 287. (Robert D'Alessandro.)

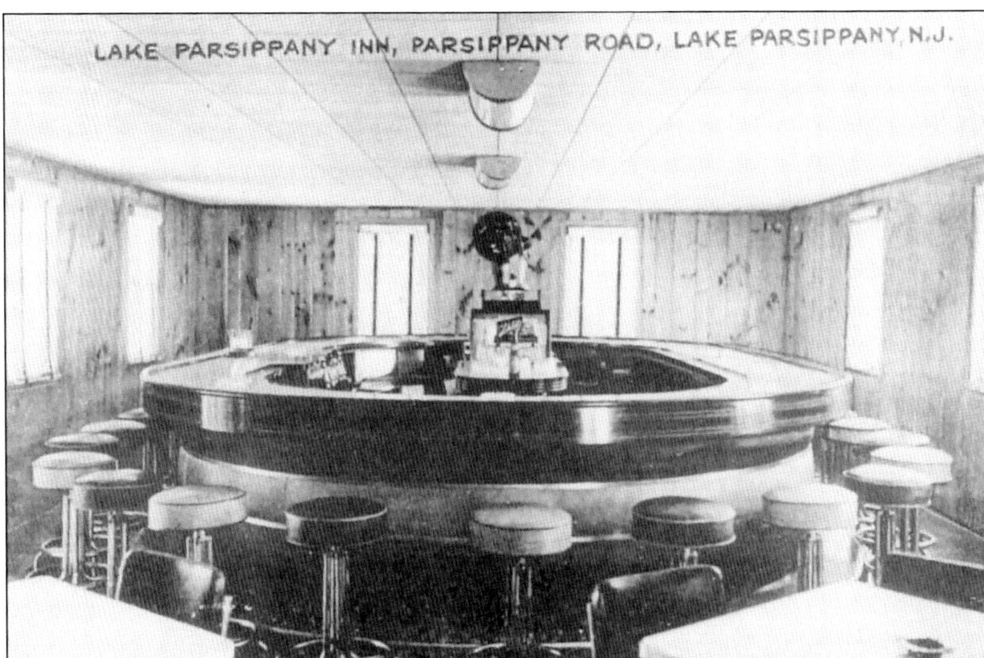

Anton Huck's Lake Parsippany Inn, 1940s. The inn was located on Parsippany Road between Carlstadt and Dorothy Roads and later became Ingrid's Rendezvous. It is reputed to have been a stagecoach stop in colonial times, and was razed in the 1990s. (Mary Purzycki.)

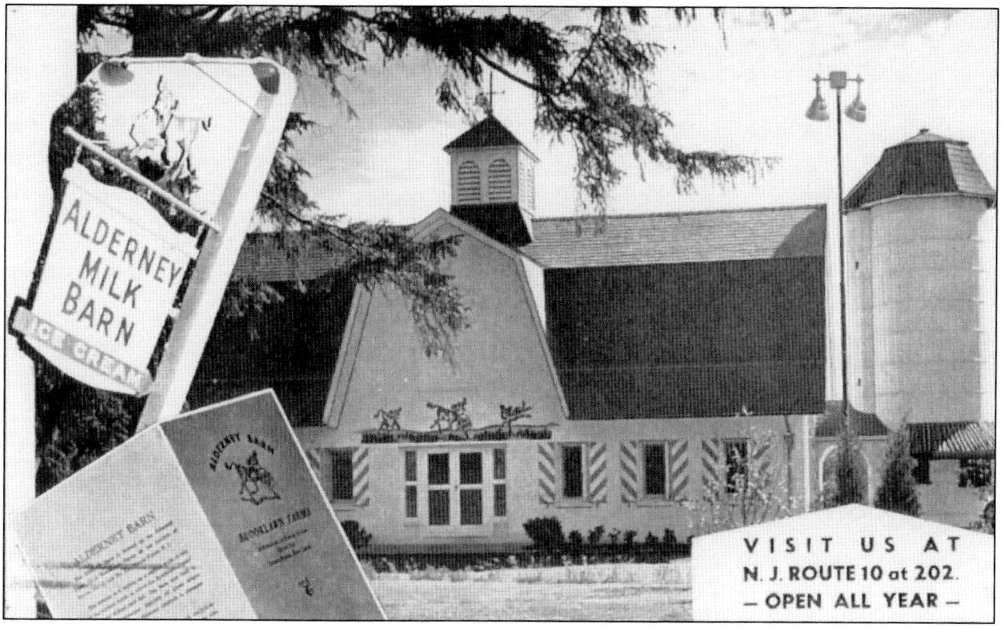

The Alderney milk barn on the northeast corner of Routes 10 and 202. The barn became the Sip and Sup Restaurant and Ice Cream Parlor before it burned down in the late 1960s. It was originally the main dairy barn for Alderney Farms. (Robert D'Alessandro.)

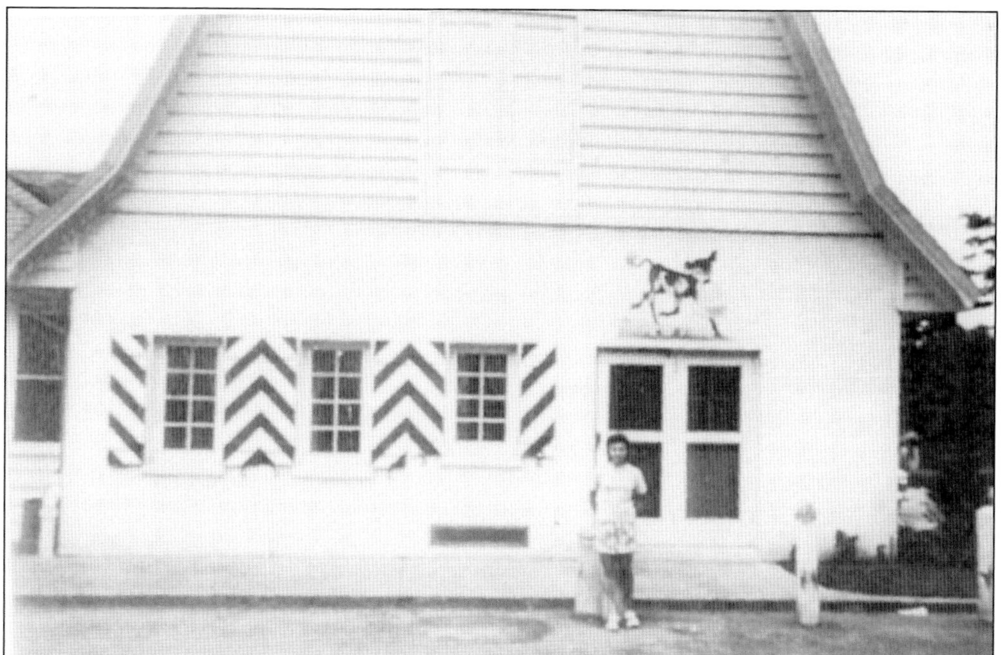
Mildred Cicala Abbate at the side of the Alderney milk barn in the late 1940s. (Ann Egan.)

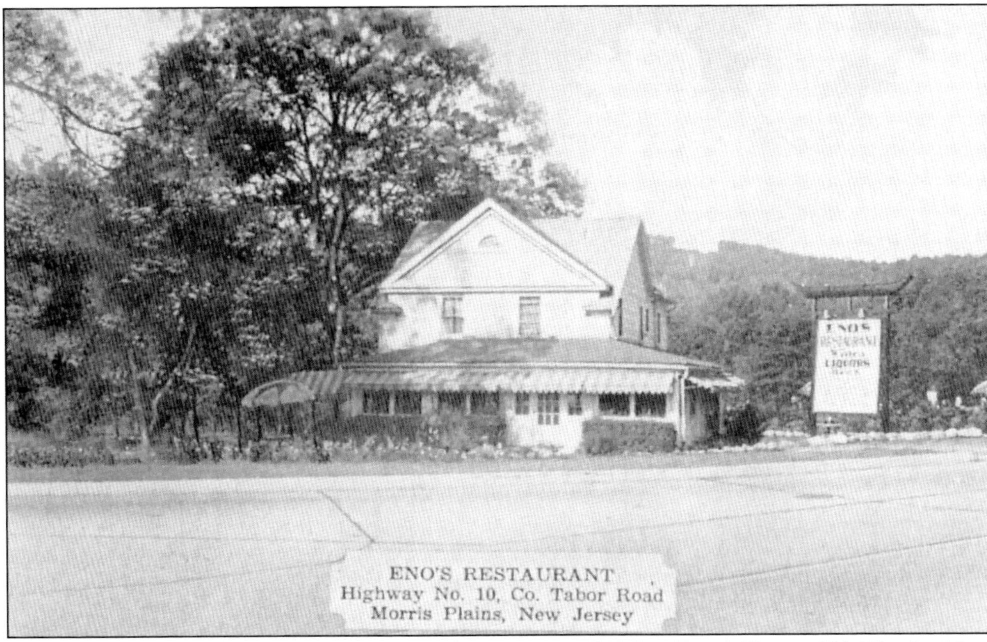

Eno's Restaurant on the northeast corner of Route 10 and Tabor Road (Route 53). The building is still standing and operating as a restaurant under a different name. (Robert D'Alessandro.)

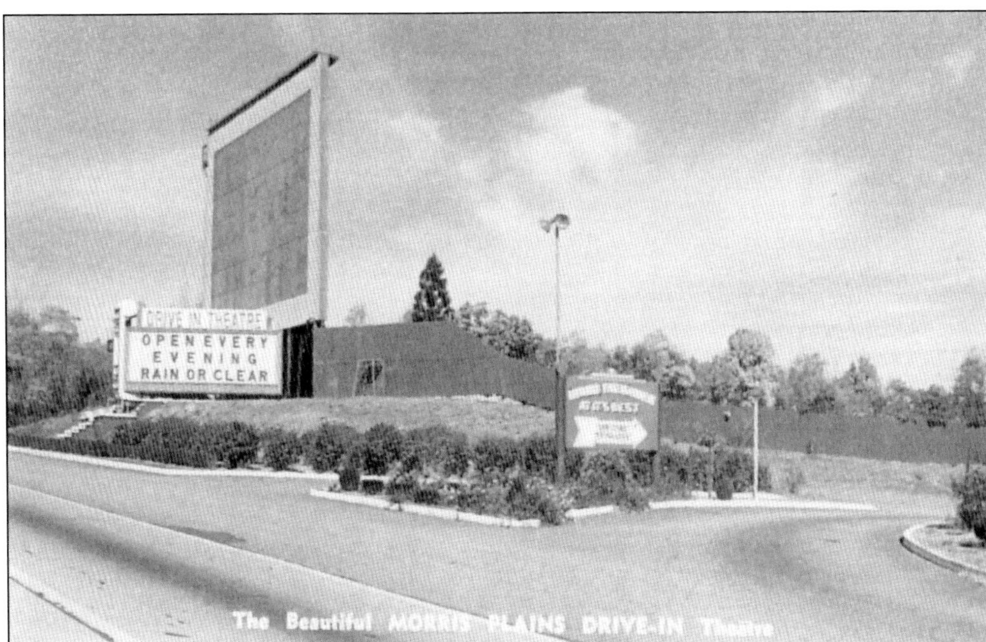

The Morris Plains Drive-In Movie Theater on Route 10 West, which was geographically located in Parsippany-Troy Hills. The theater was torn down in the 1970s; the Gatehall Office Complex presently occupies this site. (Robert D'Alessandro.)

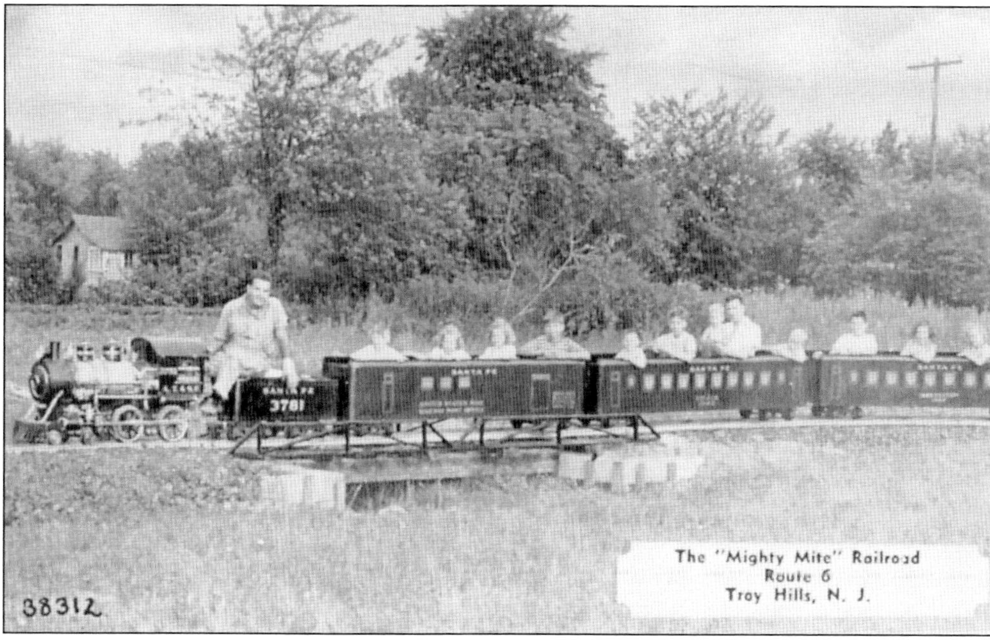

A Mighty-Mite Railroad Ride, *c.* 1950. This ride was situated adjacent to Rich's Hobby Towne, which was located about where the Holiday Inn stands today. Rich's Hobby Towne was a popular center for slot car races and hobby supplies of all kinds. (Robert D'Alessandro.)

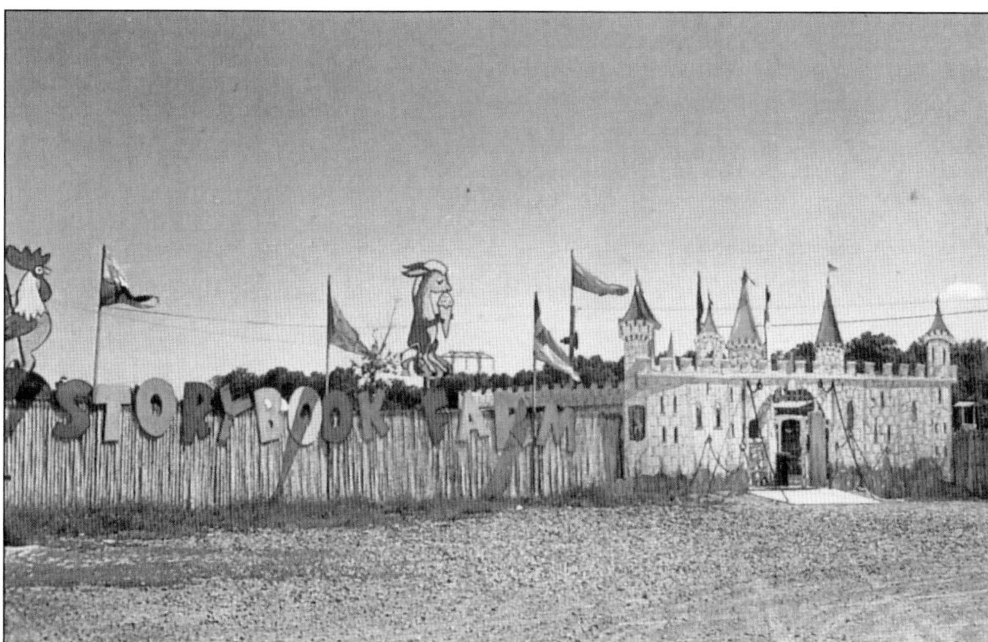

The entrance to Storybook Farms on Route 46 West, just west of Arlington Plaza. During the 1950s and '60s this was a popular kiddy attraction. (Robert D'Alessandro.)

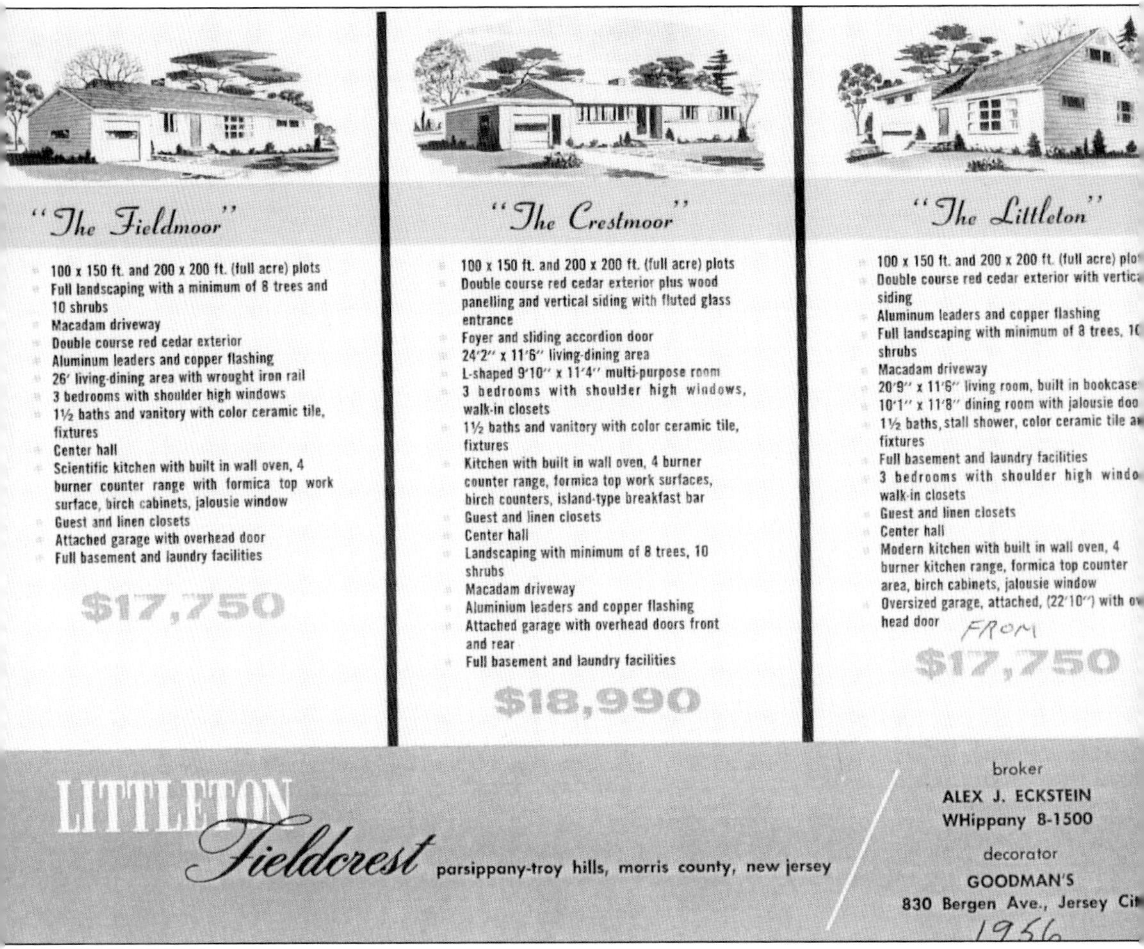

An advertisement for new homes built in the late 1950s in the Fieldcrest Road area near Route 202. Because people thought 1 1/2 bathrooms to be too extravagant, builders had to eliminate the 1/2 bath and drop the price by $1,000 before they were able to sell these homes. Parsippany-Troy Hills' population doubled during the 1960s and led to the rise of many such developments. (Art and Ginnie Hendrickson.)

Seven

Scenes around Town

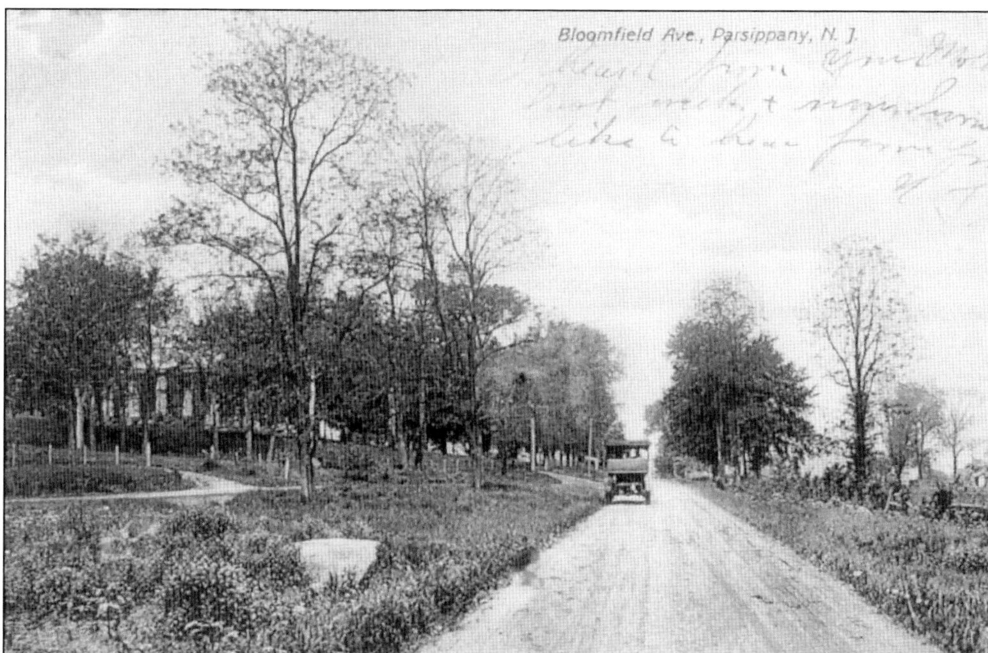

Bloomfield Avenue, Parsippany, looking west, c. 1920. The Parsippany Presbyterian Church is on the left. Bloomfield Avenue was originally a toll road. The last toll-taker was John Mead, who worked in that capacity until 1822. Bloomfield Avenue became Route 6 in 1938, and Route 46 in 1953. (Robert D'Alessandro.)

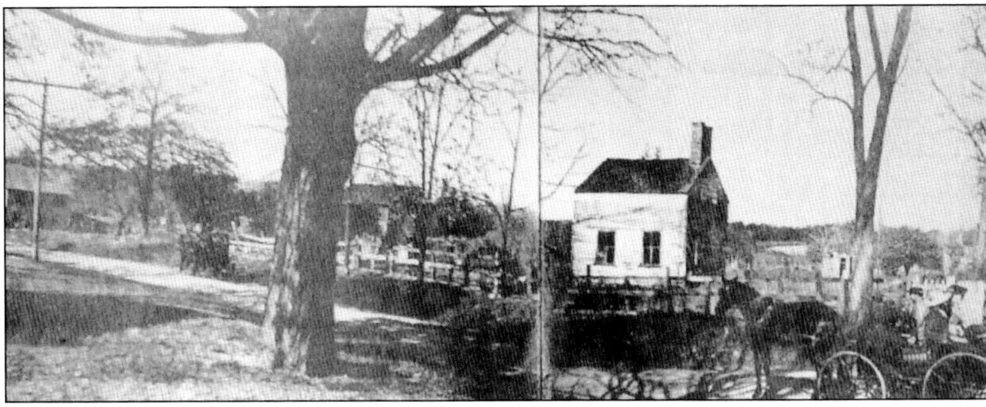

Route 46 East, c. 1910. The house and buildings are part of the Baldwin Farm. Meeker's Blacksmith Shop is on the right. (Parsippany-Troy Hills Township.)

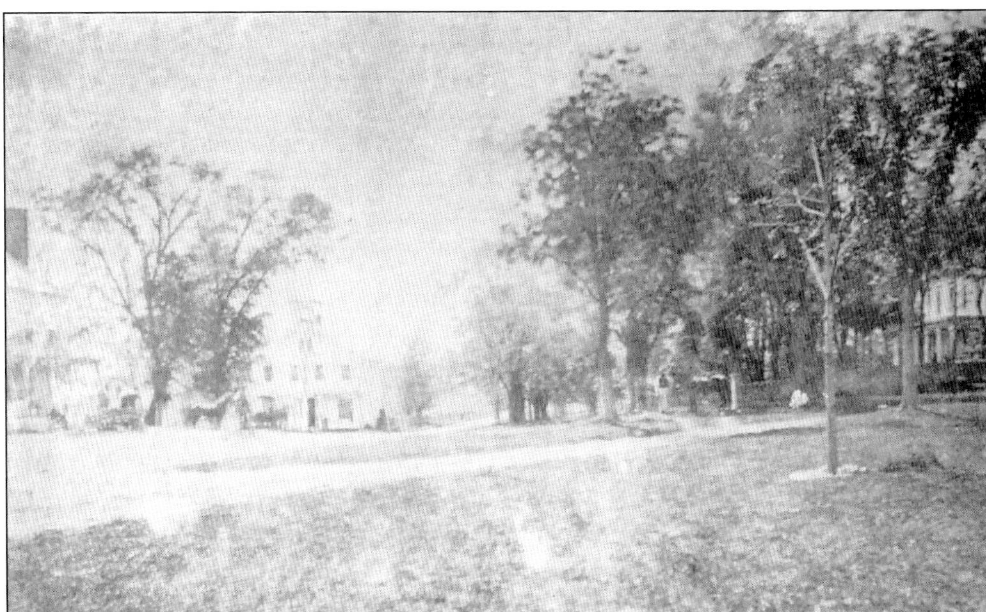

Cobb's Corner, looking west, c. 1865. This area is today's Route 46 and Parsippany Road. On the right is the Cobb House (the site of the Parsippany-Troy Hills Municipal Building). To the left is the Parsippany Hotel and a general store. The general store served both as the town hall and as the police headquarters. (Parsippany-Troy Hills Township.)

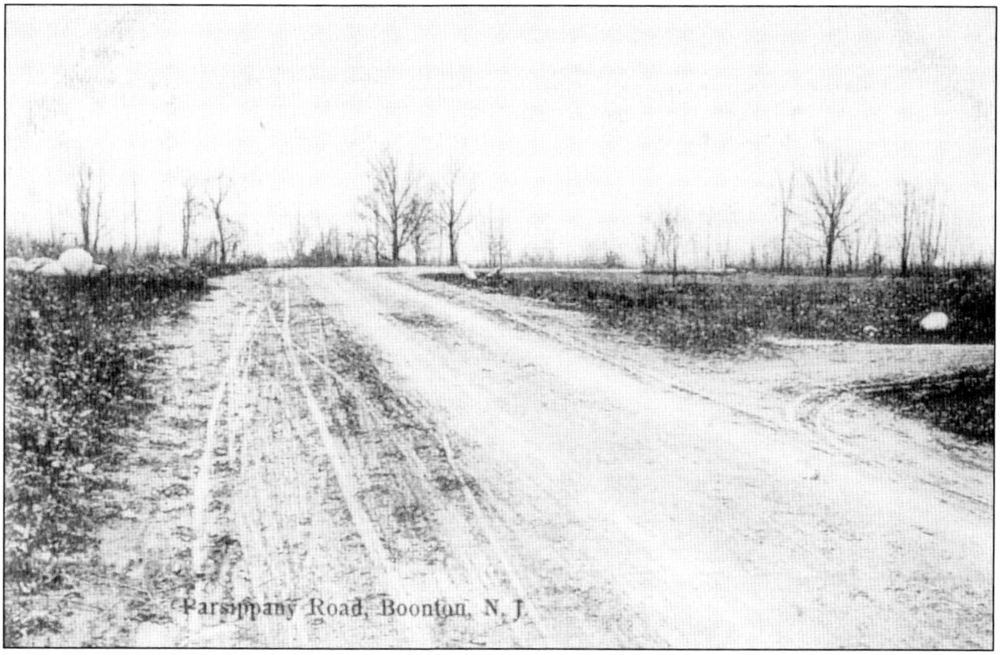

Parsippany Road, looking north toward Boonton, *c.* 1890. This area was realigned to make way for the Jersey City Reservoir. (Robert D'Alessandro.)

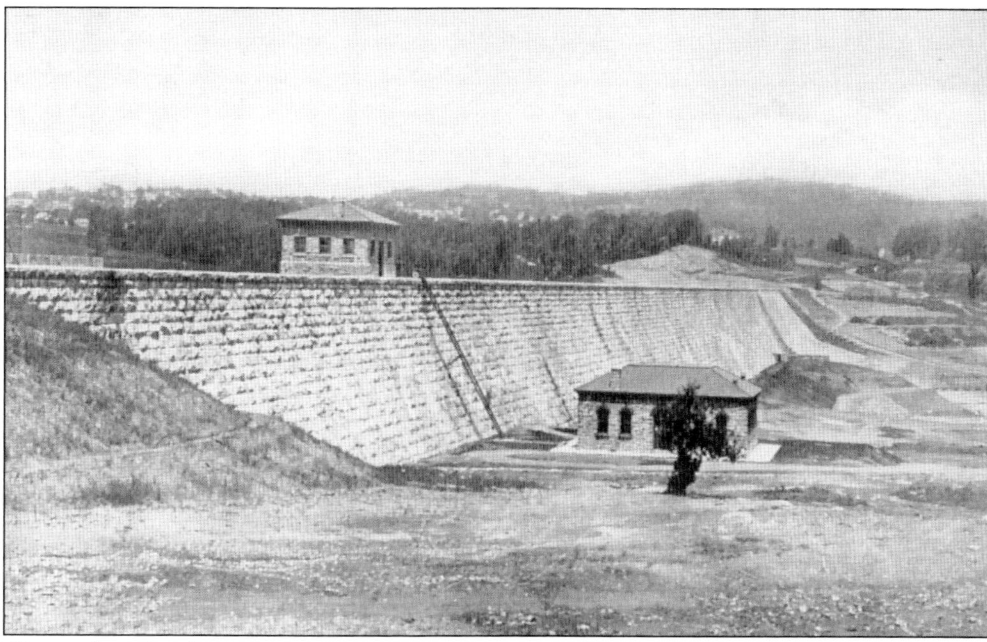

The viaduct for the Jersey City Reservoir, *c.* 1896. The viaduct was considered at the time to be one of the construction wonders of the world. People came from as far away as Japan to study this marvel of engineering. The reservoir covered 773.7 acres and held 7.5 billion gallons of water when completed in 1904. Present-day capacity has been considerably increased. (Robert D'Alessandro.)

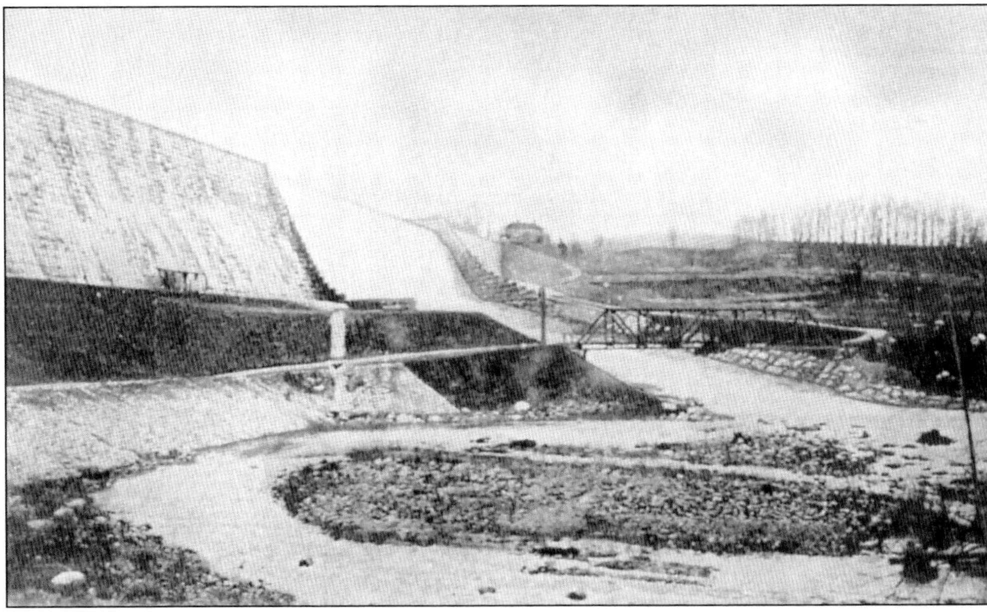

The Jersey City Reservoir's sluice, *c.* 1896. In the foreground is the Rockaway River. Today Greenbank Road runs parallel with the Rockaway River. Pipelines that are 36-inches wide transport potable water from this area to Jersey City. Parsippany-Troy Hills gets its water from artesian wells. (Robert D'Alessandro.)

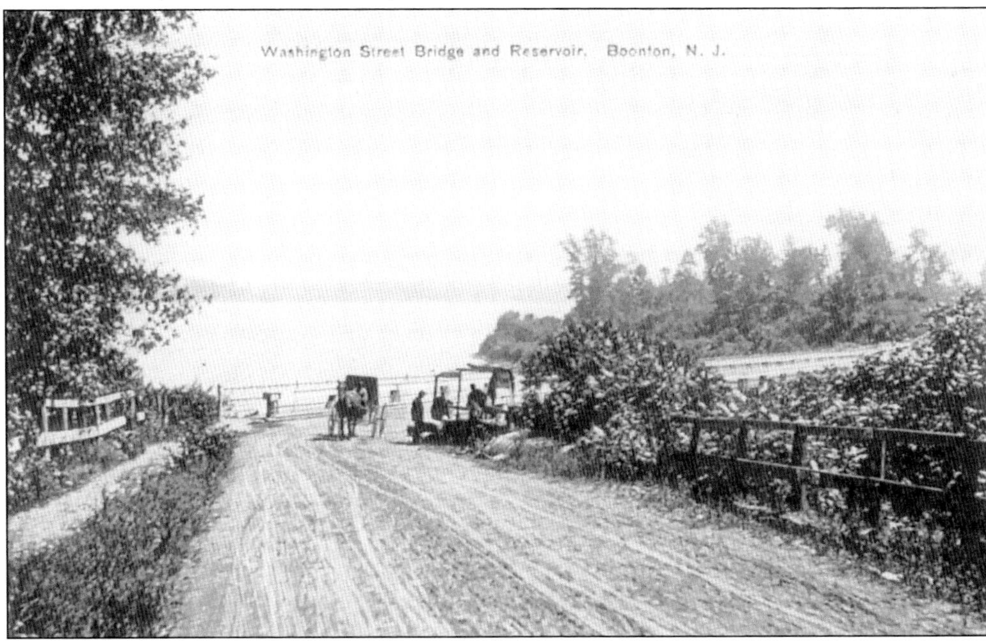

The Washington Street Bridge and Reservoir, looking south, *c.* 1896. The bridge crosses Reservoir Road to Boonton. The reservoir was built at the cost of $7,595,000 for the citizens of Jersey City after an 1890s typhoid fever epidemic contaminated their water supply. Mainly Italian immigrants and African-Americans took the jobs available as laborers at the reservoir. This was dangerous work and cost many men their lives, working as they did in the quarry and on the trestles along the dam. (Robert D'Alessandro.)

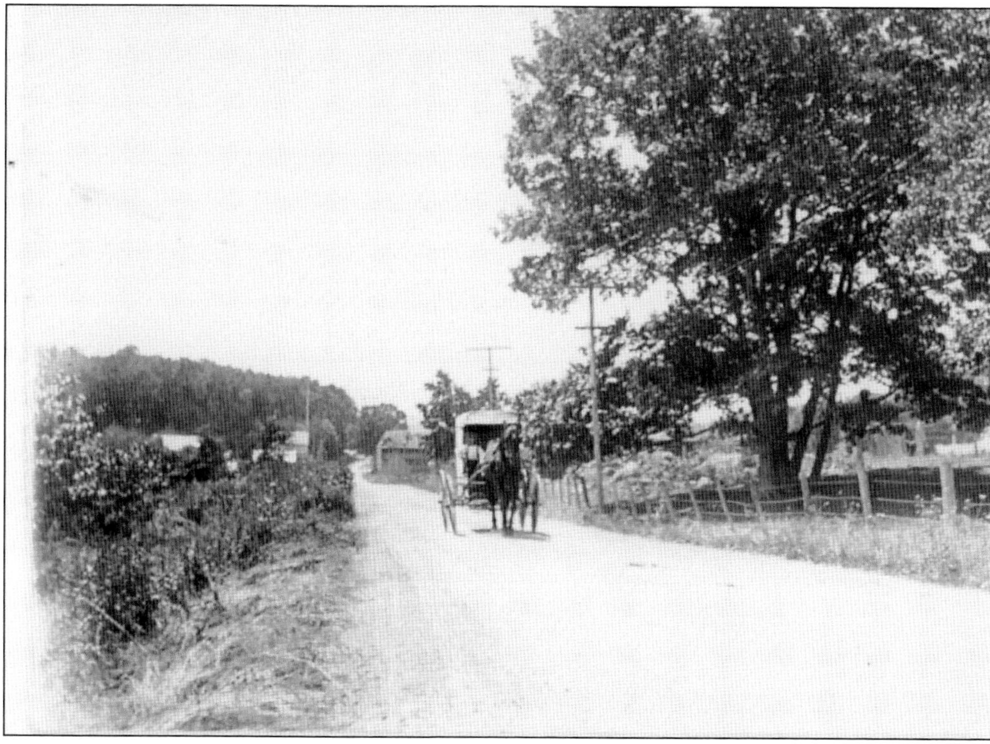

Route 53 in Mount Tabor, looking north, *c.* 1900. (Robert D'Alessandro.)

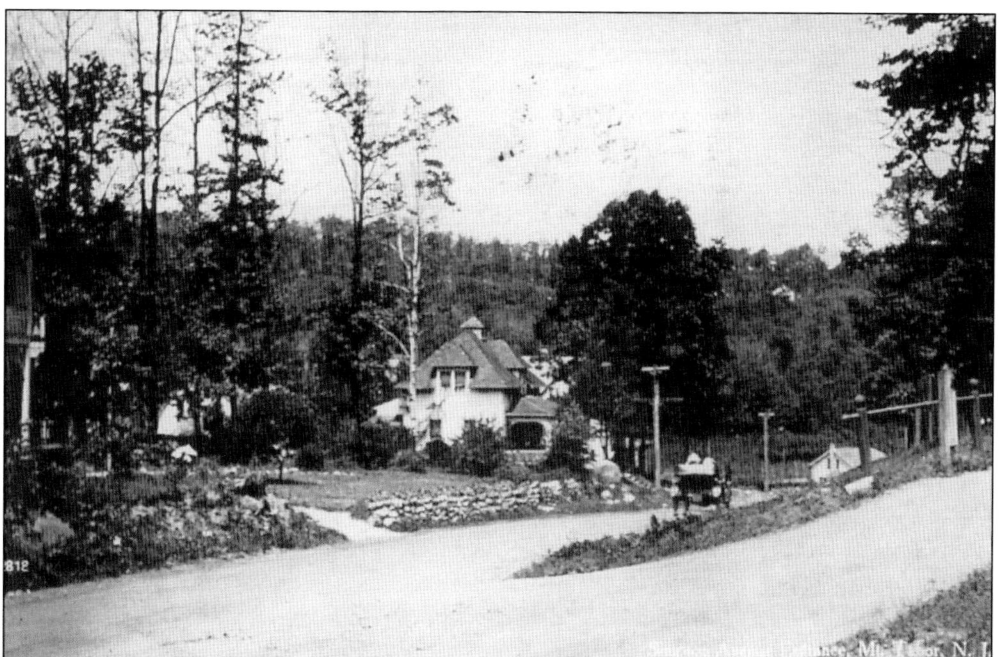

Route 53 in Mount Tabor, looking north, *c.* 1910. This is the Simpson Avenue entrance to Mount Tabor. (Robert D'Alessandro.)

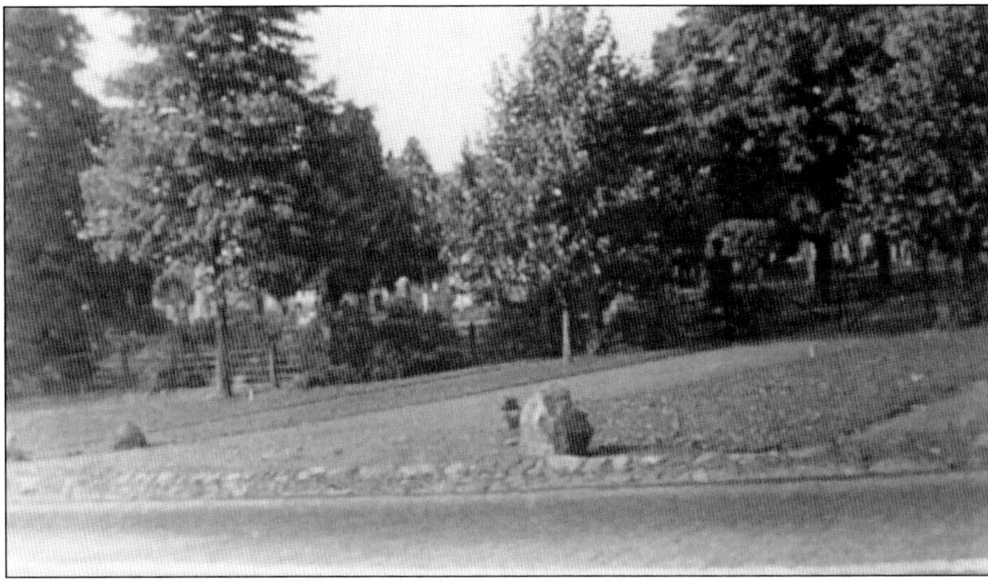

The gate of the Parsippany Presbyterian Church Cemetery, looking north across Route 6 (today's Route 46), *c.* 1937. The gate is on the original thoroughfare, which, until 1911, ran through the cemetery and separated the old section from the new. George Bowlsby deeded 2 1/4 acres of land to the church on November 30, 1745, for "2 pounds current money" during the reign of George II. Many ancestors of prominent local families are buried in both sections. The earliest extant tombstone is for Samuel Michel, son of John and Sarah, who was born in 1747 and died on August 7, 1755. *See Founding Families*. (Charles Bates.)

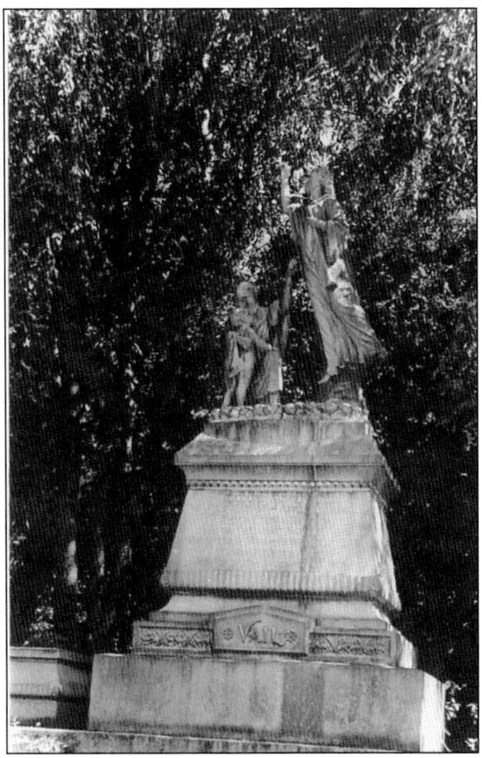

The Theodore Newton Vail Monument, located in the Vail portion of the Parsippany Presbyterian Church Cemetery. Theodore Vail (1845–1920) was the first president of American Telephone and Telegraph (from 1907–1919). He was also related to Alfred Vail, who, along with Samuel F.B. Morse, invented the Morse Code and telegraph. It is said that Bell invented the telephone, but Vail invented the telephone business. (Joint Free Public Library of Morristown and Morris Township.)

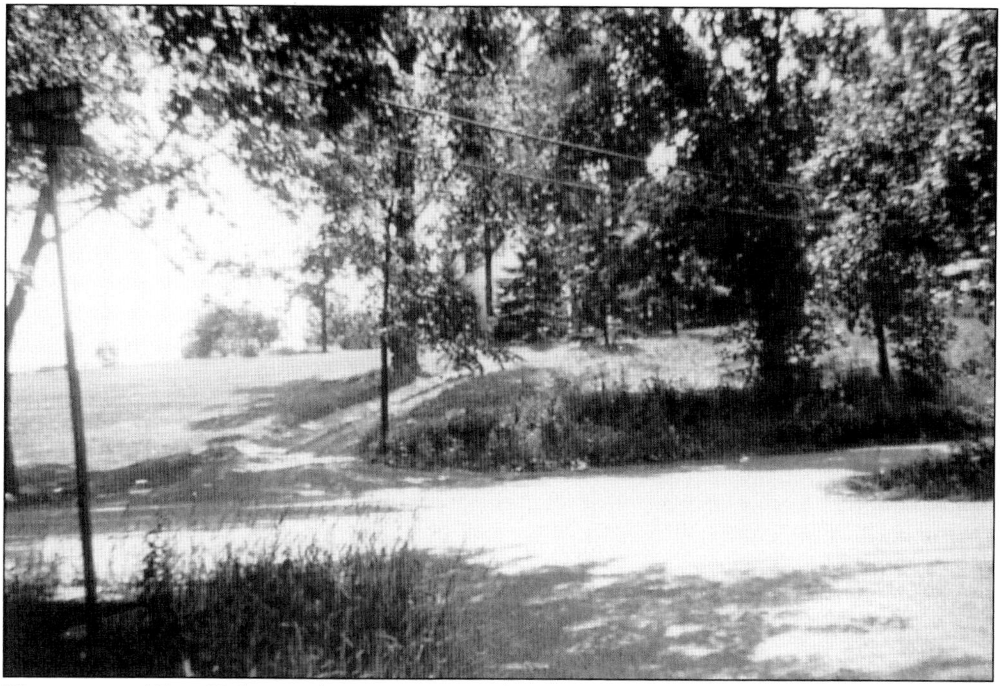

The corner of East Halsey and Parsippany Roads, *c.* 1960. This image provides a rural view of the roads. (Charles Bates.)

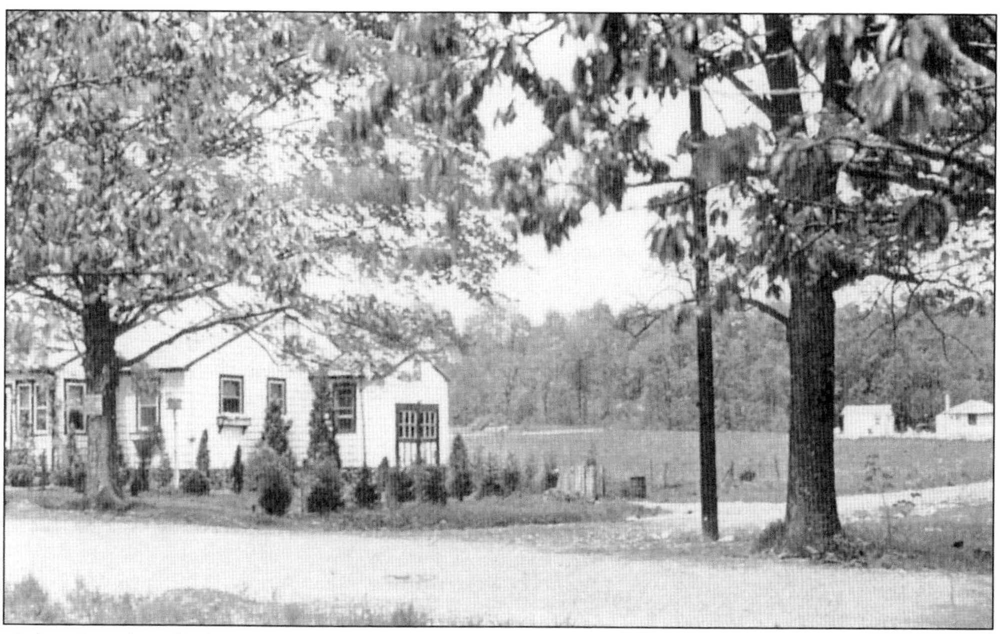

Halsey Road and Elmwood Drive, *c.* 1938, when both were dirt roads. The area is now totally developed with single-family homes. (Robert D'Alessandro.)

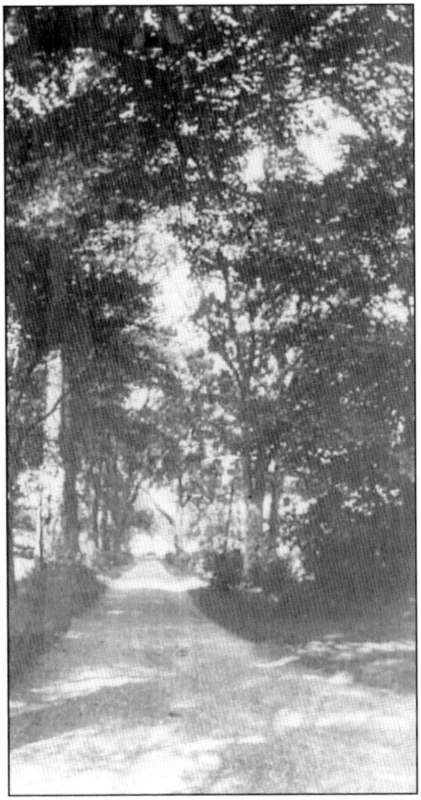

The entrance to Grossmann's Farm on Parsippany Road. This is approximately where the main branch of the Parsippany-Troy Hills Public Library stands today. (Nick Cerbo.)

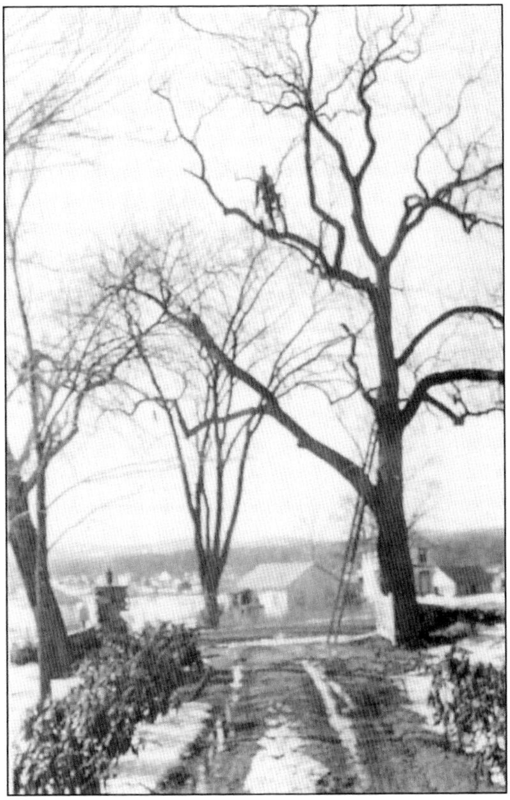

Stopping to stare at a man in a tree, c. 1930s. This view looks from the Grossmann Estate toward the newly formed, man-made Lake Parsippany. (Nick Cerbo.)

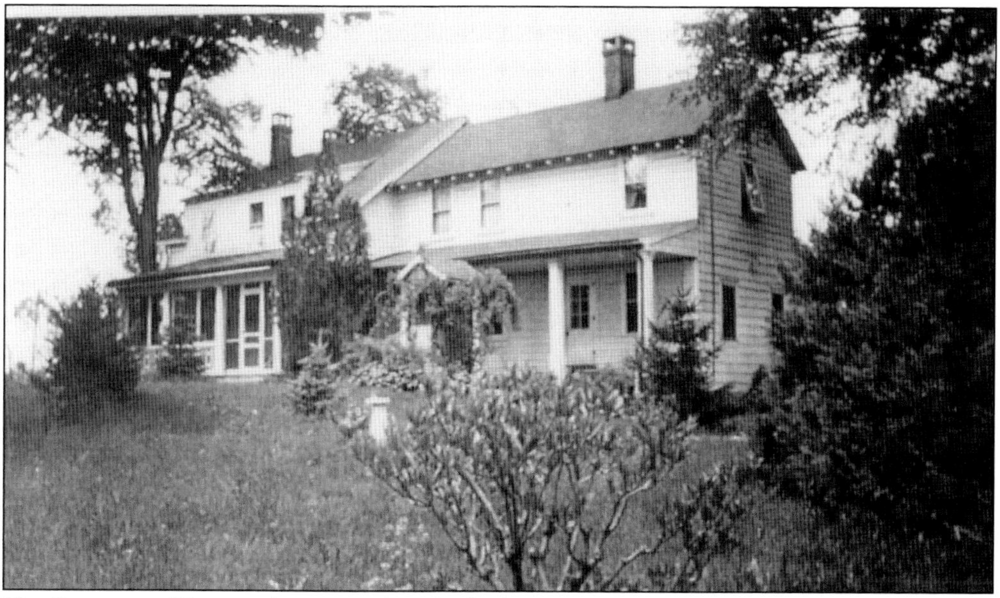

The Grossmann Home in the spring of 1935. This house was once owned by Theodore Newton Vail (see p. 108). (Nick Cerbo.)

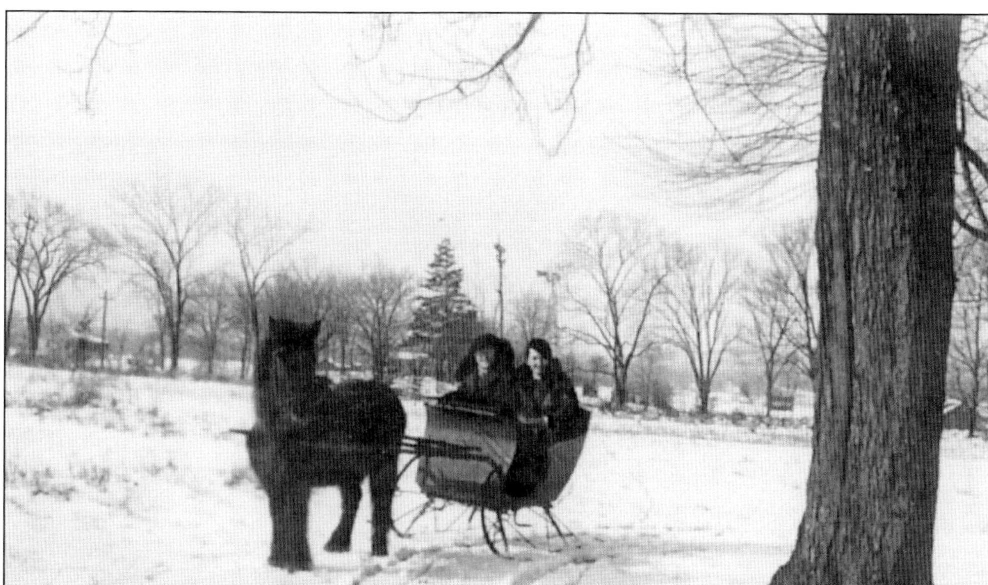

Having fun in a horse-drawn sleigh on the Grossmann estate, *c*. 1930. (Nick Cerbo.)

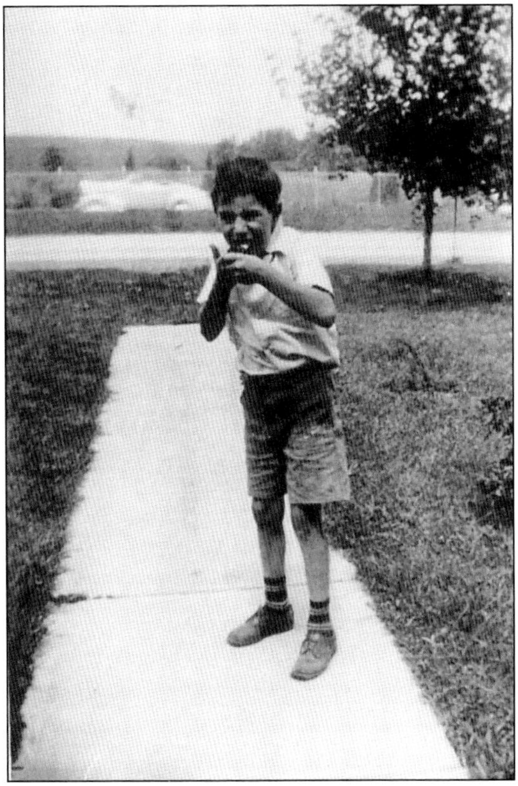

Nick Cerbo, *c.* 1930. At about nine years of age, Nick is shown eating a pizza made by his mother, Stephenina. Route 46 is in the background. (Nick Cerbo.)

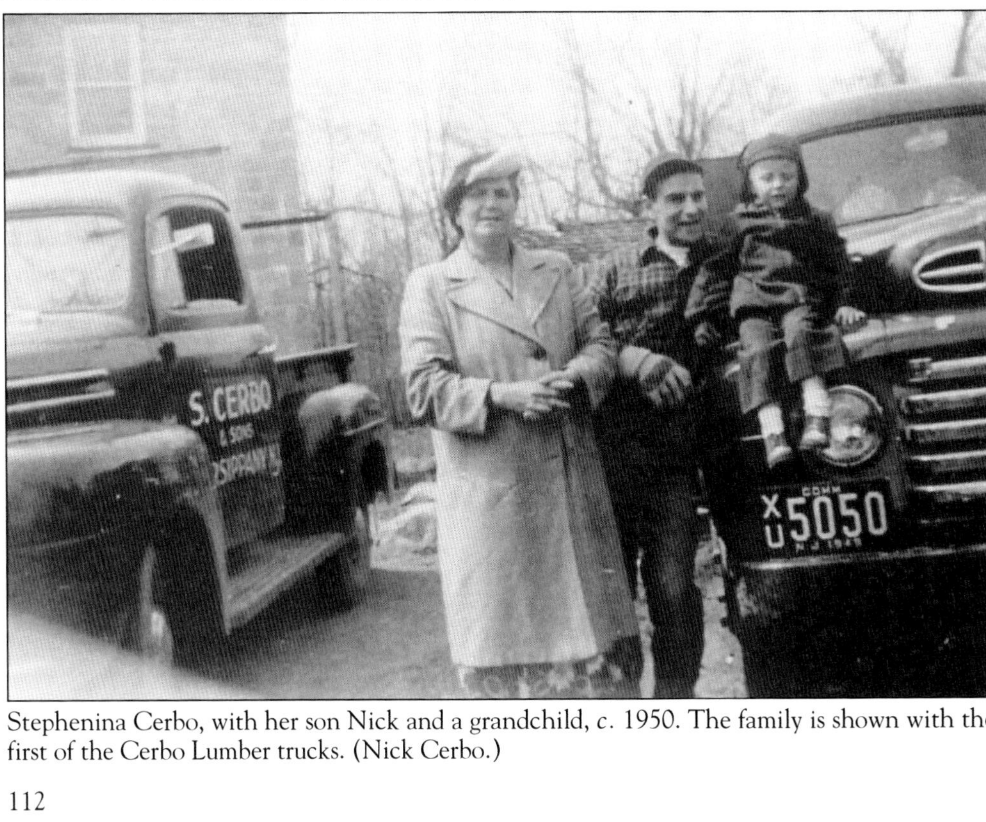

Stephenina Cerbo, with her son Nick and a grandchild, *c.* 1950. The family is shown with the first of the Cerbo Lumber trucks. (Nick Cerbo.)

Eight

Lake Communities

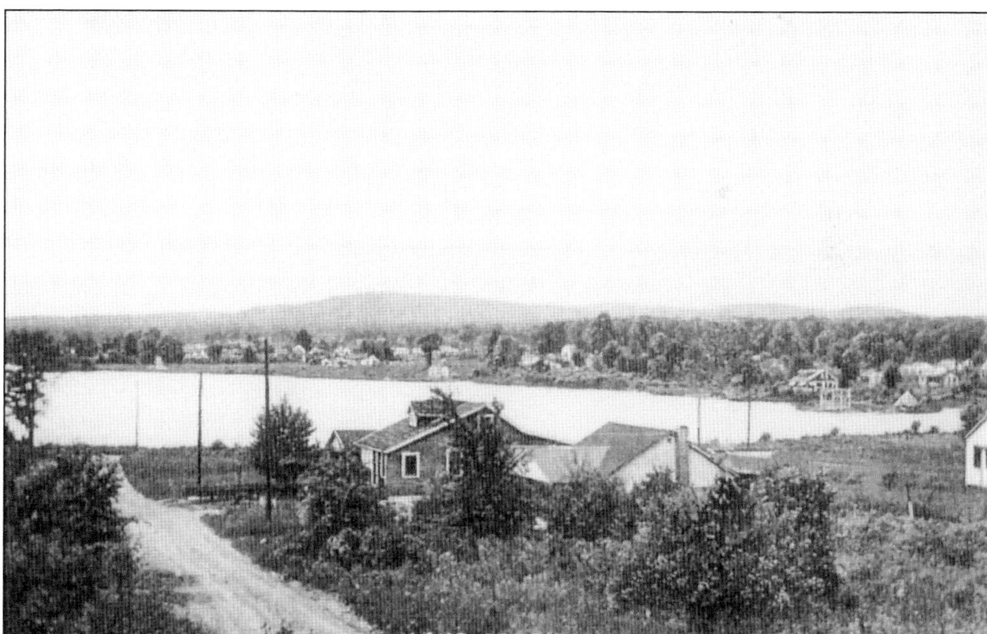

Lake Parsippany, looking south, *c.* 1930. Watnong Mountain—in the background—is the site of a large apartment complex today. (Robert D'Alessandro.)

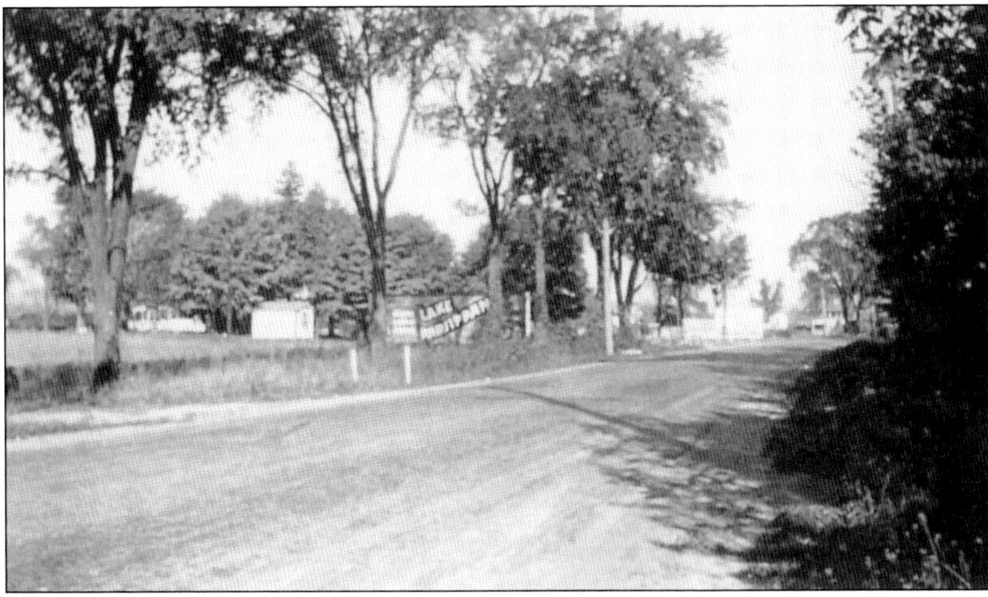

Parsippany Road, looking west from Grossmann's Farm, *c.* 1935. The sales office for Lake Parsippany lots is in the left background. The sign offers boating, bathing, and fishing amenities as an inducement to buy property around the lake. (Nick Cerbo.)

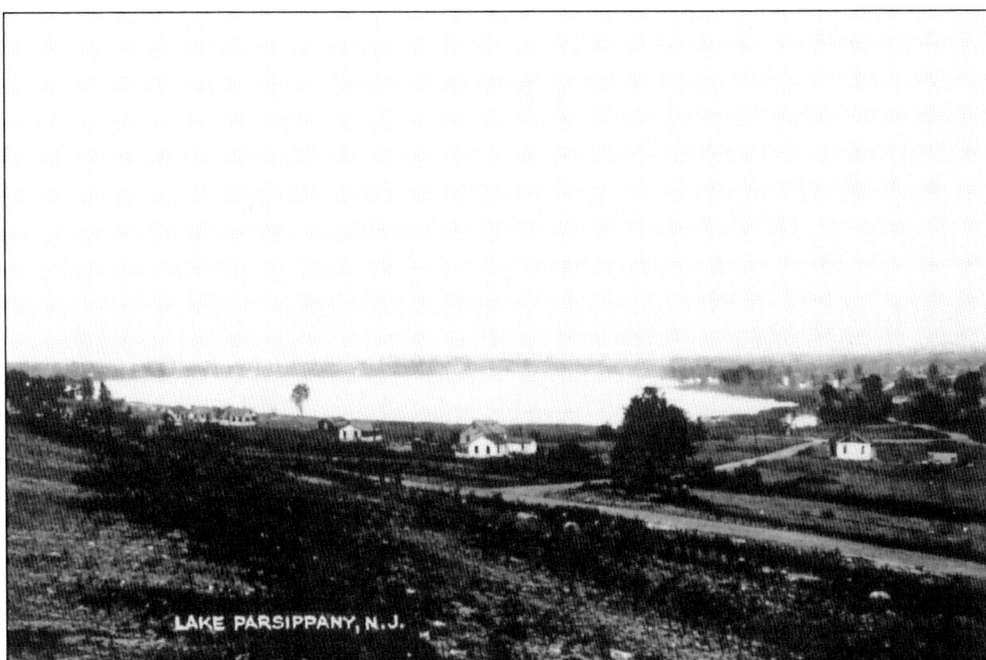

Lake Parsippany, looking east, *c.* 1930. (Robert D'Alessandro.)

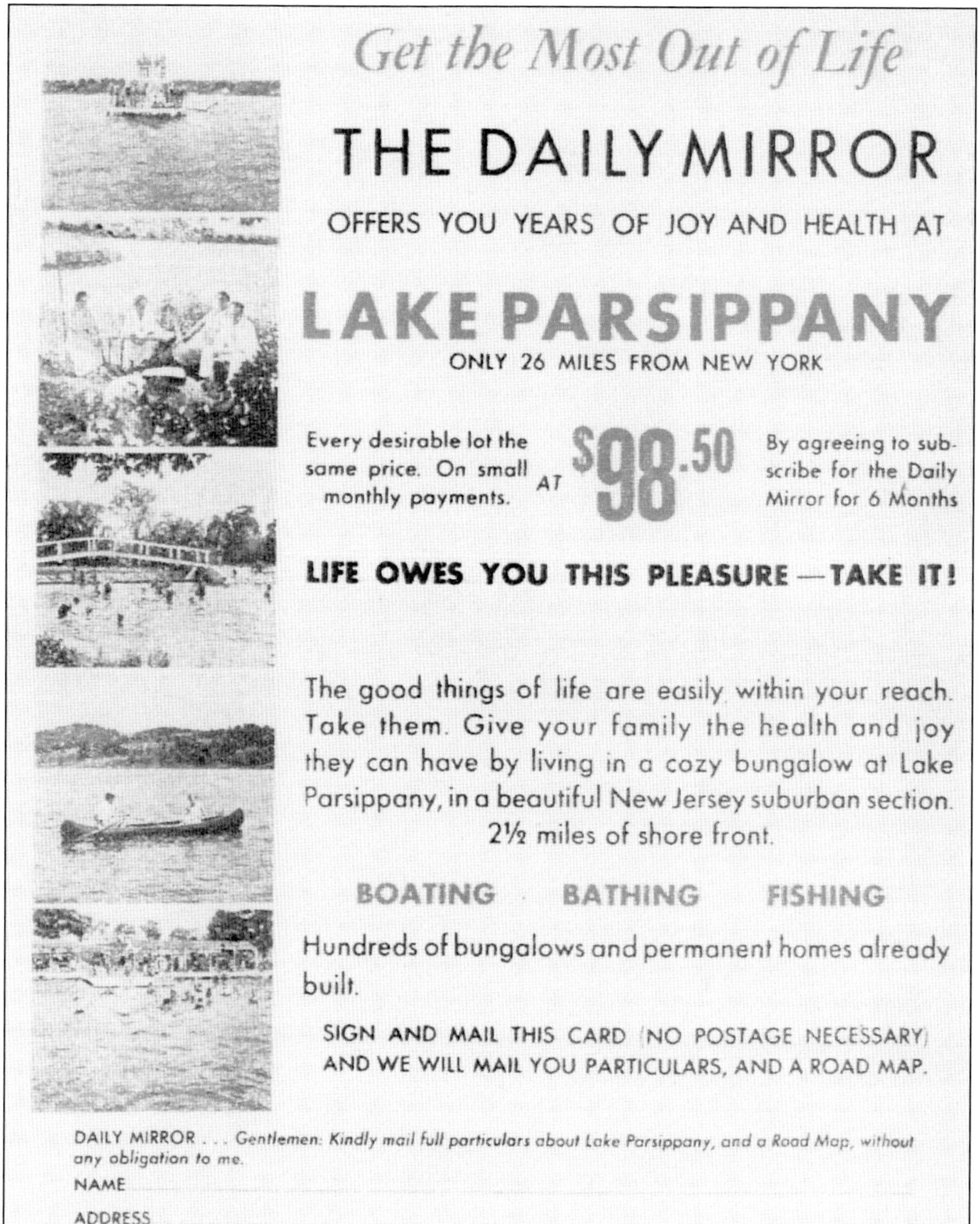

An advertisement for the sale of lots in Lake Parsippany. Lots were 20-by-100 feet. To build a dwelling required a minimum purchase of two lots. (Mary Purzycki.)

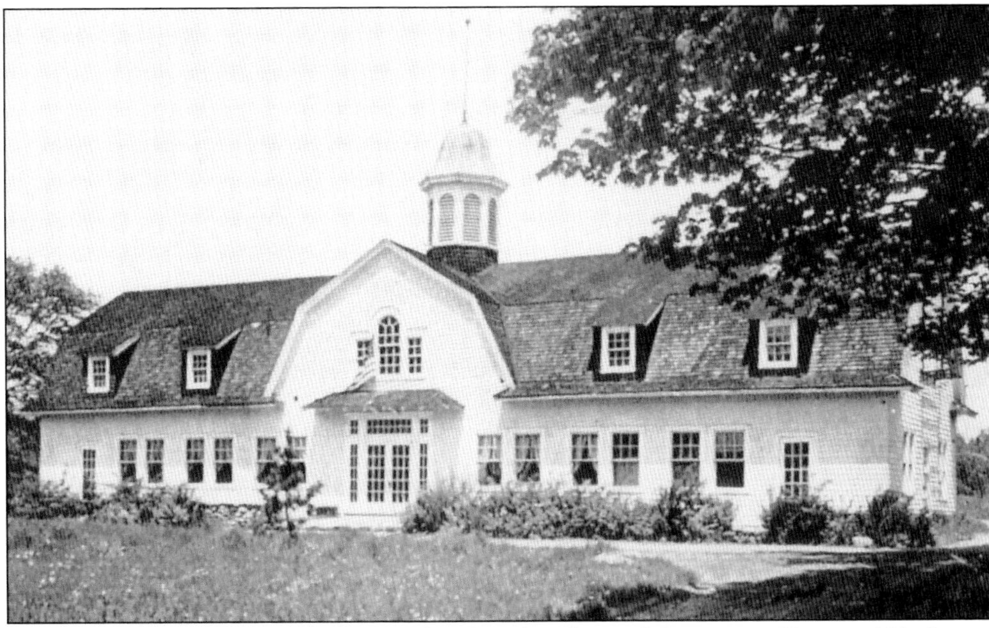

The Lake Parsippany Clubhouse on Halsey Road in front of the present District 4 Firehouse. The clubhouse is no longer in existence. (Robert D'Alessandro.)

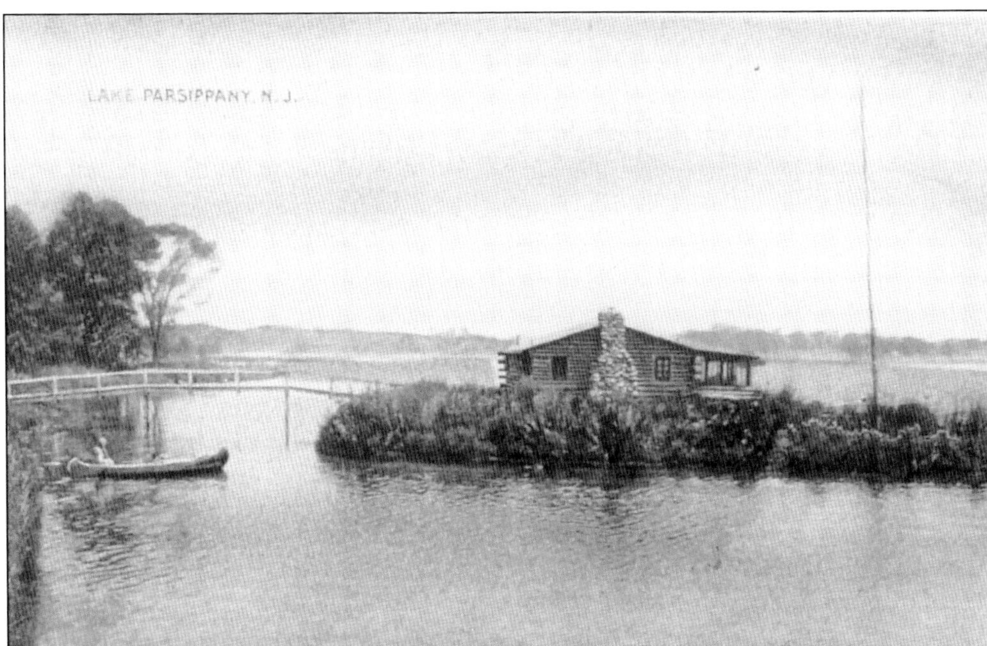

One of the two tiny islands on Lake Parsippany. This view from Halsey Road looks east. Flemington Drive is just north of the island. (Robert D'Alessandro.)

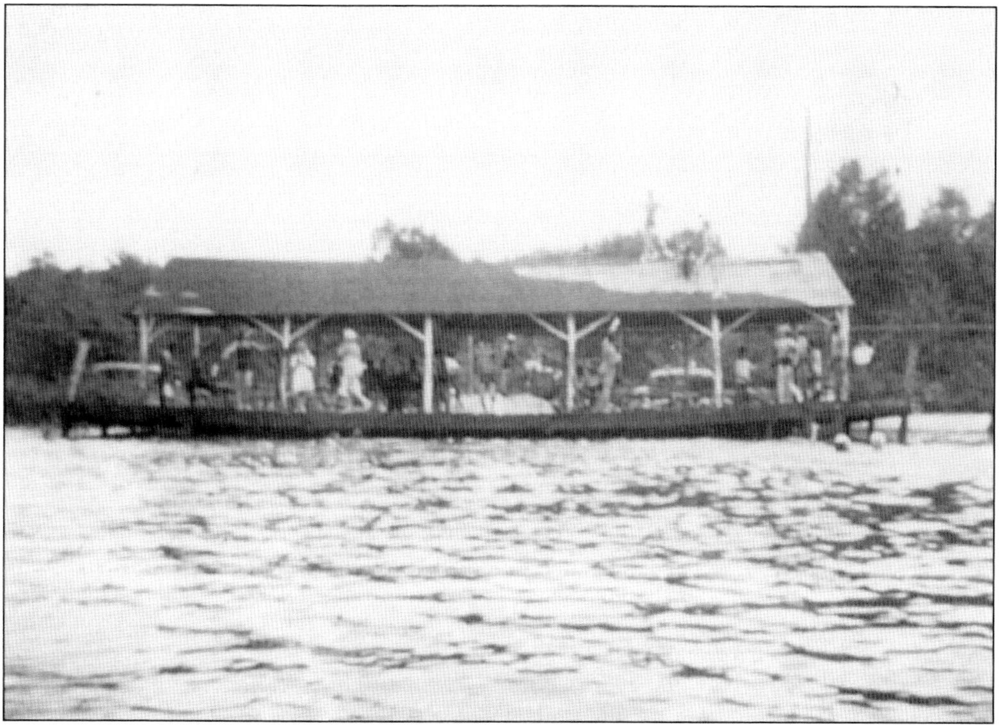

"Twelve Foot." This popular local diving pier was 12 feet deep at this point in the lake. Located across from the Beach Pub and Restaurant at 701 Lake Shore Drive, it was removed during the 1970s. (Ann Egan.)

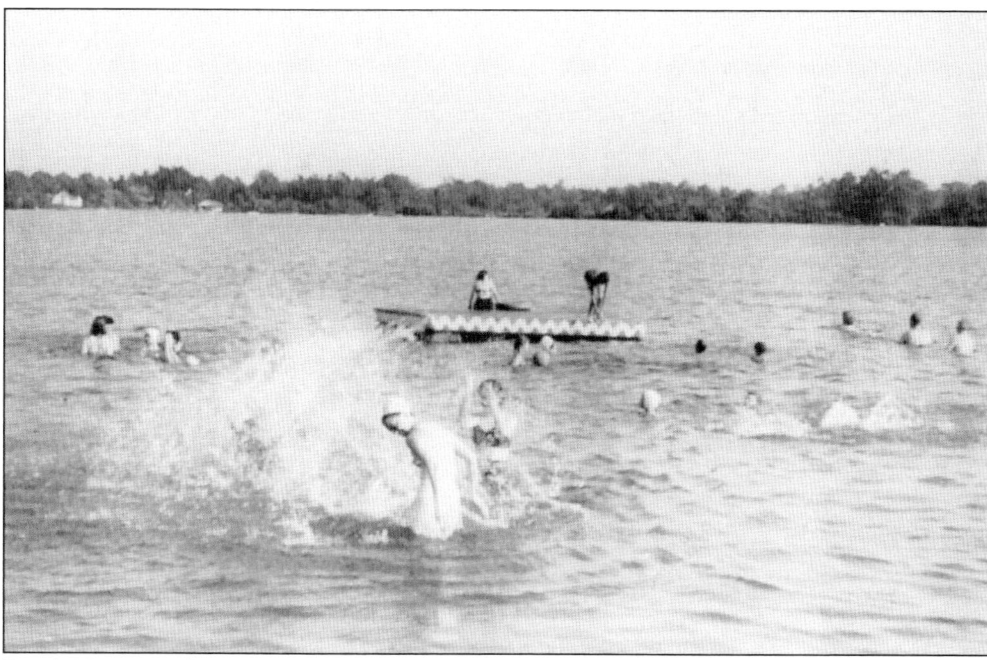

Beach No. 4 at Lake Parsippany. Shown here are Ann Cicala (Egan) and Eileen Vanderspiegel. (Ann Egan.)

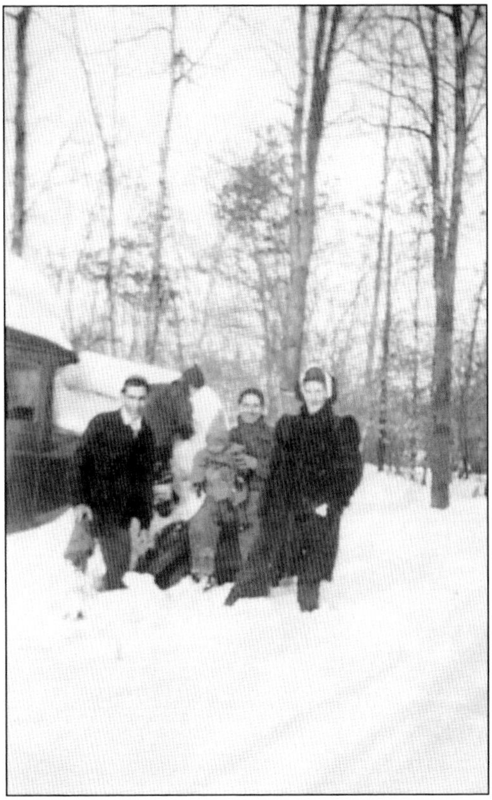

The Blizzard of 1947. It is reputed to have snowed over 3 feet. From left to right are George Beatty, Daniel Tortorello Jr., Daniel Tortorello Sr., James Piegaro (baby), and Florence Beatty Tortorello. (Randy Francis Tortorello.)

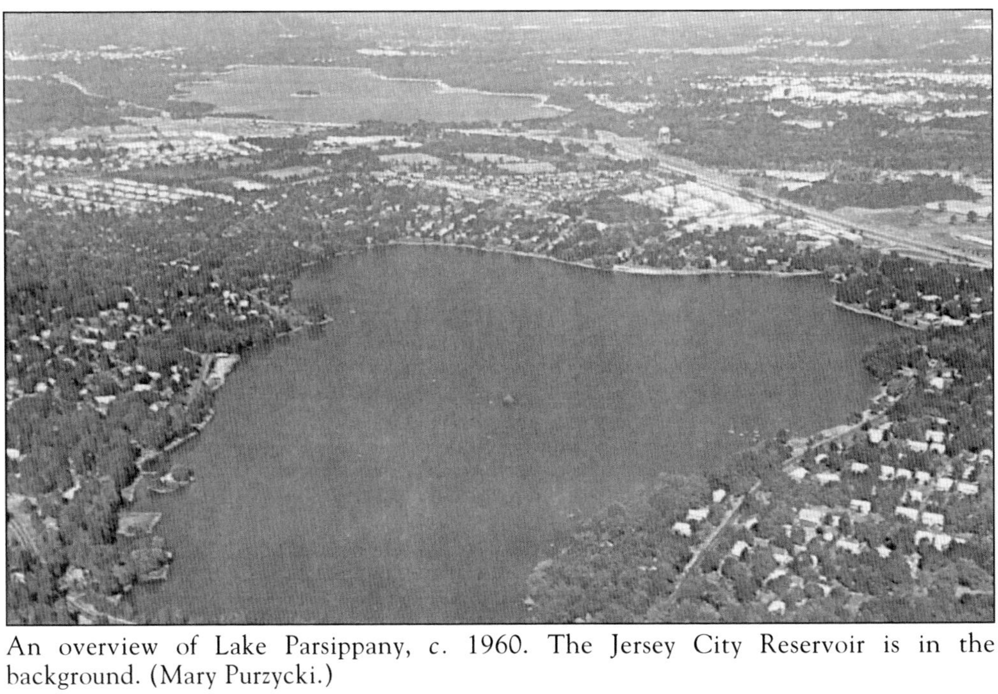

An overview of Lake Parsippany, c. 1960. The Jersey City Reservoir is in the background. (Mary Purzycki.)

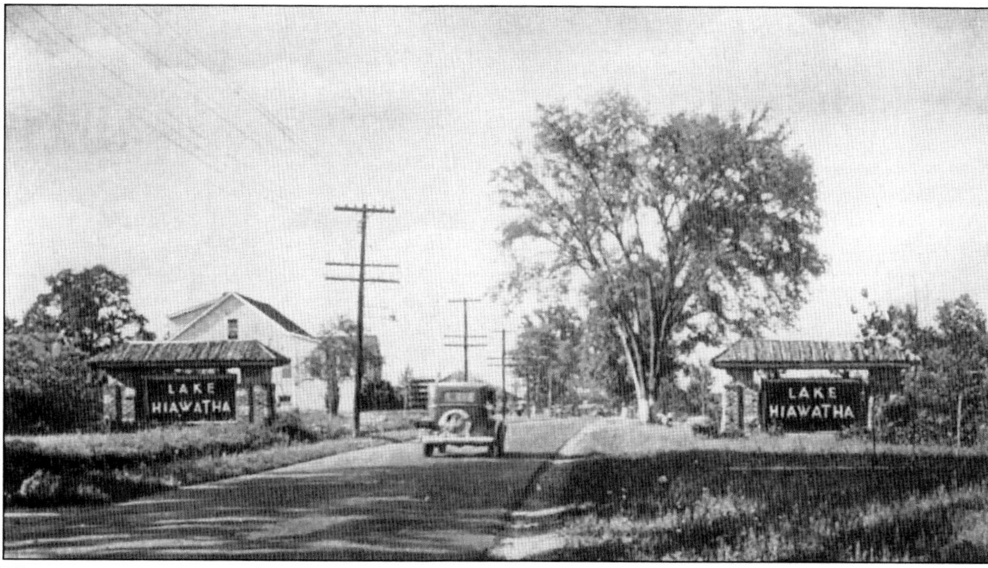

The main entrance to Lake Hiawatha through North Beverwyck Road, *c.* 1930. This view is from about where the Lake Hiawatha Post Office stands at the present time. (Robert D'Alessandro.)

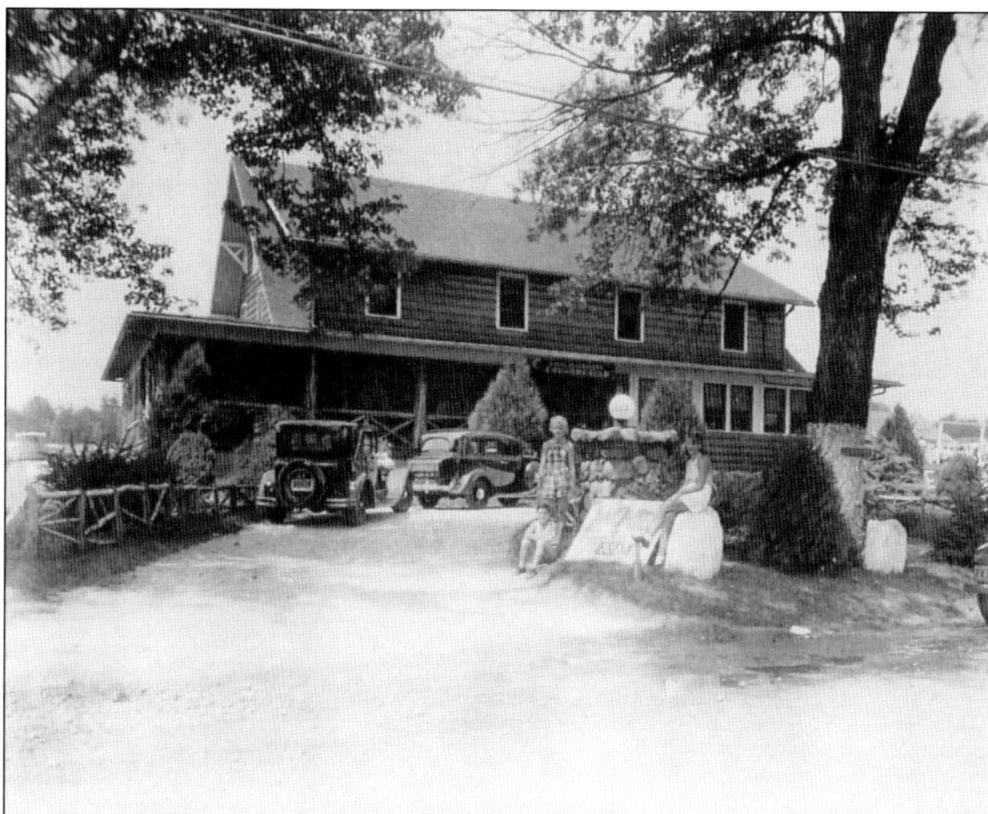

The Lake Hiawatha Clubhouse on the southwest corner of North Beverwyck Road and Minnehaha Boulevard, *c.* 1930. (Parsippany Historic Museum.)

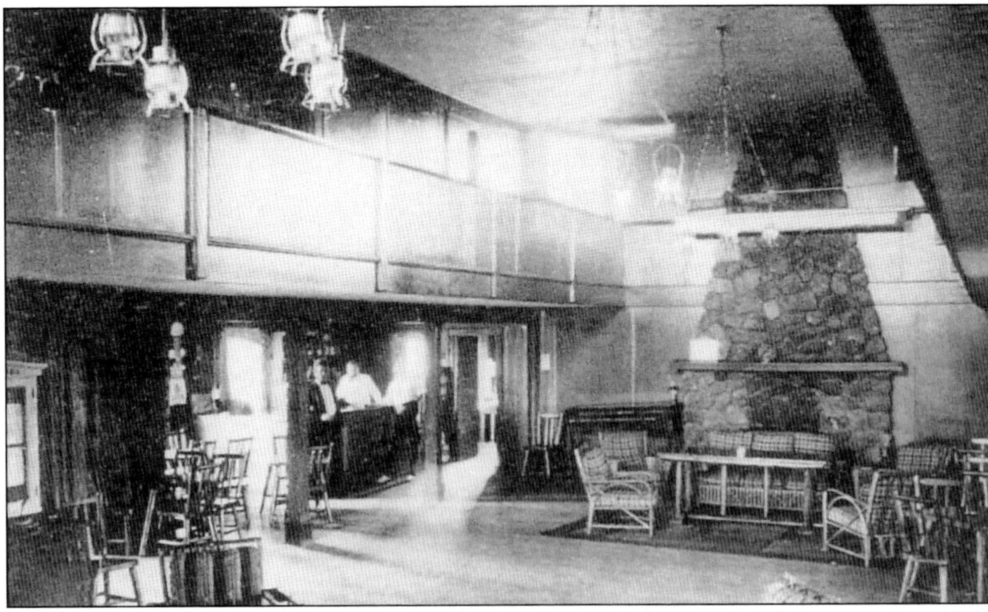

The interior of the Lake Hiawatha Country Club, *c.* 1930. The country club was replaced by a bank in the 1960s. (Fran Kaminski.)

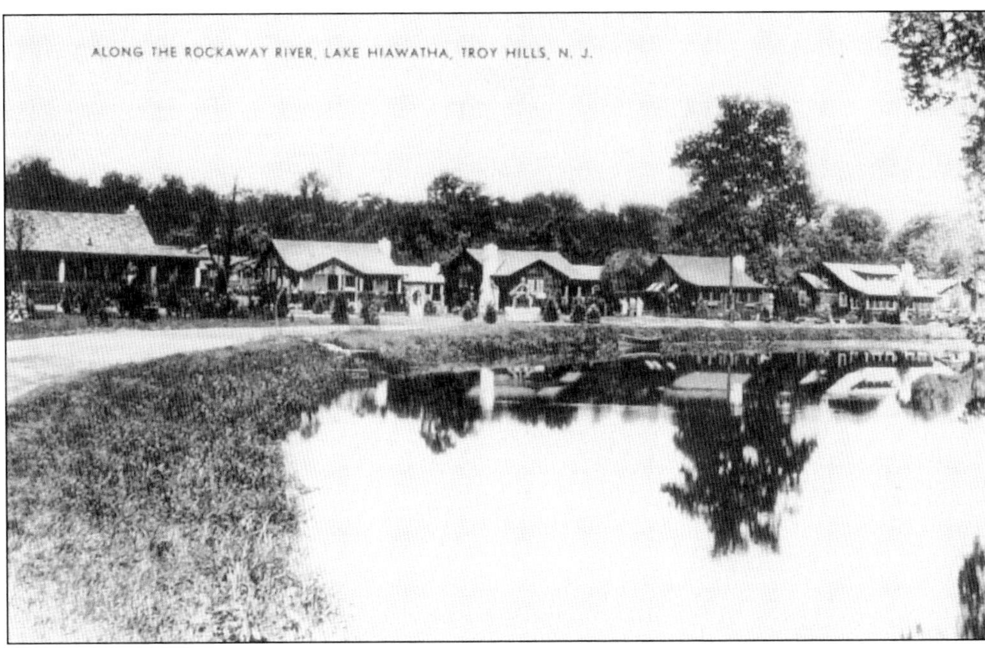

Along the Rockaway River at Lake Hiawatha, *c.* 1932. This stretch of the river has since been filled in with land, and tract homes have been built on it. (Robert D'Alessandro.)

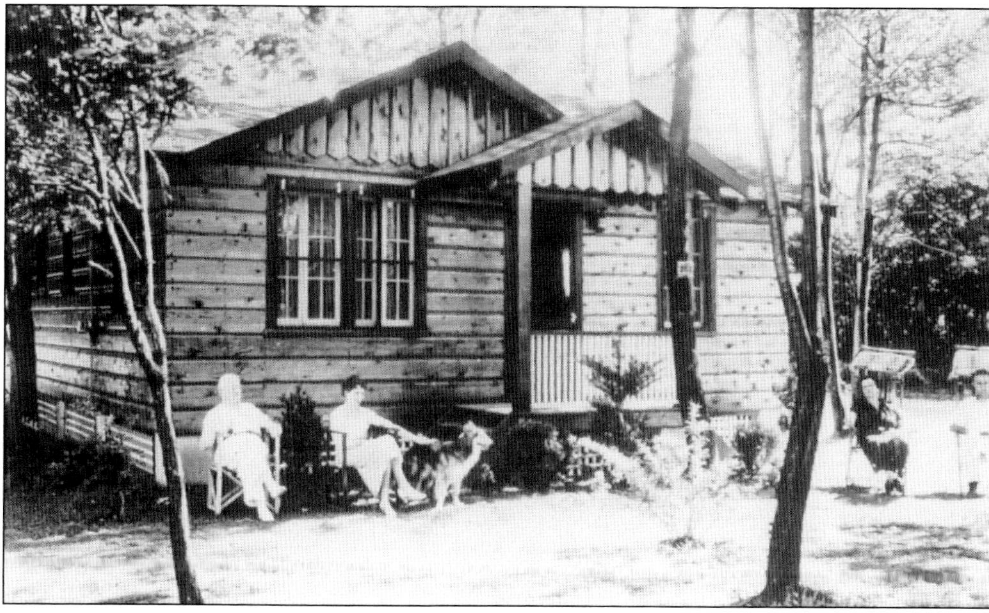

Summer cabins, *c.* 1930. The cabins were constructed by Benjamin J. Kline, builder. Many of these little cabins have since been converted into year-round homes. (Robert D'Alessandro.)

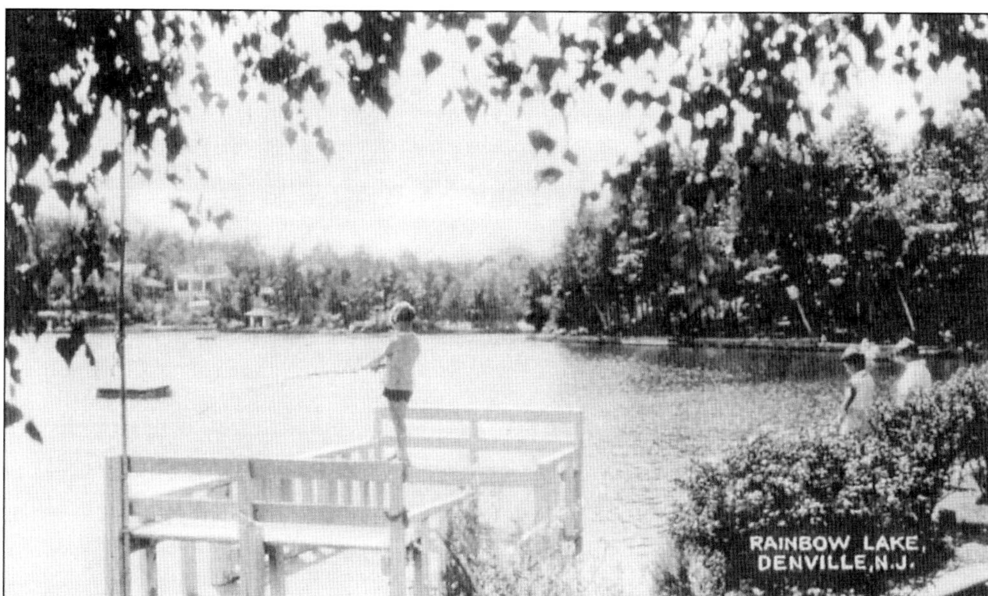

A *c.* 1930 view showing the community of Rainbow Lakes along with the lake itself. (Robert D'Alessandro.)

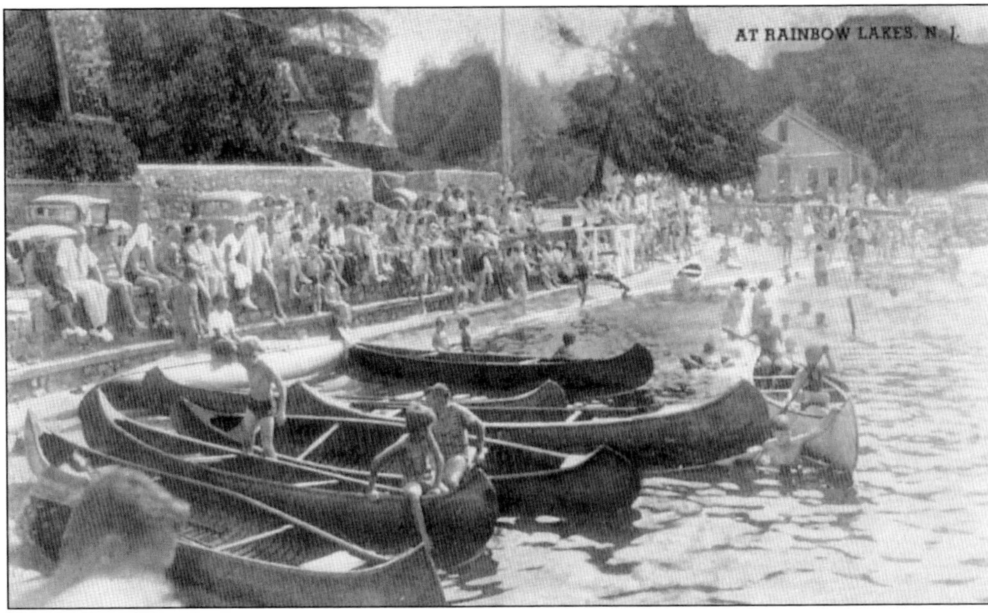

Canoeing on Rainbow Lake, *c.* 1930. Rainbow Lake was originally a bog swamp that was dredged and flooded *c.* 1913. The Park Lake Land Company developed the newly made lake for speculation purposes, and gave the area its name. The land was purchased from Monroe Howell and Edwin Kimball. The Arthur D. Crane Co. developed the rest of the community of Rainbow Lakes in 1924. (Robert D'Alessandro.)

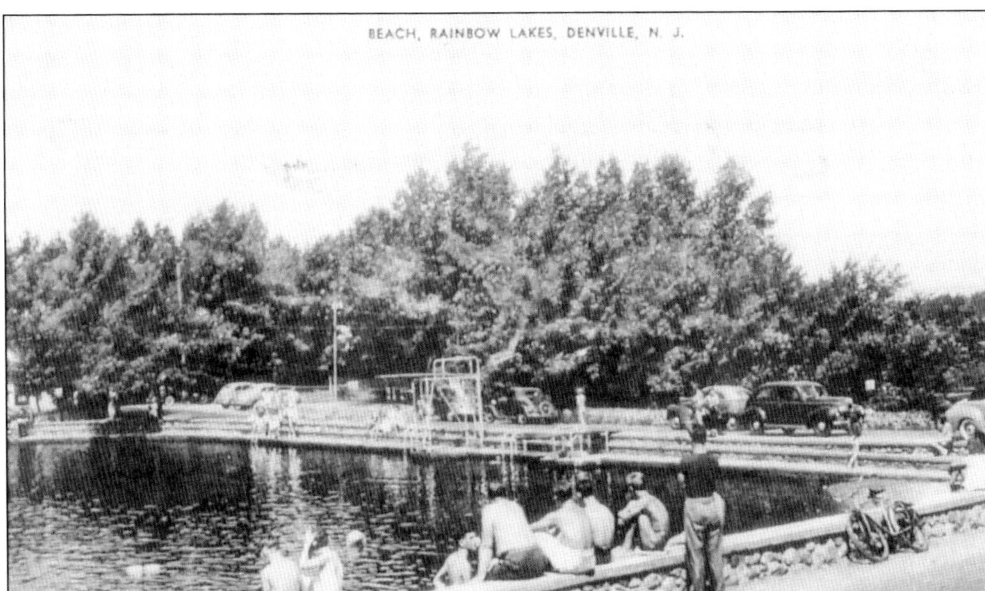

A beach scene at Rainbow Lakes, *c.* 1935. Note that the community of Rainbow Lakes is part of Parsippany-Troy Hills but has a Denville mailing address. (Robert D'Alessandro.)

Nine

Recreation

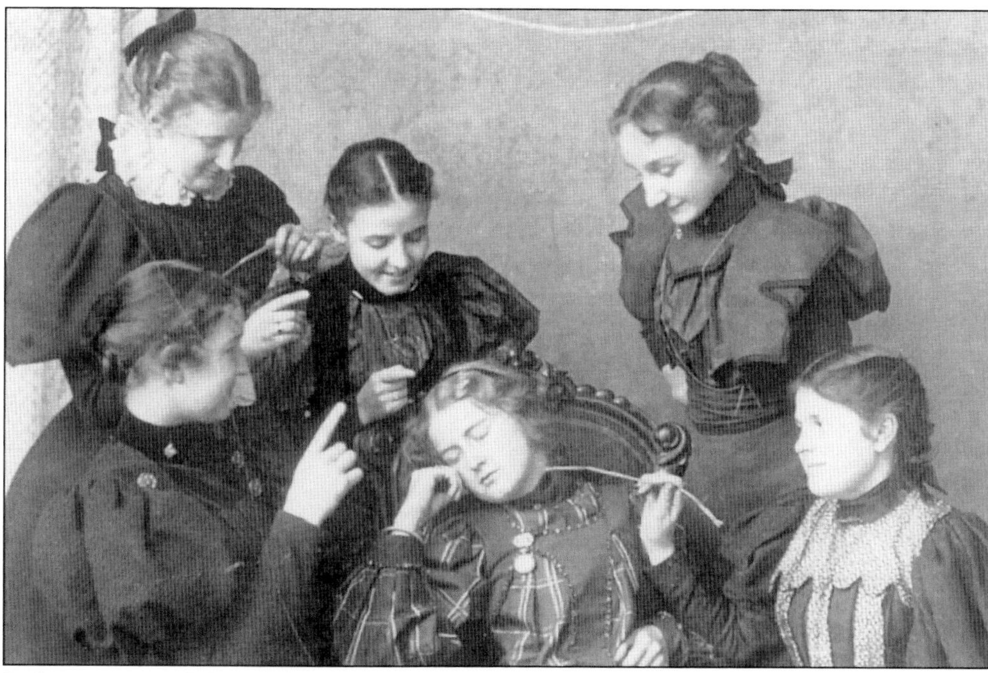

Parlor games, 1897. From left to right are as follows: (front row) Hannah Thompson, Daisy Mathis, and Estelle Turquand; (back row) Margaret Rogers, Alinda Reeves, and Alice Hazelton. This photograph comes from the collection of Estelle Bleu Turquand Condit. (Parsippany-Troy Hills Public Library, Condit Room.)

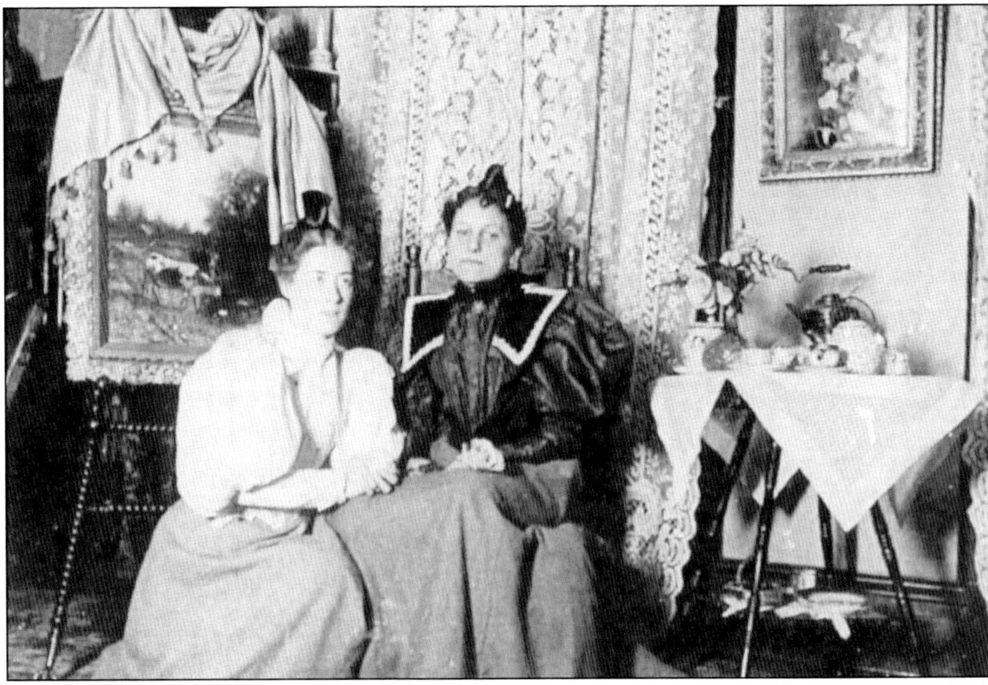

Cousin Alida Banta and friend Mabel Penney, April 11, 1895. Notice the extravagant high Victorian furnishings. This photograph is from the collection of Estelle Bleu Turquand Condit. (Parsippany-Troy Hills Public Library, Condit Room.)

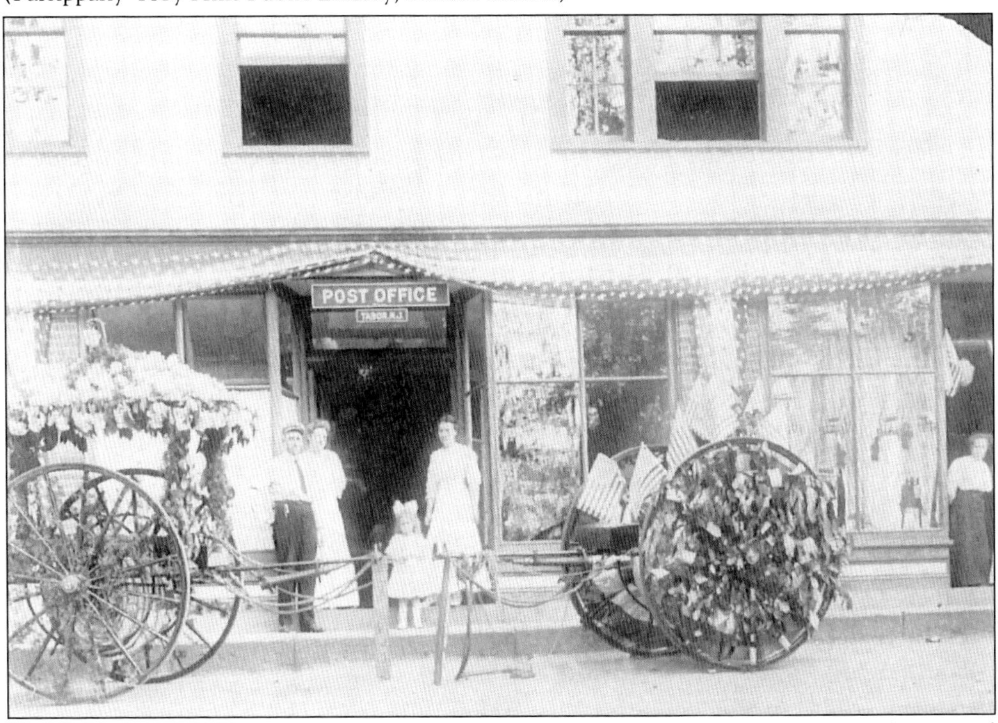

The post office at Tabor, New Jersey (Mount Tabor), *c.* 1890. The float is from the annual Mount Tabor Children's Day parade. (Linda Smith.)

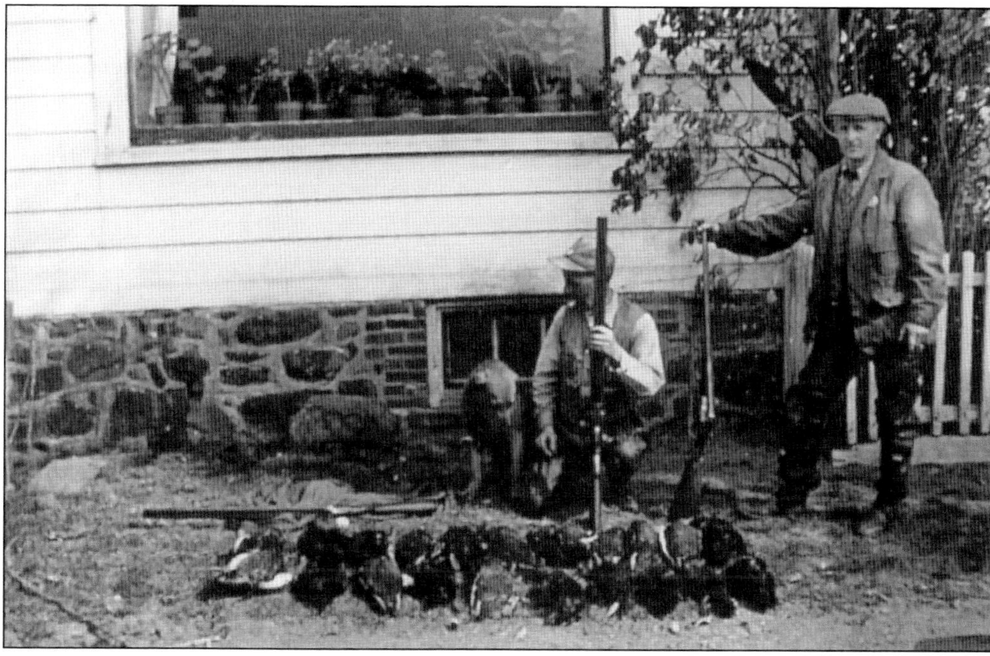

Charles Howell Bates and Will Baldwin (with the rifle). Mr. Bates was the father of Charles Bates, and a longtime Parsippany-Troy Hills' resident. Mr. Baldwin's ancestors were Abraham Baldwin and Zachariah Baldwin III, the first missionaries to come to this area (*c.* 1730). Zachariah Baldwin III (1704–1756) and wife, Rebecca Crane Baldwin (1707–1791), are buried in the Parsippany Presbyterian Cemetery. (Charles Bates.)

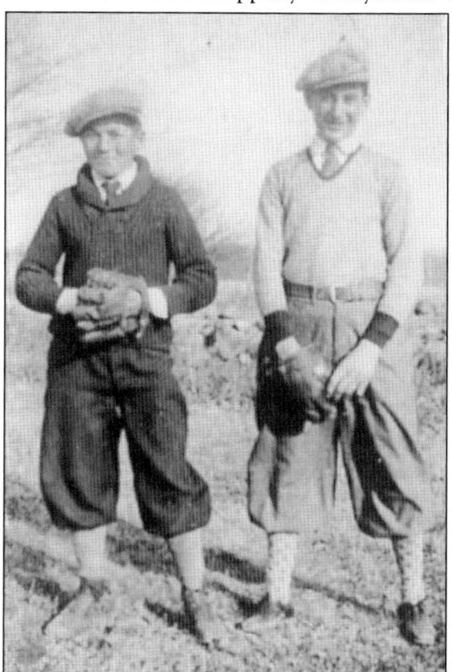

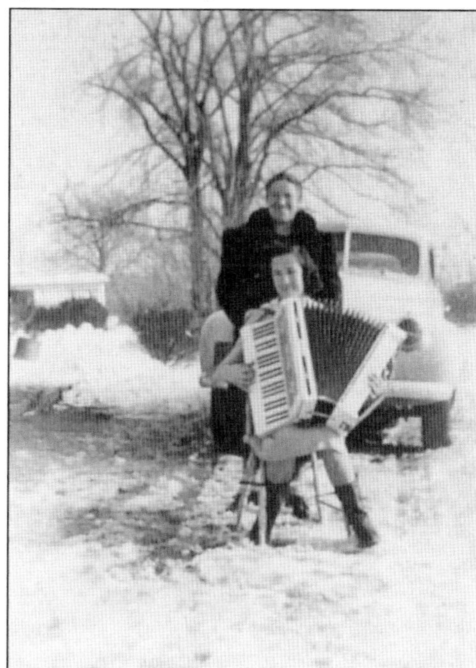

Left: George Schaible and Joe Przyhocki in 1933. Right: Mary Przyhocki and daughter Ann Przyhocki Morgenthien. (Ann Przyhocki Morgenthien.)

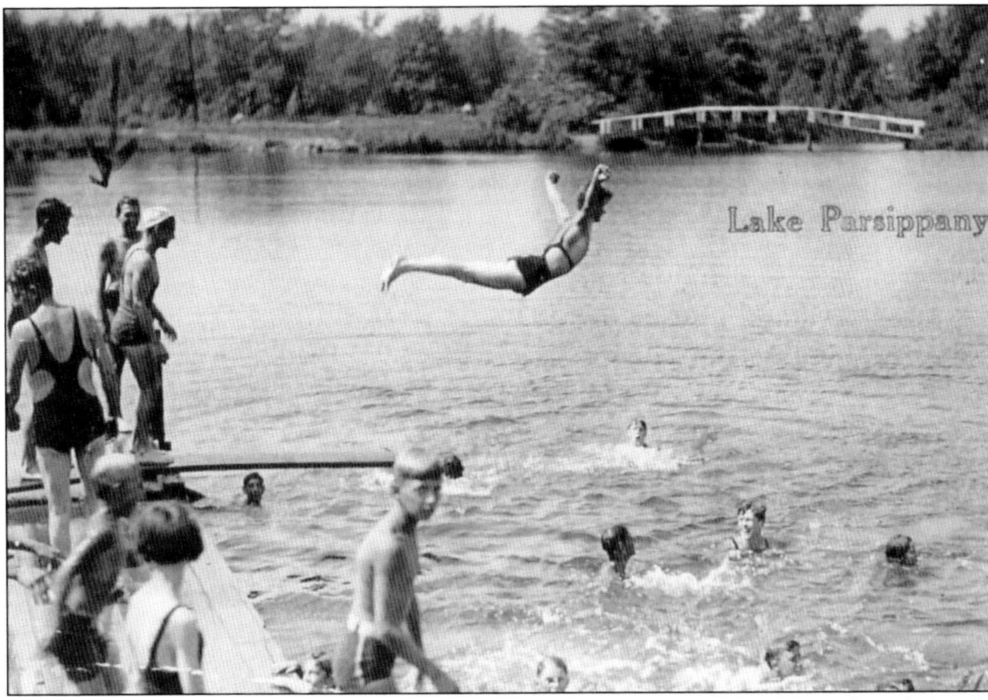

Lake Parsippany on July 17, 1941. George Beatty is in the water under the diving board. On the back of this postcard is written: "Dear Mom, I am having a swell time. Love, George XXXXX." The arrow points to Dennis James, a well-known radio and TV announcer. As a young man, James lived on Halsey Road and was the lifeguard at "Twelve Foot." (Randy Francis Tortorello.)

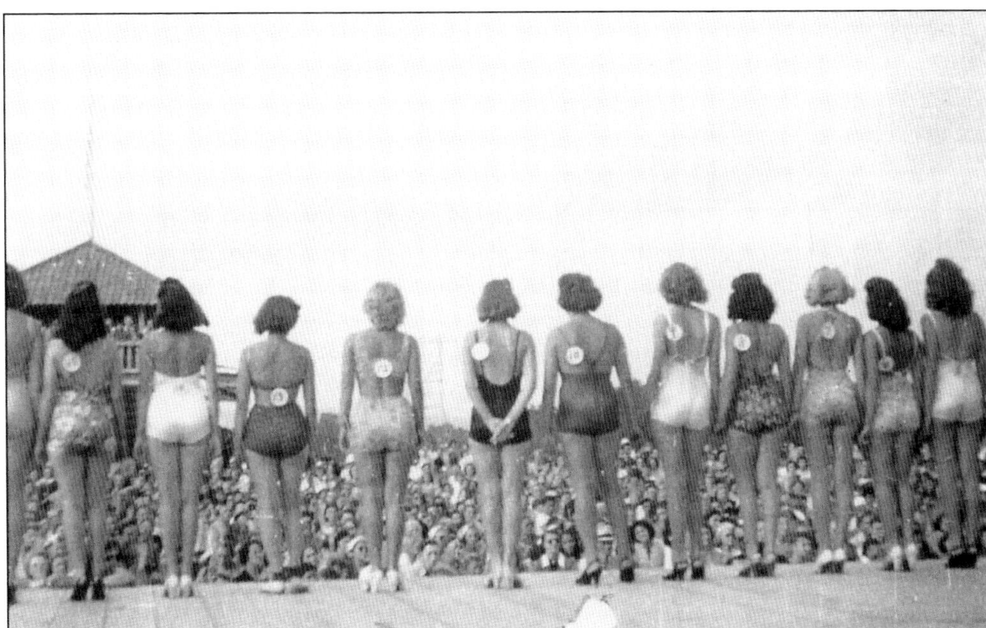

The annual beauty contest at the Lake Hiawatha Country Club, *c.* 1930. The pavilion is in the left background. Notice the ankle socks on the fourth contestant on the left. (Fran Kaminski.)

The summer of 1943. From left to right are Lucy Cucchiarra (Policastro), Irene Beatty (Piegaro), and Angela Pagano (Leonardis). Notice the lipstick markings on the girls' legs. These are the initials of their fiancés, who were on active duty during World War II. (Randy Francis Tortorello.)

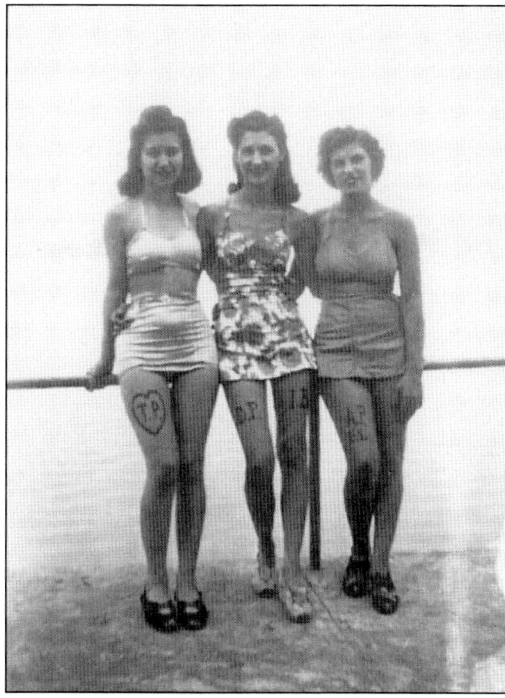

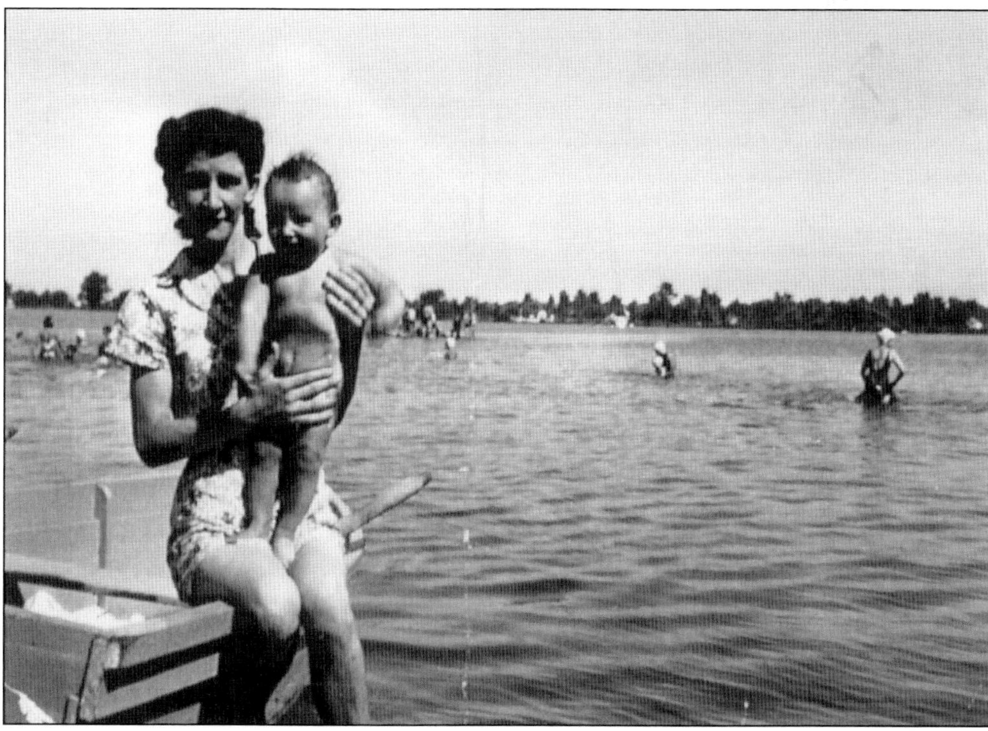

Florence Beatty Tortorello and son Daniel Jr. at Beach No. 4 at Lake Parsippany during the summer of 1942. Mrs. Tortorello's father, uncle, and brother (Charles, John, and Willie Beatty, respectively) were well drillers hired by the *New York Daily Mirror* to flood the area that became Lake Parsippany. (Randy Francis Tortorello.)

Acknowledgments

We wish to extend our thanks and appreciation to the following people and organizations for all their help and cooperation, which made this book possible.

Anita Baldwin
Howard Baldwin
Mr. and Mrs. Richard Smith Baldwin
Charles Bates
Robert Benson
Muriel Berson
Nick Cerbo
Tony Cerbo
Roberta Chopko
Diane Cicala
Will and Miriam Cohen
Robert D'Alessandro
Ann Egan
Harold O. Farrand
Bertha Feinstein
Marian Filler
Art and Ginnie Hendrickson
Joint Free Public Library of Morristown and Morris Township
Fran Kaminski
Sam Levitt
Ann Przyhocki Morgenthien
Morris County Library
Parsippany Historic Museum
Parsippany-Troy Hills Public Library, Condit Room
Parsippany-Troy Hills Township
PIP Printing: Martin Contzius and Mary Serafin
Mary Purzycki
Saint Christopher's Church
Connie Schaible
Linda Smith
Randy Francis Tortorello
Sadie Wishnick
Jack Wooton

COMPILERS:
Fran Kaminski
Barbara Laufer
Bertha Feinstein
Randy Francis Tortorello